D0058433

The Sacred Cause

A volume in the series

CORNELL STUDIES IN SECURITY AFFAIRS

edited by Robert J. Art *and* Robert Jervis

A full list of titles in the series appears at the end of the book.

The Sacred Cause

CIVIL-MILITARY CONFLICT OVER
SOVIET NATIONAL SECURITY, 1917–1992

THOMAS M. NICHOLS

Cornell University Press

ITHACA AND LONDON

First published 1993 by Cornell University Press.

International Standard Book Number 0-8014-2774-6
Library of Congress Catalog Card Number 92-34543
Printed in the United States of America
Librarians: Library of Congress cataloging information appears on the last page of this book.

♾ The paper in this book meets the minimum requirements of the American National Standard for Information Sciences— Permanence of Paper for Printed Library Materials, ANSI Z39.48-1984.

For
Nick James Nichols
and Joan Gavin Nichols

Contents

Preface

I prepared the final version of this book as the dizzying pace of events in the USSR (or the Union of Sovereign States, the Commonwealth of Independent States, or whatever it may be as you read this) began to accelerate toward their stunning conclusion. At one point I thought I might tell the story as it stood in early 1989; later, I felt compelled to wait, as the end of the Soviet state approached so unexpectedly. The final chapter of this or any similar work, I suppose, has yet to be written. It is my hope, however, that the fluid nature of Russian politics will not detract from the essential premise of this book, for it is one that bears directly on the Russian future: that the structure of civil-military politics in the Soviet era was inherently conflictual, in that it pitted an ideologically indoctrinated officer corps against an increasingly pragmatic Party elite, which in turn served to create a military of unstable and conflicted loyalties. These confused and contradictory loyalties may be among the greatest threats to the emerging post-Soviet democracies.

Central to this argument is the question of whether there is a uniquely "Marxist" nature to the Soviet military. Obviously, the Soviet military was in many ways like its counterparts in other nations, driven to opposition by policies that might well have caused tensions in any other military organization. But there is a fundamental difference between a military controlled through an institutional ideology (it needn't be Marxism) and one under more self-regulating control. The difference is that the ideologized military does not necessarily see loyalty to the State and the furtherance of military professionalism as the highest political virtues (I say political as opposed to the common military virtues of bravery, honor, etc.); instead, because they worship at the altar of the state religion, their first loyalty is to the dogmas of the state religion and not to the state itself.

This situation is especially problematic where a messianic, teleological ideology such as Marxism is involved. The legitimacy of the civil power is never above reproach; it is legitimate only insofar as it adheres to the ideology it has imposed on the military. By contrast, in a nonideological setting, the primary criterion for civil legitimacy is that the leadership gain its office through whatever sociolegal arrangements legitimately confer that office, and that the duties of the office be executed in accordance within those sociolegal norms; the military is allowed no political judgment of the leaders except to ascertain that they are in fact the legitimate holders of the mechanisms of power (as opposed, say, to usurpers or pretenders).

This involvement of the military in questions of ideological legitimacy then, is the essential difference between a Marxist military and an apolitical military. The history of Soviet civil-military relations is replete with cases from the 1950s onward where the military (and especially the Main Political Administration) came to see itself as the appropriate guardian of the Soviet national interest and, in the end, of Marxism-Leninism itself; when the MPA was forced to choose loyalty to the Party or to the ideology, more often than not it chose ideology. Upon reflection I find it remarkable that the MPA, the very body charged with transmission of the Party line to the barracks, has so many times turned on its masters, even before Mikhail Gorbachev—as the hasty attempts to shore up Party authority among the military in the late 1970s and early 1980s indicated. (Nor were the practitioners immune: the General Staff also opposed or disregarded orders it believed unwise.)

I chose to use General Dmitrii Volkogonov's words as the title of *The Sacred Cause* to reinforce the idea that the Soviet military saw its calling in the USSR as higher than the State, higher than the law, higher than the constitution. I believe the Soviet officer, in many ways, saw himself as the agent of History itself, in a way that few Western officers would understand or accept.

The result, I argue in the following pages, is that the role of Party and Army became reversed, that the Army became the watchdog of the Party rather than vice versa, raising the uncomfortable question of who, in times of trouble, shall watch the armed watchers. Military objections to Party policy went deeper than the objections to prosaic insults; they went right to the heart of the leadership's foreign policy. Here, the military (no doubt acting to some extent in self-interest, but—more important—convinced of its own rectitude as well) attempted to exercise a kind of veto over policies that were, in any state, properly the domain of the civil power.

This relationship is of more than historical or theoretical interest, of course. One reason that I felt this project was still worth pursuing even as the term "Soviet" lost all but historical meaning is that the end of the Soviet Union has not meant the end of this dangerous and untenable civil-military situation. The larger flow of events, such as the conspicuous and increased presence of officers at pro-Communist rallies in Moscow, the Russian-Ukrainian spat over the Black Sea fleet, the Georgian civil war, and the sudden escalation of the Armenian-Azeri conflict, as well as smaller episodes (including conversations with several Soviet officers throughout the winter of 1991) continues to convince me that the new regimes of the Commonwealth may soon be forced to reap what their Soviet predecessors have sown in civil-military affairs. The August 1991 coup is over, but there may be rebellions or coups to come of a different sort, especially in view of the worsening of military standards of living and growing popular disillusionment with Boris Yeltsin.

We all hope, of course, that it will not come to that. Certainly, the present situation, while difficult, is far from desperate; the pointless and disjointed nature of the August coup, in fact, may have served to awaken many Soviet officers to a new sense of duty that excludes such acts. In the midst of chaos, however, the military role in politics remains uncertain. This is not to say that the military has any better plan for, or is any better able to rule, the fractious Commonwealth than the civilians. But the history of praetorian takeovers indicates that officers sometimes act first in what they see as an intolerable crisis and leave the details of problem solving for later. And should the Russian or other Commonwealth states find themselves facing this kind of military threat from within, it will be a direct result of the methods of military control employed by the Soviets since the Revolution itself.

As every social scientist is taught, the value of good research lies chiefly in explanation rather than prediction or prescription, and accordingly my primary intention in this book has been to attempt to clarify one of the murkier realms of Soviet politics. If there is a prescriptive aspect here, however, it is this: the post-Soviet leaders must avoid replicating the mistakes of their predecessors. The officers and men of the former Soviet Armed Forces are, I believe, generally honorable soldiers. But the civilian insistence in the Russian and other post-Soviet governments on continuing to include officers in the councils of power, in the legislature, in the leadership bodies, and in the give and take of palace politics has created, and will continue to encourage, temptations among the military that even the usually well-disciplined Soviet officer corps may find impossible to resist.

I would like to express my gratitude to the two men who inspired me to begin this work and then helped me to bring it to this conclusion: Thane Gustafson of Georgetown University, who provided the inspiration for a project on civil-military relations, and William C. Fuller, Jr., of the U.S. Naval War College, whose incisive criticisms made the transition from concept to a workable manuscript possible. Their advice and friendship have been invaluable, and I owe them an enormous personal and intellectual debt.

Several institutions were instrumental in providing support. None of the work would have been possible without early financial assistance from the Department of Government at Georgetown, and my thanks go to the University and to the department chairs during my time there, Bruce Douglass and John Bailey.

I owe special thanks to the Center for Strategic and International Studies (CSIS) in Washington, D.C., to my colleagues and friends in the CSIS Soviet Studies program, under whose auspices much of the early writing and research took place, and to the former and present directors of the Soviet program, Thane Gustafson and Stephen Sestanovich, for their moral support and for the fortunate opportunity to become involved in the CSIS project on Soviet civil-military affairs.

Various stages of research and final editing were undertaken at the U.S. Naval War College in Newport, R.I. Much of the research in the first four chapters was supported by a John M. Olin Foundation Fellowship while I was in residence at the Naval War College Foundation; I returned to the War College two years later, and completed the manuscript under a Secretary of the Navy Fellowship in the Department of National Security Decision Making. I thank the Foundation's director, Robert Watts, and the chairman of the NSDM Department, William Turcotte, for the opportunity to study, write, and teach in Newport.

The crucial bridge of support came from the Burke Junior Faculty Fellowship program at Dartmouth College, without whose material aid it would have been literally impossible to finish the book. My thanks must also go to my colleagues in the Department of Government at Dartmouth for their patience while I left my duties there to go first to Washington, D.C., and then to Newport, where I put the final manuscript in order.

Several friends and colleagues have taken the time to read, comment on, and discuss various parts of the manuscript in its various incarnations. Series editor Robert Jervis made several useful suggestions and additions; other helpful criticism came from Phillip Bayer, David Becker, Richard Bryers, Daniel Goure, Thomas Hengeveld, and Theodore William Karasik. Special thanks to Larry George, who volunteered to read and critique the entire work, a professional courtesy above and beyond the call of duty which made clear improvements on the original draft.

I must also acknowledge the personal debt I owe to three teachers–George Kennedy, Robert Merkel, and Stephen Sternheimer—for their early and continuing encouragement and friendship.

Finally, many thanks to Linda Titlar, who encouraged me, and who managed to put up with me, during the sometimes arduous writing process—and agreed to marry me anyway; and to my parents, Nick and Joan Nichols, who saw me through seemingly endless years of education and writing with endless energy and enthusiasm, and to whom this book is dedicated, with love and gratitude.

Thomas M. Nichols

Wilder, Vermont
September 1992

The Sacred Cause

Introduction:
"Our National and Sacred Cause"

It is sometimes said scornfully that literature on the contemporary Army is little more than bureaucratic literature. But surely,
has the defense of the Fatherland ever been a departmental
matter? It is not simply a matter for the Ministry of Timber
Industry. The defense of the Fatherland was, and remains, our
national and sacred cause.
— Col. Gen. Dmitrii Volkogonov, January 1988

"They must not be capable of unconstitutional gambits"

It lasted only three days, but when it was over, the Soviet Union, in
fact and then in name, was gone. For the officers of the Soviet Armed
Forces, however, the end of the brief and botched coup of August
1991 was only the beginning of a new and more painful stage in their
halting march toward reform. The new defense minister, Air Force
Col. Gen. Evgenii Shaposhnikov, announced that no less than 80
percent of the most senior officer corps would have to be dismissed
due to their uncertain loyalties. The new officers, he said, "must be
younger than the ones we have had, more loyal, and not capable of
unconstitutional gambits."[1] As he spoke, Shaposhnikov's predecessor, Marshal of the Soviet Union Dmitrii Yazov, was in prison
awaiting trial with his fellow conspirators for the capital offense of
high treason. Another senior officer, the well-known and widely respected Marshal S. F. Akhromeev, himself a former chief of the General Staff, had been found hanged in his Moscow apartment the day
after the collapse of the coup. And the commander in chief of the
Soviet Ground Forces, Gen. Army Valentin Varennikov, for a time on

[1] Bill Keller, "Secession Widens," *New York Times*, August 26, 1991, p. 1.

[1]

the run, has been identified as a key figure in the conspiracy to depose President Gorbachev. Other prominent Soviet officers, such as former Chief of the General Staff Mikhail Moiseev, were retired under a cloud of suspicion.

How did the Soviet Armed Forces, once thought among the most professional militaries in the developed world, find themselves at this impasse? Even if the coup was, as reports now seem to indicate, hatched primarily in the hallways of the KGB and the Interior Ministry, how could it have involved so many of the senior officers of the Soviet military? This painful and humiliating question has forced the remaining leaders of the armed forces of the former USSR to confront the legacy of seventy years of Party control of the military. That legacy is the subject of this book.

Soviet (and Post-Soviet) Civil-Military Relations

This book examines the development of the civil-military relationship in the Soviet Union from the 1920s to the early 1990s, and seeks to describe the causes and effects of more than a generation of tenuous and shifting control of the armed forces. And while it is not my purpose here to consider in detail the drama of August 1991, patterns emerge in the examination of the Soviet civil-military relationship which may serve to clarify the path that led the Soviet military—or at least its most senior officers—to disgrace at the penultimate moment in Soviet history.

Despite the fascinating events of the coup, why study "Party-military" relations at all? In the 1990s, very little of either institution is left to study. Certainly, the Soviet Armed Forces had fallen upon hard times, even before the August events; the Party itself is quite literally dead, an unexpected arrival in the dustbin of history.

First, the Soviet nightmare is not quite yet at an end. Early evaluations of the performance of the military during the coup have led many Westerners to assume that Soviet officers were in fact opponents of the putschists, rather than co-conspirators. But Stephen Sestanovich is right to point out that the pattern of reticence among senior officers "emerged only *after* the scale of popular opposition to the coup became clear."[2] This, I would argue, suggests that the loy-

---

[2] Stephen Sestanovich, "Foreword," in Bruce Porter, *Red Armies in Crisis* (Washington, D.C.: CSIS, 1991), p. viii, my emphasis.

alties of the remaining members of the armed forces are, at best, untested, and that the possibility of a Soviet version of the Yugoslav tragedy, perhaps played out with federal troops embroiled between warring ethnic factions, is not out of the question. Indeed, in early 1992 reports began to arrive that fighting between Armenia and Azerbaidjan had escalated, and there were accusations from Azeris that Commonwealth of Independent States (CIS) forces were aiding the Armenians (the CIS 366th Regiment, trapped between the two combatants, had been ordered, according to officials in Moscow, to leave the area). Marshal Shaposhnikov claimed that the escalating conflict posed a "direct threat" to the 11,000 Commonwealth troops in the area, warning, according to Western reports, that "if his soldiers are harmed, full-scale war will result."[3] In time, the 366th extricated itself, but similar situations continue to confront CIS forces in several former Soviet republics.

In any case, the former Soviet states will for years be faced with the problems of dismantling the post-Soviet military, the military-political apparatus, the resettlement of the thousands of servicemen still in Europe, the formation of national militias, and the like. If the new leaders of the post-Soviet order are to avoid the mistakes of their ill-fated predecessors and create a reliable, professional, stable military organization from the debris of the former Soviet empire, the need to reconsider the scope and nature of military involvement in Soviet politics should be one of the most fascinating and pressing issues in post-Soviet reconstruction.

Moreover, the position of the military in other communist and recently post-communist polities remains unclear, and the Soviet case may provide insights into the mechanisms of civil-military interaction in these nations—many of which, like Yugoslavia, are in the midst of the convulsions of change. As Bruce Porter cogently put it in the wake of the Soviet coup, the military threat in the communist world "may not be direct military intervention—which implies decisive planning and execution—but rather the inexorable fragmentation and demoralization of armed forces whose ranks reflect the crisis of their societies."[4] In the years to come, the remnants of the Soviet Armed Forces, and their former comrades in arms from Germany to Nicaragua, will be confronted with new oaths and new loyalties; before

[3] Shaposhnikov did not name the likely opponents in that full-scale war. Paul Quinn-Judge, "Armenian Forces Attack Azeri City," *Boston Sunday Globe*, March 1, 1992, p. 16.
[4] Porter, *Red Armies in Crisis*, p. 93.

[3]

this military excursion into post-communist *terra incognita* takes place, it is worthwhile to consider the why and how of military opposition to Party supremacy during the Soviet experience.

Civil-Military Conflict in the Soviet Era

If study of the party-military relationship may serve to illuminate possibilities for the future of the Soviet successor states, it also may shed some light on the past. A central theme of this book is that the Western view of Soviet civil-military relations dominant among policymakers and scholars since the 1970s—that is, of generally undisturbed amity—is inaccurate. Civil control of the military in the USSR was imperfect and tense after Stalin's death, and this realization implies that our understanding of the very nature of Party authority, not least as it pertains to control of the military, has been based on assumptions of questionable accuracy or utility.

This book is primarily concerned with national security policy, the arena in which the Soviet military most clearly and consistently challenged the CPSU for thirty-five years. It is here, in the largest questions of national defense, that the military leadership not only opposed various Party policies, but in doing so thereby challenged the authority of the Party itself. These challenges became pronounced under Gorbachev, but they were not new. What was new was *glasnost'*; the previously muted exchanges between soldiers and civilians became, by comparison, noisy and insulting battles. Although the major focus of civil-military conflict since the 1950s has been the creation and execution of national security policy, a new era opened in Soviet politics after 1988, one in which the military apparently saw itself (rather than the Party) as one of the last sources of cohesion and order in the rapidly decaying USSR.

The Nature of the Military Challenge

Some may object that there was nothing unique or interesting about Soviet civil-military affairs, a criticism that arises from a more general Western belief that modern industrial states rarely experience genuine or substantive civil-military conflict. (Stephen Meyer, for one, has even gone so far as to suggest that the search for civil-military friction in the USSR was merely part of the American tendency to "hunt for dark forces that are gaining sway over the forces of good" whenever Soviet policies displeased Washington.)[5] Even in the wake of the August putsch, there are indications that some Western analysts rushed to the wrong conclusions and focused on the small part of the high command that resisted the coup. Certainly, many would argue that the coup was a special situation; until faced with the destruction of the USSR, the reasoning goes, the Soviet military was as loyal as any other. After all, they ask, aren't all military men the same?[6] Don't they all paint frightening pictures of the world as they seek to protect their privileges (and their budgets)? Don't they all complain whenever meddlesome civilians tell them to change their war plans or tighten their belts? In other words: wasn't civil-military "conflict" in the Soviet Union of the same type seen every day in the United States, with sullen generals forced to sit before congressional committees?

In some ways, military men are in fact alike. Research on military sociology (particularly the work of Morris Janowitz) long ago suggested that "experts in violence" share something in common, and it is therefore to be expected that these experts experience similar feelings toward policies they perceive as civilian interference. As Janowitz put it, "The military establishment as a social system has unique characteristics because the possibility of hostilities is a permanent reality to its leadership. . . . The unique character of the military establishment derives from the requirement that its members are specialists in making use of violence and mass destruction."[7] But even if there are attributes and attitudes shared generally by officers of every nation, there are significant differences in the inclination or the opportunity to act on such attitudes. In the West, the boundaries between politicians and officers are clear, and soldiers who overstep those boundaries are rare.[8] (When they appear—as officers such as Billy Mitchell and Douglas MacArthur attest—they are removed.) The

[5] Stephen Meyer, "The Army Isn't Running Gorbachev," *New York Times*, May 8, 1990, p. 29.

[6] This attitude runs deep in Western society; I am reminded of an exchange I witnessed between a U.S. colonel and his Soviet counterpart in which the American noted with aplomb, "You're just like us; you just follow orders." The Soviet colonel concurred.

[7] See Morris Janowitz, *Sociology and the Military Establishment* (New York: Russell Sage, 1959), p. 18.

[8] Even in the German case, where officers play more of a role in political life than in most other industrial nations, the guidance (the *Innere Führung*) given to military personnel is meant to instill an understanding of the obedience to law and to the civil power.

Soviet case, however, is not comparable to the American or British or French cases, for the USSR has never experienced any of the legal or cultural mechanisms that provide the kind of virtually complete civil control over the military enjoyed in the West. Moreover, one of the chief instruments of military control in the USSR, ideology, proved to be a double-edged sword rather than a safeguard of civil dominance. Military opposition to Party policy therefore carried much broader implications for Soviet political stability than similar discontent among officers of the democracies.

This is a difficult idea to accept, accustomed as Westerners have been to thinking of the Soviet Union either as a modern industrial state or as an autocracy under strict control. In fact, the Soviet state included elements of both; nonetheless, in military affairs Soviet leaders never experienced either the constitutional autonomy of a modern state or the immediate and direct control of an autocracy. Put another way, the Soviets never succeeded in creating a politically "modern" military in the Western tradition, one guided *by* politics without participating *in* politics, and throughout Soviet history the Party and the military were both partners and competitors in an uneasy symbiosis. As a result of this arrangement between these two allied but very different groups, control over national security policy (and by extension, over aspects of foreign policy more broadly) was a forced compromise between civil and military authorities. Thus, a situation developed in which the Soviet Union had a technically advanced First World military organization and a Third World system of military control.

This conflictual picture of the Soviet civil-military relationship carries several analytical and practical implications. Most important, it means that the West has accepted a distorted vision of the Soviet policymaking process, which implies an erroneous understanding of the nature of Party authority itself. Soviet foreign and defense policies were not merely the product of Party pragmatism (or Party *diktat*), any more than they were the pristine deliberations of the military professionals. Moreover, the realization that there was significant civil-military friction on high-level issues suggests that the practical mechanisms of Party control, as well as the foundations of Party legitimacy, were not as strong or as all-encompassing as previously thought, especially if—as I will argue—the ideological militancy of the armed forces stood in opposition to the pragmatism of the Party, rather than vice versa.

[6]

THE SOURCES OF PARTY-ARMY CONFLICT

Samuel Huntington recognized more than three decades ago that "military policy cuts clearly across the usual distinction between foreign policy and domestic policy," and that military policy in any country is necessarily a function of civil-military interaction.[9] In the Soviet case, the crosscutting nature of the debate takes on added significance, because it was conducted in an environment ostensibly structured by the scientism of Marx, the Party discipline of Lenin, and the rigid hierarchy of Soviet military doctrine. When the Soviet military dissented on issues of national defense and foreign affairs, there was more at stake than policy: the legitimacy of the Party itself was called into question. Senior Soviet officers who advocated policies contrary to those of the Party leadership—as they did in several instances since the 1920s—were in essence arguing that they, responding to a higher duty and sanctioned by a higher authority, were the true guardians of the state and the Revolution.

The sources of Party-military friction can be traced to four aspects of the Soviet political system: the structure of ideology, the consequent rigidity of Soviet military doctrine, the nature of Soviet political culture, and the institutional role of the Soviet officer.

The Dilemma of Ideology

Among these factors, by far the most important is that the Soviet Communist Party was the victim of its own success insofar as the senior Soviet officer corps were (and remain) well-indoctrinated Marxists.[10] Soviet officers themselves agree; indeed, when sociologist Bengt Abramsson suggested in the early 1970s that all militaries, including the Soviet Union's, were by natural inclination "conservative," Soviet officers huffily responded in several works that Abramsson misunderstood the class character of military organization. Predictably, they argued that the Soviet military, as the product of a

[9] Samuel Huntington, *The Common Defense* (New York: Columbia University Press, 1961), p. 1. This interrelationship is not a uniquely American phenomenon; Andrei Gromyko has also written of the constant political interaction between Soviet foreign and defense policies. See A. Gromyko, *Pamiatnoe*, vol. 1 (Moscow: Politizdat, 1988), p. 374.

[10] Party membership among the officer corps in the 1980s was close to 80 percent. See Ellen Jones, *Red Army and Society* (Boston: Unwin-Hyman, 1984), chap. 5.

Marxist state, was a Marxist military rather than a conservative or militaristic one.[11] Recent events in Eastern Europe and in the USSR itself suggest that this claim was more than bluster and that in fact the Soviet military rather than the Communist Party has proved to be the ultimate repository of orthodox Soviet Marxism-Leninism. As one Soviet military writer put it, Marxism-Leninism serves to define the very *world view* of Soviet society, and especially of the Soviet military; thus, the senior officer corps unavoidably saw the world through the prism of Marxist thought.[12] (The traumatic effects of the breakdown of this cognitive prism were dramatically illustrated by Marshal Akhromeev's suicide, before which he reportedly penned a note saying that he could not live when "everything I have worked for my entire life is crumbling around me.")[13]

What this creates in practice is a fusion of the traditional virtue of military loyalty and the politically transcendent aspects of Marxism. As Huntington pointed out, most military officers see their profession as "a 'higher calling' in the service of the state."[14] What this meant, however, was that Western officers saw their "higher calling" as a duty to the wishes of political leaders, the representatives of the state. The Soviet officer, however, schooled in Marxism-Leninism and enveloped by the omniscience of the Party, believed in a loyalty to the State in the more abstract, even Hegelian sense, a loyalty to the idealized Party-State that stands above the bureaucrats in the Council of Ministers or the rabble in the Congress of People's Deputies. It was no contradiction for a Soviet general to accept in his heart that he was a servant of the CPSU and the USSR while still opposing the policy of the leadership. (This is not inherently contradictory: by analogy one might point to liberation theology Jesuits who fervently affirm their

---

[11] For two examples of direct attacks on Abramsson's thesis, see Maj. Gen. E. Sulimov, "Zashchita sotsialisticheskogo otechestva—zakonomernost' razvitiia novogo obshchestva," *Kommunist Vooruzhennykh Sil* 7 (April 1971), p. 21; and Cols. V. Konoplev and V. Kovalev, "O roli vooruzhennykh sil v sovremennom obshchestve," *Kommunist Vooruzhennykh Sil* 4 (February 1971), p. 29.

[12] V. Khalipov, *Voennaia politika KPSS* (Moscow: Voenizdat, 1988), p. 22, and Dmitrii A. Volkogonov, ed., *Marksistko-leninskoe uchenie o voine i armii* (Moscow: Voenizdat, 1984), p. 12.

[13] These words appeared in early reports from Moscow, but the story was quickly quashed at the time by Soviet authorities. The actual text of the note has not yet been released.

[14] Samuel Huntington, *The Soldier and the State* (Cambridge: Harvard University Press, 1957), p. 8.

loyalty to the Holy Father and to the Church while simultaneously espousing doctrines they themselves know to have been declared heretical.) Marshal Yazov perhaps reflected this conflicted loyalty after his arrest, when he was interrogated on videotape. "I may have betrayed Gorbachev," he said, sitting erect and in full uniform and medals, "but I never betrayed my Motherland."[15]

Naturally, for some members of the Soviet military ideology was and will always be merely a convenient rationalization for personal or institutional aggrandizement. This, however, is irrelevant: years of indoctrination and lifetimes of service rationalized in the terms of the Revolution are powerful forces regardless of the cynicism of this or that officer. (As Kurt Vonnegut once wrote, we are what we pretend to be, and so we must be careful what we pretend to be.) Whatever doubts and disillusionment there may have been among the senior ranks, in the end it is clear that the Soviet officer conceived of his duty as duty to Party and State in their highest, even transcendental incarnations.

One of the more paradoxical aspects of this sense of duty is the fusion it created between the explicit internationalism of Marxist thought and the hypernationalism inherent both in Imperial Russian culture, with Moscow as the "Third Rome," and Soviet culture, with Moscow as the defender of the Revolution. There was not, however, any apparent tension in military thought between Soviet nationalism and Marxist internationalism, any more than there was tension between the humble Christian roots of Russian Orthodoxy and the relentlessly arrogant messianism of the Russian Empire. In each case, the parochial defense of Moscow is seen as furthering the larger interests of a world to be bettered in the long run.

This is a dangerous ideological mixture with which to nourish the military, for it creates a closed system of thought in which conflict is always assumed to be present and the position of the State (as an expression of the will of the proletariat) always assumed to be just. In the end, it leads to a military that may prove difficult to control when civilian desires conflict with what the military perceives as the national interest. In the Soviet case, it elevated the defense of the socialist fatherland to, in the words of Col. Gen. Volkogonov at the opening of this chapter, a "national and sacred cause."

---

[15] Cable News Network broadcast, October 28, 1991.

The Power of Doctrine

The influence of Marxism extends far beyond the attitudes and indoctrination of the Soviet military. In the earliest days of the Soviet state, it served to create an aura of scientific legitimacy around military policy, which was described as the result of an objective Marxist evaluation of, and collective Party deliberations about, international and domestic conditions, the end result of which is called *military doctrine*. Because the Party was the source and arbiter of Marxist "science," the inclusion of military doctrine as an extension of Marxism served to bind the legitimacy of the Party, the military, and Marxism itself together in a politically potent mixture.

What is "military doctrine," and why was it central to the civil-military relationship? The concept itself (for which there is no Western analog) was all-encompassing: what Westerners would call "national security policy" the Soviets called only one aspect of military doctrine. Officially defined as "the system of views adopted by a state at a given time on the essence, goals and character of a possible future war, on the preparation of the nation and of the armed forces for it, and on the means of its conduct," military doctrine (promulgated through the speeches and writings of senior Party and military figures) addressed fundamental questions about the nature of the international environment, the proximate and underlying causes of war, the probable opponents, the duration of conflict, the type of weapons to be used, and so on.[16] In theory, the CPSU and the General Staff worked out military doctrine together, with the Party taking the leading role in the process.

Because military doctrine was conceived of as the scientific evaluation of the environment, its conclusions had to be heeded hierarchically: doctrinal pronouncements drove strategy, manpower policy, weapons development, and a host of other important policy areas. Harriet and William Scott captured the overarching nature of Soviet doctrine in this way: Soviet doctrine "is a concept quite different from Western military doctrine, which is merely a set of principles for the use of armed forces in combat. *Soviet military doctrine transcends the Soviet Armed Forces. It [has an impact] on all aspects of Soviet life,* whether it be the military-patriotic education of Soviet youth, the location of new industries, or scientific exchanges with the noncom-

---

[16] S. F. Akhromeev et al., eds., *Voenno-Entsiklopedicheskii Slovar'* (Moscow: Voenizdat, 1986), p. 240.

munist world. Soviet military doctrine provides the overall framework for preparing the country against the possibility of future war."[17] One Soviet general pointed out in 1991 that military doctrine "is rightly considered the 'holy of holies' of a state's defensive system."[18] By its very nature, then, control of doctrine entailed control of resources, making military doctrine a tempting political target. The problem: if the Party was the source of Marxist science, and therefore of doctrine, how could military thinkers challenge doctrine, or hope to gain control over it, without challenging the Party?

The answer is that they couldn't, and so disagreements about doctrine in the Soviet period always carried as a subtheme the issue of legitimacy. Consequently, the word "doctrine" itself became a politically loaded term in the USSR from the moment it was introduced in the 1920s. In the United States, by comparison, the president stands at the apex of command, but he does not stand at the apex of thought, and so American military officers and experts can debate defense policy without necessarily debating the authority of the president either as the chief executive or as the commander in chief. In the Soviet Union, opposition to military doctrine was *by definition* opposition to the Party leadership, a conflict that is the basis for much of this book.

The Constitutional Complication

Another factor that contributed to this difficult situation was an almost complete lack of constitutional norms regulating the civil-military relationship. This was not a dysfunction peculiar to the military; rather, it underscores the more general lack of constitutionalism in Soviet political culture. To be fair, the Soviet Armed Forces could only take the USSR Constitution as seriously as anyone else did in the Soviet state—and until recently that wasn't very seriously—and maybe even less so, because of their belief in a duty that transcended something as ephemeral as a Party-manufactured constitution. To take a common example, the discussion of the sources of military policy in a 1984 volume in the "Officer's Library" series lists the USSR Constitution fourth, after the Party program, Party congresses, and

[17] Harriet Scott and William Scott, *Soviet Military Doctrine* (Boulder, Colo.: Westview, 1988), p. 254, my emphasis.
[18] I. Vorob'iev, "Vse li vzveshno v nashei doktrine?" *Krasnaia Zvezda*, January 26, 1991, pp. 2–3. Unless otherwise noted, all translations are mine.

the plenums of the Central Committee.[19] Nor was there much reason to be concerned about the constitution; only 2 out of 174 articles of the Constitution of 1977 dealt with national defense, and those 2 (articles 31 and 32) said next to nothing.[20] Efforts to impose a legal-constitutional order on the armed forces got under way for a time in the Congress of People's Deputies, but in the end they were few and made little headway.

The lack of constitutional norms served to exacerbate the already delicate balance between military obedience and Party legitimacy. Without a firm legal or historical tradition (as embodied in a constitution) available to adjudicate the dispute, the constitutional complication created the possibility of an endless cycle of disagreement between conflicting notions of duty and patriotism. There were few informal norms to supplant this dearth of legal mechanisms. Like all Soviet political institutions, the civil-military relationship suffered from blurred lines of authority, a result of Stalinist methods of political control.

Worse, this area of Soviet politics remained among the most "totalitarianized," because subsequent Soviet leaders found it tempting to try to inherit the complete control over the military briefly enjoyed by Stalin. This persistence of the totalitarian pattern in civil-military affairs meant that the limits on military participation were kept purposely vague, even when other areas of the society and the economy underwent reform. More important, it also meant that civil intrusions into military affairs were, after the 1930s, the rule rather than the exception in the USSR.

These efforts were unsuccessful. Stalin's successors are not Stalin, and the Soviet military never again allowed itself to be subordinated to the center as it was during the 1930s. Instead, attempts at "totalitarian" control of the armed forces backfired as the military actively used this poor definition of its political role to attempt to influence the defense agenda, both by changing the environment of debate as well as through willful distortions or evasions during the implementation of policy.

The Dual Role of the Soviet Officer

A fourth factor that complicated the civil-military relationship, and served especially to undermine Party authority, is the fact that senior

---

[19] Volkogonov, *Marksistko-leninskoe uchenie o voine i armii*, p. 8.

[20] See Robert Sharlet, *The New Soviet Constitution of 1977* (Brunswick, Ohio: King's Court, 1978), p. 86.

Soviet officers were able to act as legitimate players within the political structure and actually engage in the politics of national security. As Zhores Medvedev wrote in 1983, "the professional military are well-represented in the Central Committee," and although they "form a smaller lobby than the regional Party secretaries or the technocrats . . . they are far more united."[21] This sort of "lobbying" is not the same thing as providing advice (even prejudicial advice), or formulating options, or even expressing disapproval. (In other words, it is not the same thing as what is sometimes called "institutional pluralism.")[22] It is more serious: it is taking part in the political process, seeking allies, influencing opinion, and occasionally even defying the wishes of the political leadership. The top military leaders in the USSR were, after all, members not only of the Central Committee, but of the Supreme Soviet, the Congress of People's Deputies, and occasionally even of the once powerful Politburo.

This kind of interconnection should not be underestimated; how much more importance would Americans attach to the process of national security policy formulation if the chairman of the Joint Chiefs, the service heads, and dozens of other active-duty officers were also U.S. representatives and senators? This is the uniquely Soviet aspect of the problem, and it provides perhaps the strongest basis for rejecting the assertions that Soviet soldiers were obedient officers like any other in the industrial world. They lived in the boardroom as well as the barracks, a situation described perfectly by Andrei Gromyko in his recollections of meetings with then-Minister of Defense Marshal Rodion Malinovskii:

> Malinovskii remained above all a military man, as he himself often emphasized. But the important post entrusted to him by the party and the government, of course, opened before him the possibility to prove himself in the capacity of a state figure as well. And I should say that he coped quite well with this important assignment.
>   Malinovskii sometimes began a meeting like this:
>   "I will speak with the directness of a military man . . ."
>   And this he did.[23]

---

[21] Zhores Medvedev, *Andropov* (New York: Norton, 1983), p. 106.

[22] A useful refinement of the concept of political participation in the Soviet polity may found in Philip Roeder's discussion of the difference between "participation" and "coproduction." See Philip Roeder, "Modernization and Participation in the Leninist Developmental Strategy," *American Political Science Review* (September 1989).

[23] True to form, Gromyko declines to describe the conversation that followed, although on subsequent pages he seems to suggest that he found Marshal A. A. Grechko less imperious, more able, and generally less difficult to deal with than Malinovskii—a

This is not praise; Gromyko was quite resentful of military interference in foreign affairs, even referring at one point to Soviet officers as "martinets."[24]

In 1990, the chief of the Soviet airborne troops used his position as a people's deputy to lambaste government policies (on behalf of his constituents, of course) from agriculture to ethnic affairs—all the while disingenuously claiming that soldiers only execute the wishes of politicians![25]

In the last few years of Soviet rule, even the Soviets themselves began to show more evident discomfort with this arrangement. When a prominent Soviet officer, Col. Gen. Albert Makashov, excoriated the leadership's foreign policy at the June 1990 Russian Republic Party Congress, several observers questioned whether the general even had the right to render such political judgments in public. A military spokesman, crystallizing the political duality of the Soviet officer in a single sentence, responded by saying that Makashov had as much right as anyone else to speak "as a communist."[26] (Makashov was relived of his command in the postcoup purge of the military leadership.)

These failures to create clear boundaries on military participation in politics in the USSR, the results of the Soviet insistence on a Marxist military, provided Soviet officers with political privileges and options that are not available to their Western counterparts and created an environment in which civil-military conflict would be both chronic and unresolvable.

EVOLUTION OF THE SOVIET CIVIL-MILITARY RELATIONSHIP

How did this unusual situation come about in a polity that was in so many other respects a "modern," albeit authoritarian, state? The

---

recollection at odds with foreign policy adviser Georgii Arbatov's depiction of Grechko, as will be seen in chapter 4. A. Gromyko, *Pamiatnoe*, 1:373–376.

[24] According to defector Arkady Shevchenko, Gromyko "hoped to bring the Soviet armed forces command around to thinking in terms of limiting weaponry, not just acquiring more." Gromyko told him: "The more contact they have with the Americans, the easier it will be to turn our soldiers into something more than just martinets." This runs counter to the deprecating evaluation Gromyko gives of American military officers in his memoirs, however. See A. Shevchenko, *Breaking with Moscow* (New York: Knopf, 1985), p. 203, and Gromyko, *Pamiatnoe*, 2:304–306.

[25] Earlier the same officer had claimed that his political agenda reflected the wishes of his voters. See "Chto zabotit deputatov v pogonakh," *Krasnaia Zvezda*, May 20, 1990, p. 1, and "Airborne Commander Views Military Reform," FBIS-SOV-90–112, June 11, 1990, pp. 75–77.

[26] "Po telefonu obratnoi sviazi," *Krasnaia Zvezda*, June 22, 1990, p. 1.

historical origins of the Soviet civil-military problem can be traced back to two major events. The first was the creation of a hierarchical military doctrine in the 1920s, and the second was Stalin's ascendance shortly thereafter. The formal power attached to this concept of military doctrine (indeed, the fact that such a concept even exists), and the manner in which it developed, has been central to the struggle between civil and military elites in the Soviet Union. It is even fair to consider whether other shortcomings in the Soviet system of civil control might have been overcome were it not for the existence of a formal military doctrine. The essential point to bear in mind is not that there was conflict over the substance of defense policy (conflict otherwise to be expected), but rather that the structure of doctrine and of Party supremacy itself created a pervasive habit of political disobedience among the officer corps.

Frunze, Stalin, and the Development of Soviet Military Thought

Ironically, the creation of a formal military doctrine of such wide scope was originally intended as part of a series of mechanisms of Party control, designed to ensure that the new Soviet military would be a force for progress and not reaction. Instead, military doctrine became the source of civil-military struggle as each side realized the inherent power of the concept. Instead of a leash, the early Bolsheviks created a scepter, which successive generations of officers and Party leaders have struggled to wield, with inconclusive results and a fair amount of damage to both contestants. How did this happen in a system that supposedly gave more thought to the issue of civil control than almost any other modern state?

Early Soviet thinking about the structure of the military was a product of the Bolsheviks' Marxist approach to the question, an ideological orientation that combined a mistrust of standing armies with the desire to produce a "scientific" system of military thought. Lenin's thinking on civil control of the military is directly derived from the class determinism of Marx, evident in his admonition in *State and Revolution* that "every revolution, by shattering the state apparatus, demonstrates to us how the ruling class aims at the restoration of the special bodies of armed men at *its* service, and how the oppressed class tries to create a new organization of this kind, capable of serving not the exploiters, but the exploited."[27] Lenin's warning represented the problem of remaking a standing military in the socialist image and likeness (although, in the wake of the *Potemkin* incident of 1905, he

---

[27] V. I. Lenin, *State and Revolution* (New York: International Publishers, 1971), p. 11.

also recognized the potential for revolution within the ranks).[28] The Bolsheviks were concerned that a professional standing army, by the very traditions embedded in military values and training, would inevitably become, in Lenin's words, "a weapon of reaction." The purpose of Soviet military doctrine, then, was that the army would be organized hierarchically, with the scientific wisdom of the Party interpreting reality and translating that reality into concrete guidance for the military, thus ensuring that military thinking would always occur within the confines of Party ideology.

This functional approach to doctrine was also paralleled by a heated theoretical debate between Leon Trotsky and M. V. Frunze (a leading Soviet military figure until his death in 1925) on the necessity of a scientific body of military guidance, which in the 1920s came to be known as the debate on "a unified military doctrine."[29] After the narrow defeat of both Allied and indigenous enemies—and when it was clear that the communist millennium was not quite at hand—Trotsky and Frunze, commissar and soldier, led the debate on the ramifications and requirements of national defense.

Frunze argued that the Soviet military must be guided by scientific, overarching principles. This orthodox Marxist-Leninist orientation was complemented by Frunze's adherence to the Clausewitzian virtues of civil control he learned from a tsarist mentor in his early training. True to character, Trotsky made the more orthodox but less practical objection about the anathema of professional standing armies in a socialist state and denied that there could even be a Marxist science of war; for Trotsky, war was a trade, like welding or pottery, to be mastered like any other. Many factors aided Frunze (international tensions, the frightened sentiments of the revolutionary victors, and even Lenin's incapacitation) and his vision of an authoritative and unified doctrine eventually won out. This early Soviet theorizing provided conceptual authority to the adoption of formal "doctrine," a concept that was quickly enshrined as the summit of Soviet military thought.

If Frunze created the theoretical basis of doctrine, it was Stalin who

---

[28] See A. S. Bubnov, *Grazhdanskaia voina, partiia, i voennoe delo, sbornik stat'ei* (Moscow: Izdatel'stvo "Voennyi vestnik," 1928), p. 64.

[29] See M. V. Frunze, "O Edinoi Voennoi Doktrine," in M. Gareev, ed., *M. V. Frunze: Izbrannye proizvedeniia*, (Moscow: Voenizdat, 1984); P. A. Zhilin, *Problemy voennoi istorii* (Moscow: Voenizdat, 1975), pp. 141–153; Maj. Gen. M. Shushko and Lt. Col. V. Koslov [sic], "The Development of Marxist Leninist Teaching on War and the Army," *Voennaia Mysl'* 4 (1968), Library of Congress microform, Washington, D.C.; I. A. Korotkov, *Istoriia sovetskoi voennoi mysli* (Moscow: Nauka, 1980).

wedded theory to practice. Stalin took Frunze's reasoning to its logical end: if doctrine (like ideology) was the expression of the Party's wisdom, and the general secretary was the personification of the Party, then only the general secretary could properly enunciate doctrine. Early on, Stalin had cannily recognized the power and legitimacy to be gained through the control of doctrine (the fight over doctrine, after all, had helped to lead to Trotsky's downfall), and under Stalin military doctrine became the private preserve of the Party leadership. The original purpose of military doctrine was to create political parameters within which the professional military could serve the state; Stalin, however, subverted this goal and instead turned military doctrine into a tool of civil intervention in military matters. And while Stalin could have had his orders obeyed through sheer coercion, he chose in military affairs (as he had in other fields) to rationalize his dicta in the language of a preexistent concept that already had the glow of legitimacy about it.[30] Although Frunze provided the intellectual rationale behind a unified military doctrine, it was the Stalinist system that finally gave doctrine its practical muscle—albeit in ways its framers probably never intended.

Civil-Military Affairs under Khrushchev: Stalinism without Stalin

The alacrity with which the military approached the reform of defense policy after Stalin's passing indicated the scope of Stalin's control. However, there was more to the post-1953 reassessment of doctrine than a simple undoing of Stalin's mistakes. The unlacing of the Stalinist strait jacket came during a period of severe technological and political change in the international environment, one that presented the new Soviet leaders with a series of hard decisions for which Stalin had left them unprepared. In his memoirs, Nikita Khrushchev candidly spoke of the fear and uncertainty among the leadership that resulted from Stalin's jealous control of defense matters; not only were the new leaders untutored in conducting future military development, they were unsure even of the basic details and condition of their own forces at the time of Stalin's death. The military could provide little help, for they had been kept as much in the dark as

---

[30] This sort of rationalization was not, of course, unique to military affairs. One parallel that comes immediately to mind is Stalin's involvement in nationality issues; his writings, though often simplistic, were clothed in the language of a kind of Marxist anthropology—representing Stalin's acknowledged "expertise" in the field of national relations.

anybody else. New challenges required study, and both the Party and the military set out to consider questions long ignored.

Unresolved at this point was the appropriate balance of power between the Party and the military in the formation of national security policy. The future of a defense policy without Stalin's imprimatur was an important political question, since foreign and defense policies would no longer spring fully formed from Stalin's mind. The circle of policymaking in defense, as in all other spheres of Soviet politics, widened from one to several (including participation by the military), and the arrival of oligarchic consultation necessarily signified the departure of automatic unanimity.

The new leadership, however, saw a usefulness in the kind of control over the military Stalin had established, and Khrushchev acted quickly to try to forestall the erosion of the Stalinist pattern. Khrushchev's eventual attempt to seize military doctrine represented a willful attempt to return undiluted control of military affairs to the civilians, from whom it had been slipping from the moment of Stalin's death. Khrushchev needed to integrate military policy into the broader concerns of Soviet foreign and domestic policies (as is always the lot of the civilian leadership), as well as into his own political concerns, and these requirements made the Stalinist method of military control attractive to him.

Military disagreements with Khrushchev, voiced in both the open and the restricted Soviet press of the day, were significant as much for their content as for the fact that they represented the military's understanding that the death of Stalin had led to the opening of a political Pandora's box. Military participation in national security affairs was now legitimate and possible, and Khrushchev never succeeded in turning back the trend of military involvement in debate on the highest issues of foreign policy.

Brezhnev's Retreat

Leonid Brezhnev apparently did not disagree with military criticism of Khrushchev's intervention in security matters. Until at least 1977 the Brezhnev leadership retreated from defense policy, leaving the business of military planning to the soldiers, whose influence in foreign and security affairs consequently grew by default. For a time, it seemed (at least superficially) that the USSR was heading toward a more modern division of labor, with civilians making policy and military officers making plans. It is not clear that this was actually the case, however, and in any event the modus vivendi between the

[18]

Party and the military was short-circuited by the combination of re-source stringency and the unchecked growth of military influence on defense and foreign policy matters. Even as economic growth was sputtering to a halt, military arrogance and influence grew. [31]

Civil-military conflict might have been expected to arise during the war in Afghanistan, and it is reasonable to ask why the war against the *mujaheddin* is not covered in more detail here. Generally, I have left aside that war because it failed to generate serious civil-military contention.[32] There are three reasons for this lack of conflict. First, because the war was jointly approved by a small triumvirate of senior Party and military officials—thus obscuring the origin of the whole misbegotten adventure—there could be no recrimination from either side. Shared guilt meant shared silence, and once the original culprits in the Brezhnev leadership had passed on, all that was left was to honor the valiant dead and bring the whole escapade to closure.

Second, the military never came to see Afghanistan as a complete defeat. The civilian leaders joined in the charade and acceded to a kind of Soviet version of "peace with honor," glorifying the veterans while leaving aside the issue of victory or defeat. This fiction did much to turn General Boris Gromov's final walk across the bridge from Afghanistan from a forced retreat to a dignified exit; there would be no final, struggling helicopters drifting from the roof of the Soviet Embassy. Finally, there is no evidence to suggest that Afghanistan ever displaced Europe and the United States as the center of Soviet national security policy. Rather, the war seems to have occupied the status of a sideshow, engaging great energies but never forcing its way to the top of the larger agenda.

In the end, Brezhnev's reign was marked by a long civil-military truce not because the political questions of defense policymaking were resolved, but rather only because they had been avoided. The civil-military Cerberus, held at bay by being gorged on money, fell into a period of torpor. Once it was clear (probably as early as 1975) that resource stringency would force military cutbacks, these old animosities were roused from slumber. This time, however, the military

[31] One such example is found in the well-known story of the Soviet military SALT negotiators who would not discuss certain matters in front of their own civilian colleagues, for the very good reason that the civilians were not privy to information shared even with the Americans. John Newhouse, *War and Peace in the Nuclear Age* (New York: Knopf, 1989), p. 225.

[32] The failure of Afghanistan to emerge as a civil-military issue is covered thoroughly in Bruce Porter, "The Military Abroad," in Timothy Colton and Thane Gustafson, eds., *Soldiers and the Soviet State* (Princeton: Princeton University Press, 1990), from which this brief discussion is taken.

had the upper hand, for it had used Brezhnev's pliancy to take control of these issues. By 1982, there were few sources of alternatives to the military's views, and it seemed that even under conditions of financial duress the military professionals would succeed in managing Soviet defense policy as they saw best. Neither Iurii Andropov (who had the potential to challenge the military establishment) nor Konstantin Chernenko (who did not) lived long enough to put forward any sort of vision for the future of the Soviet Armed Forces and military doctrine, if they had one.

The Gorbachev Endgame

Mikhail Gorbachev obviously had such a vision, represented by his call for "New Political Thinking" in international affairs and the "new doctrine" unveiled in Berlin in 1987. But he lost precious time in the mid-1980s struggling with the legacy of Khrushchev's impulsiveness and Brezhnev's reticence. He had obviously learned from history: while his desire to reassert civilian control over security policy paralleled Khrushchev's efforts, he sought to avoid Khrushchev's mistakes. Rather than attempting to rule by fiat, he began his assault on the Soviet military with a rhetorical campaign designed to reintroduce and reinforce the notion of political dominance in both the theory and practice of security affairs. Gorbachev lost the battle but won the war, in that the military remained defiant, but it was largely Gorbachev's policies—some successful, some disastrous—that prevailed, not the military's. The struggle continues even today, as elements of the former Soviet military attempt to defend a position gained over the course of almost thirty years.

The Soviet military remains as one of the last vestiges of the Soviet (and, yes, Russian) multinational state, a disturbing situation when coupled with a senior officer corps that is thought by many to be, in John Erickson's words, "conservative in essence, hawklike and xenophobic in the extreme."[33] Other analysts believe that the military is in final eclipse, and that the current civil-military squabbles (and the trauma of the August coup) may actually only be the birth pangs of a genuinely modern military. According to this line of thought, the military leadership will eventually be tamed—even at the cost of large-scale dismemberment—as part of the general Soviet (or Russian) evolution toward a state based on the rule of law.

---

[33] John Erickson, "On the March for Tsar Mikhail," *London Sunday Times*, News Review, March 4, 1990.

[1]

Bureaucrats or Bonapartes?
Western Views of the Soviet Military

This was precisely what the United States and Canada thought:
the military governs policy here, not the other way around. But
if you believe that Khrushchev, Brezhnev, and Chernenko were
military, who, in that case, was a politician?
—Maj. Gen. G. Kirilenko to Georgii Arbatov, April 1990

INTRODUCTION

The study of Soviet civil-military relations, more than most other
areas in Soviet studies, still suffers from scholarly disagreement over
first principles. Were Soviet soldiers Party members in uniform, or was
the Party a group of militarized politicians? Is it even useful to speak
of "Party-Army" relations in a socialist polity led by an interlock-
ing elite? Observers of the Soviet scene often questioned even the use
of the term "civil-military" relations, arguing that the high command
was part and parcel of the leadership, and that therefore the relationship between the senior officer corps and the top politicians was no
more or less interesting than cleavages among the leadership generally. Indeed, some argue that differences among officers and appara-
tchiks are so narrow as to be among the least interesting divisions
within the Soviet elite. Others accept the idea of a civil-military division, but disagree over the source and depth of those divisions.[1]
Unfortunately, most of these assertions about the nature of Soviet
civil-military relations have remained a matter of religion rather than

[1] See, for example, the multiple treatments given the issue of civil-military politics in
Ted Karasik and William Green, eds., *Gorbachev and His Generals* (Boulder, Colo.: West-
view, 1990), and in Timothy Colton and Thane Gustafson, eds., *Soldiers and the Soviet
State* (Princeton: Princeton University Press, 1990).

[21]

research. There has been little work done on Soviet civil-military affairs since the 1970s, and most analyses treat the issue only in passing. What work there is on the subject revolves around the basic issue of control, phrased in terms of the likelihood of a coup d'état.

Many of these divisions among analysts of the Soviet case date back to debates from the 1950s about the nature of civil-military relations in general, and a brief review of that debate will help to frame the issue more clearly. It will also serve to define the vocabulary of civil-military politics that remains in use even now.

What Is Civil-Military "Theory?"

The study of civil-military relations is not guided by a single theory, but rather by a series of competing assumptions about the dynamics of the relationship between civilian leaders, the representatives of the governed, and soldiers, in whom the instruments of legitimate force are vested. Traditionally, it is assumed that there is an inherent tension between civilians and military professionals, and so civil-military theory as a subdiscipline has tended to concern itself almost exclusively with the potential for domestic violence, with the natural temptations to use the advantage provided by the control of weapons. Indeed, the study of civil-military relations has long been framed by S. E. Finer's famous reflection: "Instead of asking why the military engage in politics, we ought surely ask why they ever do otherwise."[2]

At first reading, Finer's comment may seem only a roundabout form of institutional or organizational analysis, in that it treats the military as just another group competing for power. But the civil-military relationship defies simple institutional theory. The military is not just another bureaucracy; after all, most bureaucrats do not carry automatic weapons. And despite the similarities in the values of military men, there are telling differences among militaries that make comparison difficult. The functioning, for example, of two parliamentary systems such as the Israeli Knesset and the Japanese Diet may seem quite comparable, but few would argue similar comparability between the Israeli and Japanese militaries. The result, as Timothy Colton pointed out in 1990, is that even today there is no accepted "global" theory of civil-military relations.[3]

[2] S. E. Finer, *The Man on Horseback: The Role of the Military in Politics* (New York: Praeger, 1962), p. 2.
[3] See Colton's introduction in Colton and Gustafson, *Soldiers and the Soviet State*, p. 6.

But while there is no strict "theory" of civil-military relations, in the sense that there is no mechanistic civil-military model, there are nonetheless groups of competing hypotheses about the nature of the interaction between soldiers and civilians. The civil-military perspective, if not a strict theory, usefully broadens the focus of analysis to allow consideration not only of specific institutional problems, but also of the larger interaction between the competition for domestic power and the struggle for international security. In short, the study of civil-military affairs provides one of the elusive links between the fields of international relations and comparative politics, because it is in the civil-military arena that the problems of domestic politics and foreign policy collide most directly.

Huntington and the Professional Soldier

Samuel Huntington's 1957 *The Soldier and the State* continues to define the basic vocabulary of civil-military analysis. Huntington was particularly fascinated by the experiences of the major belligerents in World War II, where military organizations obeyed civilian directives even in cases where officers thought those directives to be dangerous or even disastrous. A basic typology of modes of control emerged from his analysis, defined by the means and degree of coercion needed to assure military loyalty. Huntington's essential distinction was between "objective" and "subjective" control, with each type of control a function of the level of military professionalism. According to Huntington, a truly "professional" soldier recognizes, like any other professional, the necessity of the social division of labor. He sees himself as a specialist, distinct from other specialists in other fields, particularly from the specialists in politics. Indeed, Huntington's professional soldier not only accepts political supremacy, but actually *desires* it, for it is part of the natural diversification of duties, an expression of the right order of society. Where soldiers are highly "professionalized," control is "objective"; it is self-maintaining, with the boundaries between soldiers and statesmen respected by both sides. Maximize the military's autonomy over specifically military issues (what Huntington calls "militarizing the military"), and the military will continue to see itself as a tool of policy rather than as a source of policy.[4]

The antithesis of objective control, "subjective" control, defines a

[4] Samuel P. Huntington, *The Soldier and the State* (Cambridge: Harvard University Press, 1957), pp. 83–84.

[23]

situation in which military power is checked by civilian power, a situation Huntington believes more accurately describes the majority of the world's civil-military systems. Military participation in politics in such a system is taken as a given, but circumscribed by the greater political power of the various civilian groups, gained through means ranging from class politics to institutional arrangements. Huntington suggests, in a passage especially but unintentionally relevant in the Soviet case, that this undesirable outcome is not usually the result of military officers seeking greater political power, but rather due to civilians trying to "maximize their power in military affairs."[5] A subjective system of control is closer to an interest-group view of the military, in that it treats the officer corps as participants in the political game. In Huntington's view, objective control is the normative goal, subjective control the empirical reality.

Of the three major schools of thought about civil-military relations in the USSR, two describe a system of subjective control while one—the dominant paradigm in the West today—depicts the Soviet situation as one of objective control.

WESTERN VIEWS OF SOVIET CIVIL-MILITARY RELATIONS

The study of civil-military relations in the Soviet Union suffered from a "decade of neglect" in the late 1970s and early 1980s. Although the works of pioneers such as Samuel Huntington and Morris Janowitz were initially concerned with the United States and Germany, civil-military theory eventually, and naturally, became focused on the continual instability and military interventions in the new nations of the Third World. Studies of civil-military affairs, therefore, overwhelmingly have been concerned with that region, and much of the literature is inapplicable to the developed world.[6]

This regional focus had an unfortunate intellectual side effect. Because the areas studied were highly coup-prone, civil-military theory reflected the agenda of the day; it became narrowly concerned with only the largest question of military involvement in politics, as research pursued the question of why and how civilian leadership falls to military dominance. This served to compound the lack of scholarly interest in the USSR, due to the prevalent belief in the West that the

[5] Ibid., p. 84.

[6] For a useful comparative synthesis of the various schools of thought of the 1950s and 1960s, see A. R. Luckham, "A Comparative Typology of Civil-Military Relations," *Government and Opposition* (Winter 1971).

Brezhnev era represented something of a "golden age" in Soviet civil-military relations, and that therefore the issue in any case had been rendered moot.[7] Still, there have been some efforts since the late 1960s to consider the nature of civil control in the Soviet Union, and those studies have defined the parameters of debate into the 1990s. Three authors in particular represent the dominant strains of Western thought about Soviet civil-military relations.

Kolkowicz and the Conflict Model

Roman Kolkowicz presented the conflict-centered model of Soviet civil-military relations in his 1967 work *The Soviet Military and the Communist Party.* At the center of Kolkowicz's analysis is the idea of inevitable conflict between the Soviet military and their civilian masters, expressed as a conflict between Party control and military professionalism. The result of this tension, according to Kolkowicz, is that the history of party-military relations in the USSR is "a study in distrust and occasional conflict rooted in a certain incompatibility between the hegemonial holder of power in the state and one of its main instruments of power."[8]

Kolkowicz argues that "many of the Soviet military's characteristics are those of all large professional establishments, regardless of their political-social environment."[9] In this version of the civil-military struggle, the pragmatic military constantly chafes under the control of the ideological party, and Kolkowicz describes the tension between the Party and the military as a function of clashing traits, some "natural" to the Soviet (or any other) military, others desired by the Party and a function of the Party's ideology.[10] Where the military values elitism, the Party desires egalitarianism; where the military is nationalistic, the Party is internationalist, and so on. Kolkowicz claims

---

[7] Jeremy Azrael uses the expression "golden age" in referring to the late 1960s and early 1970s, and Timothy Colton rightly claims that there is near unanimity among Western analysts on this view of the Brezhnev era. See Colton's introduction in Colton and Gustafson, *Soldiers and The Soviet State,* and Jeremy Azrael, "The Soviet Civilian Leadership and the Military High Command, 1976–1986," RAND R-3251-AF, June 1987, p. 2.

[8] Roman Kolkowicz, "Toward a Theory of Civil-Military Relations in Communist (Hegemonial) Systems," in Roman Kolkowicz and Andrzej Korbonski, eds., *Soldiers, Peasants and Bureaucrats: Civil-Military Relations in Communist and Modernizing Societies* (London: Allen and Unwin, 1982), p. 233.

[9] Roman Kolkowicz, *The Soviet Military and the Communist Party* (Princeton: Princeton University Press, 1967), p. 21.

[10] Ibid., p. 21.

[25]

that the "military" traits are indeed natural, a fact proven by their tendency "to emerge whenever the Soviet military has been in a position which permitted it some freedom from the coercive controls of the Party."[11]

Kolkowicz sees Soviet civil-military friction, therefore, as an inevitable product of the basic structure of Soviet political life. Kolkowicz elaborated on three of his basic assumptions in 1978:

> (1) That the political leaders, the basic political values [of Soviet life] and the ideology are inherently antimilitary, i.e., there is a profound distrust of the professional military men who possess the weapons and technology of war, the "experts in violence"; (2) that the political norms of the Soviet system reject any particularistic interests—whether institutional, functional, ethnic, or other—if such interests are articulated outside the norms and practices of the Party; (3) that this rigid insistence on Party hegemony and suppression of expression of group interests has been undergoing a progressive transformation brought about by several forces of change.[12]

For Kolkowicz, then, only successful Party control ensured that the Soviet military remained ineffective challengers to civilian rule, and these Party controls (specifically, the Main Political Administration) were themselves both the source of tension and the guarantor of obedience.

Kolkowicz's *Soviet Military and the Communist Party* was the first and most extensive articulation of Soviet civil-military relations as a system of subjective control. Huntington's influence is clear, particularly in Kolkowicz's assertion that political power kept the Soviet military "compliant," lacking any kind of useful national "constituency" through which it could affect Soviet politics.[13] Published in the wake of Khrushchev's stormy tenure, his book offered a model that seemed to make sense in the context of recent events.

Over time, however, Kolkowicz's depiction of the Soviet military on the edge of insubordination came under fire; the more time that passed without gross military intrusion into Soviet politics, the less accurate the conflict model seemed to be. Despite its intuitive appeal,

---

[11] Ibid., pp. 21–22. Much of Kolkowicz's view is based on Huntington's early theories of civil-military affairs. See Huntington, *The Soldier and the State*, esp. pp. 7–97.

[12] Roman Kolkowicz, "Interest Groups in Soviet Politics: The Military," in Dale Herspring and Ivan Volgyes, eds., *Civil-Military Relations in Communist Systems* (Boulder, Colo.: Westview, 1978), p. 10.

[13] See Kolkowicz, "Toward a Theory," p. 233, and "Interest Groups" p. 24.

Kolkowicz himself admitted the doubts raised by lack of any serious challenges to Party rule by the military.[14] The continued quiescence of the senior officer corps suggested to some that the compliance of the Soviet armed forces rested on grounds other than sheer political dominance.

Colton and the Participatory Model

It was precisely this compliant attitude that Timothy Colton set out to explain in his seminal 1979 work, *Commissars, Commanders and Civilian Authority*. Colton's challenge to the conflict model also reflected the times, particularly the continued apparent amity of the Soviet civil-military relationship under Brezhnev. Colton proceeded from the observation that, whatever else might be said about it, the Party's relationship with the Soviet military had been remarkably stable. This stability led Colton to rephrase the agenda of research on the civil-military relationship: he argued that the Soviet "military continues to possess major unexpended political capabilities," and but then admitted that this "gives rise to a further question: why have Soviet officers not exercised these capabilities?[15]

Colton answers this question by reorienting it to ask why it should be assumed that coercive control is always the ultimate question. Why not look at the dimensions of military participation in politics, rather than the potential for military takeover of the political process? "The concept of participation," he writes, "predisposes us to make more useful assumptions about military politics, and thus to ask more useful questions, than does the concept of civilian control."[16]

In seeking to broaden the conceptualization of "Soviet civil-military relations," Colton presents overt military intervention or takeover as both an unreasonable expectation and an unlikely event. As he put it in 1987, "When all is said and done," the Soviet military and the CPSU "have gotten along quite well over the years."[17] Colton suggests that there is a far greater congruence of interests between civilian and military leaders than previously believed, and that the rela-

[14] In 1982, Kolkowicz responded to Colton's observations in Kolkowicz's "Military Intervention in the Soviet Union: Scenario for Post-Hegemonial Synthesis," in Kolkowicz and Korbonski, *Soldiers, Peasants and Bureaucrats*, p. 128.

[15] Timothy Colton, *Commissars, Commanders and Civilian Authority: The Structure of Soviet Military Politics* (Cambridge: Harvard Univ. Press, 1979), pp. 231–232.

[16] Ibid., p. 232.

[17] Timothy Colton, "Civil-Military Relations in the mid-1980s," in Alexander Dallin and Condoleeza Rice, eds., *The Gorbachev Era* (Stanford, Calif.: Stanford Alumni Assoc., 1987), p. 109.

[27]

tionship may even be one of outright cooperation. "Clearly, both army and party have benefited from the relationship. The party, on the one hand, has been spared the challenges from an aroused officer corps that have beset civilian regimes in so many other political systems, particularly in modernizing societies." On the other hand, the army's "ideological, material, status, and professional interests [are] maintained and enhanced by party policy."[18] In other words, Colton believes that there are grounds for civil-military tension in the USSR, but such tensions are averted because the regime satisfies basic military demands.

Despite apparent differences between the two, Colton, like Kolkowicz, describes a system of subjective control. Although generally supportive of the leadership, Colton's military still needs to be held in check through satisfaction of its priorities. And although it was more subtle than Kolkowicz's dire account, *Commissars, Commanders and Civilian Authority* still presented a civil-military relationship dominated by a military that did not accept the inherent rectitude of political obedience, a recognition that is the hallmark of Huntington's "professional" officer.

Odom and the Symbiotic Model

The third party to this debate, Lt. Gen. William Odom, has attacked both Kolkowicz and Colton precisely on the grounds that they depict a military under only tenuous control, and he counters with a defense of the bureaucratic view of the Soviet military predominant in American policymaking and academic circles today. Odom bluntly rejects the idea that there are substantive institutional conflicts between Soviet civil-military elites, arguing that the Soviet military should not even be considered as an "interest group," however pliant or cooperative it may be. To Odom, the military is merely one of many executors of the Party's will. Odom maintains that the Soviet military does not have "interests" of its own, an assertion that is part of his broader attack on the concept of interest group analyses of Soviet politics.[19] In the end, Odom sees little difference between Kolkowicz and Colton; he argues that Colton shares Kolkowicz's basic paradigm, whatever the disagreements between them.[20]

---

[18] Colton, *Commissars*, pp. 279–280.

[19] For Odom's general critique of the interest group approach, see "A Dissenting View on the Group Approach to Soviet Politics," *World Politics* 28, no. 4 (July 1976).

[20] William Odom, "The Party-Military Connection: A Critique," in Herspring and Volgyes, *Civil-Military Relations*, p. 47.

Odom criticizes two of Kolkowicz's key assumptions. The first is the idea that professional soldiers develop a sense of identity, purpose, and professional competency that necessarily leads them to view Party involvement as adversarial. This critique amounts to an attack on Huntington's view of professionalism; Odom takes that attack further, questioning the Huntingtonian idea that military autonomy is somehow essential to an efficient defense organization, that "professional autonomy is the *sine qua non* of military efficiency, and both are inversely related to political control."[21]

More specifically, Odom sets out to dismantle the dichotomy between Kolkowicz's "Party" and "military" values. He dismisses, for example, the idea that the military is somehow "nationalistic," in a way that the leadership is not:

> Perhaps Kolkowicz merely means that military officers have more deeply visceral feelings of national patriotism than party leaders. But if this is his point, can he be sure that a young technician in the Soviet rocket forces reacts any more viscerally to the call of patriotism than an older, less educated party *apparatchik*? A much more compelling argument would be that the privileged military elite and the party elite both have an equal stake in the Soviet state and the present political order.[22]

Nor does Odom believe that Colton has somehow avoided accepting this schism. Colton's "participation" is to Odom simply the obverse of Kolkowicz's "control"; both are predicated on a belief in potential conflict. Odom even suggests that Colton's explanation—that the military somehow got what it wanted, otherwise it would have intervened in politics more strongly—is "a tautology built on Kolkowicz's categories and assumptions."[23] To be fair, Odom is right to criticize as tautological Colton's argument that a lack of military intervention implies military satisfaction, yet Odom himself does no better by arguing that the same lack proves the complete absence of conflict. Each is a case of post hoc ergo propter hoc, and it is unclear why Odom believes that the missileer and the apparatchik cannot both have a stake in the system but still oppose each other.

[21] Indeed, Odom claims that Huntington's concept of professionalism, vague and difficult to operationalize, is analogous to "phlogiston," the mythical substance once thought to be responsible for fire. William Odom, "The Party Connection," *Problems of Communism* (September-October 1973), p. 13.

[22] As Odom also points out, Kolkowicz's assumption is also made questionable by anecdotes such as Anwar Sadat's observation that Brezhnev enjoyed retelling his wartime experiences. Ibid., p. 15 and n.

[23] Odom, "The Party-Military Connection," p. 47.

In place of a model of institutional conflict in Soviet civil-military affairs, Odom presents the Soviet military as an obedient bureaucracy. He finds it difficult to accept traditional notions of cohesion among the Soviet (or any other) military, a surprising attitude considering that Odom himself is a career military officer. Odom instead describes a "military-bureaucratic ethos" under which the Soviet military functions as "a large public bureaucracy, a hierarchical organization that operates in peacetime not altogether differently from other public agencies."[24]

Odom is careful to note that this bureaucratic approach is not the same as an interest-group approach: "Personal cliques and coalitions of cliques take shape in bureaucracies, but they differ generically from interest groups. They cannot formalize themselves and thereby institutionalize the pursuit of an interest. . . . What remains more or less constant—the key factor in social cohesion and the source of roles and norms—is the bureaucratic structure in both its formal and informal aspects."[25] In the end, this leaves the Soviet military elite free only to act as "executants," unable to "frame the issues," and capable only of responding to "the way issues are framed above them." Thus, the Soviet system "is dominated by military policymaking but not by marshals."[26]

Odom, then, distinguishes himself from Kolkowicz and Colton by arguing that the Soviet system is one of objective control. Odom, it should be noted, does not choose to phrase his conclusions in this way and has even attacked Colton's reliance on Huntington's terms. He rejects such terms as "professionalism" or military "interest" as "rubbery" and difficult to operationalize, at one point even asking Colton what he means by them.[27] Yet, Odom's explanation of the Soviet civil-military relationship seems directly derived from Huntington's terminology (which in turn owes a clear debt to Max Weber):

[24] Ibid., pp. 36 and 45–48. Odom bases much of this argument on the idea of continuity in the Soviet and Russian militaries. Although he discusses the tradition of the Guards in Imperial times, he notes that they never usurped power for themselves. Furthermore, the crushing of the Decembrists and the ensuing, often militarily eviscerating reforms that followed it, ensured that the military remained politically docile. "During the last century of the Empire," he notes, "the military elite played no role in Imperial succession," a break with the earlier tradition of the Guards (p. 36). William Fuller, however, has tackled the problem of military professionalism in the Imperial military, and he reaches quite different conclusions about the importance of the tsar's army. See William C. Fuller, *Civil-Military Conflict in Imperial Russia 1881–1914* (Princeton: Princeton University Press, 1985), esp. pp. 3–7 and 46.

[25] Odom, "The Party-Military Connection," p. 44.

[26] Ibid., pp. 44–45.

[27] Ibid., p. 47.

the Soviet marshals are not would-be Bonapartes, but rather good executives who know their place in the bureaucracy. Moreover, they understand that the Party is the guarantor of their interests: The Party "is not paying off the military corporate interests to get the marshals to behave; rather, it is emphasizing military power to cope with political realities."[28] Huntington said much the same thing when he wrote in *The Soldier and the State* that "objective civilian control not only reduces the power of the military to the lowest possible level vis-à-vis all civilian groups, it also maximizes the likelihood of achieving military security."[29]

Neither the passage of time nor recent events in the USSR have dissuaded Odom from his position. "Western observers," he wrote in late 1990, "have repeatedly anticipated conflicts and fissures in party-military relations, and they have tried to see them where they do not exist."[30]

SUBJECTIVE CONTROL AND THE SOVIET MILITARY

Although the Kolkowicz-Colton-Odom debate provides the raw material for thinking about the structure of Soviet civil-material politics, all three share a problem of focus. At the center of their discussion is the question of why the military has not intervened in Soviet politics, and this has obscured the valuable descriptions of less dramatic civil-military interaction. Must the evidence confirm a potential military takeover, or does the absence of outright manipulation then mean that the Soviet military is merely a "public bureaucracy?" In practice, this means that the objective-subjective distinction is crucial: if the Soviet civil-military system was one of subjective control, then the politics of defense in the USSR must be viewed as a conflictual process in which the Party enjoyed nowhere near the legitimacy it once claimed, even without evidence of a coup. By contrast, objective control would mean that civil-military conflict was merely part of the normal bureaucratic give and take that inevitably surrounds complicated policymaking structures, reflecting success on the part of the Party in creating an objective loyalty to its vision of governance.

Odom's view of the obedient bureaucracy, an understandable product of the times, has not been borne out in the 1980s. In 1978, he

[28] Ibid., p. 48.
[29] Huntington, *The Soldier and the State*, p. 85.
[30] William Odom, "Smashing an Icon: The Soviet Military Today," *National Interest* (Fall 1990), p. 63.

wrote that "the marshals cannot afford the luxury of corporate military interests; they are in the same political boat with the CPSU."[31] In 1991, Mikhail Gorbachev apparently decided to jump that ship, and this alone would force a rethinking of Odom's assertions.

Odom's criticisms notwithstanding, I argue that the Soviet military was not simply a typical bureaucracy, and that the Soviet civil-military relationship was one of subjective, rather than objective, control. The Soviet military was kept in check by political mechanisms, despite Odom's generally correct observation that the military and the Party had many shared interests. The consistent pattern of civil intrusions in military affairs, from the mayhem of Stalin to the political struggles of Gorbachev, however, nonetheless created an environment of mistrust and competition between Party and Army that undermined the growth of attitudes conducive to objective control.

But if Odom is mistaken about the sources of Soviet military obedience, Kolkowicz is inaccurate in his evaluation of the sources of Soviet military dissent. Kolkowicz's depiction of civil-military tension is correct but for the wrong reason: it is not a Marxist party versus a pragmatic military, but rather, as will be seen in following chapters, a Marxist military opposing a pragmatic Party. In their efforts to ensure the reliability of the military, the leaders of the CPSU created a core of true believers, a cadre of officers whose very raison d'être was irrevocably tied to ideological rationales which were eventually no longer accepted by anyone except the most ossified Party ideologists. This was a dilemma of the Party's own making, of course, for it was the Party that insisted that professional military men could serve the State best by embracing Marxism-Leninism. Unfortunately, the Party did not consider the ramifications of a situation in which the military remained committed to Marxism while the Party did not, or in which the Party ceased to rule the USSR. The foundations of this adherence to ideology were laid in the theoretical debates of the 1920s, whereas the pattern of civil interference—itself the very definition of subjective control—was the result of the political traumas of the 1930s that shaped both the Soviet military and Soviet military thought. These early years are the subject of the next chapter.

[31] Odom, "The Party-Military Connection," p. 48.

[2]

Setting the Stage:
Stalin and the Military

To conduct a whole War, or its great acts, which we call campaigns, there must be an intimate knowledge of State policy in its higher relations. The conduct of the War and the policy of the State here coincide, and the General becomes at the same time the Statesman.

—Clausewitz, *On War*

"And Stalin?" I asked.
Taking care not to show surprise at the question, Konev replied, after a little thought: "Stalin is universally gifted. He was brilliantly able to see the war as a whole, and this makes possible his successful direction."

—conversation between Milovan Djilas
and Marshal Konev, 1944

THE TOTALITARIAN PATTERN

Stalin established the pattern of civil-military control that haunted the remainder of the Soviet era. By establishing himself as the nation's supreme ideologist, chief military officer, and the ultimate source of military thought, the dictator laid the foundations of an enduring system of subjective control, thereby forcing later Soviet leaders (and especially Gorbachev) to wrestle with the legacy in military affairs of a Stalinist system without Stalin. Stalin's actions represented a gross intrusion of civil authority into military affairs; like all other branches of society in the totalitarian system, the military felt the continual presence of the leader in all aspects of their activity.

In the social and political arena, Stalin's intrusions represented the "omnipresence of the center", a hallmark of the totalitarian system.[1] In the military arena, however, Stalin's actions represented the maximizing of the military authority of the civilians while destroying the political power of military; in other words, Stalin's military policy was the purposeful creation of a system of subjective control.

Stalin's successors have approached this inheritance with mixed intentions, seeking to exert similar control while at the same time attempting to dismantle many of the instruments of the totalitarian system that facilitated such effective civil intervention in military affairs. Thus, Stalin's legacy was to force later Party leaders either to retain the mechanisms of the totalitarian system, or to endure a situation in which civil-military conflict was inevitable. His successors tried to maintain a middle way, resisting the de-Stalinization of military politics while still attempting to involve the military in the formation of policy. (Although Khrushchev's later involvements in military matters came to be known both at home and abroad as unacceptable "meddling," his actions were in keeping with the tradition of civil intervention in military affairs established by his own predecessor.) In the end, no Soviet leader ever achieved the goal of complete military control as they saw it in the past under Stalin, or as they saw it in the present in the democracies.

STALINISM AND MILITARY DOCTRINE

To understand the Stalinist method of control of the military, it is necessary to understand the development of the concept of Soviet military doctrine. The creation of a military doctrine as something with autonomous authority and great political potential was intimately bound to Stalin's relationship with the Soviet military leadership. In the 1920s, the Trotsky-Frunze debate provided a theoretical rationale for an authoritative doctrine; in the 1930s, Stalin sought to appropriate that doctrine and thus corner his opponents among the military intelligentsia. As Stalin's powers grew, the process came full circle, from a coherent debate on military doctrine conducted by knowledgeable experts, to a "doctrine" that had little clear definition except to reflect Stalin's complete control of military and national security matters. Power over the soldiers had been consolidated by a civilian pretender among the ranks, as the Statesman sought to become the General.

[1] See Seweryn Bialer, *Stalin's Successors* (Boulder, Colo.: Westview, 1980).

The Implications of Doctrine

Despite renewed interest in Soviet military doctrine in the 1980s, the concept in general remains misunderstood in the West, in part because the very idea of a formal "military doctrine" sounds foreign to American and European ears. Defense policy in the Western democracies is a conglomeration of concepts: some are operationalized, others are followed haphazardly, and some serve merely rhetorical purposes. Even in the nineteenth century, "classical" military doctrine denoted a range of primarily wartime issues, such as strategy, tactics, and logistics. Since World War I, neither the United States nor the European states can claim that their security planning has been based on consistent, scientific guidelines designed to provide continuity in a critical area of national policy in both war and peace—in other words, that they possess a coherent and promulgated military doctrine.

The Soviet Union was unique among the small fraternity of great military powers in this professed adherence to a formalized, binding military doctrine. In the Soviet usage of the term, "military doctrine" is more than a mere compilation of methods and norms of the art of war. It is, in Soviet words, "a system of views adopted by a state at a given time on the essence, goals and character of a possible future war, on the preparation of the nation and of the armed forces for it, and on the means of its conduct."[2] Doctrine is divided into two parts, the political-social and the military-technical: the former is concerned with the rationale of war, the latter considers the means of war. In theory, Soviet military doctrine is all-encompassing, describing both abstract beliefs and concrete plans. Officially, it drives strategy, operational art and tactics, as well as procurement, training, and almost anything else connected with the military defense of the Soviet Union.[3] Questions answered by doctrine include the moral character of war, its causes and probable antagonists, as well as more detailed issues, such as the duration of the conflict, the weapons to be used, the theaters of combat, and so on. When Soviet civilian or military leaders speak on these questions, whatever their ostensible subject or other context, they are also speaking about military doctrine.

The concept itself dates from the earliest days of the Revolution. By

[2] S. F. Akhromeev et al., eds., *Voenno-Entsiklopedicheskii Slovar'* (Moscow: Voenizdat, 1986), p. 240.

[3] *Strategy* denotes the overall military direction of the war; *operational art* (a term for which there is no Western equivalent) is the use of military assets on a large scale—such as the blitzkrieg—to achieve the ends of strategy. *Tactics*, as in the Western sense, are the conduct of immediate, small-scale battle.

1920, the Soviets had fought off White counterrevolutionaries, skirmished with foreign interventionists, and had a close scrape with the Poles, and the new Bolshevik regime quickly recognized the necessity to consider the nature of its future army. In the 1920s, debate began on the future of the Soviet Armed Forces and a possible military doctrine. The outcome of this debate, primarily a clash between Civil War hero and Red Army commander Mikhail V. Frunze and War Commissar Trotsky, created the framework of modern Soviet military doctrine. The importance of this debate lies not in the policies that it established at the time; it is of little interest today how various tactical issues were solved. Rather, the significance is that the debate created a concept that then served to place all security-related questions in a highly structured and politically charged framework.

The establishment of a "military doctrine" as the source of defense planning in the USSR had three results. First, from the 1930s on, it was Soviet canon that military planning was a result of the Party's scientific interpretation of reality. Military officers were not free to evaluate international developments outside of the parameters of official doctrine, usually expressed in the foreign policy pronouncements of the general secretary or in the relevant sections of the Party Program. This claim to exclusivity was perhaps too much to ask—what military leader doesn't think about foreign policy?—and in practice, of course, Soviet officers did consider such questions. Thus the declaration that military doctrine, particularly in its foreign policy aspects, was a Party prerogative set up a situation in which military officers were almost forced into continual heresy, and it was this overly structured approach to doctrine that created a small but pervasive habit of disobedient thinking among the Soviet military. The structure of doctrine itself meant that the high command was continually contravening the most basic tenet of civil control, and it is little wonder that the Party's prerogative in this area quickly eroded after Stalin's death.

Second, the development of so structured a doctrine meant that resources rested on ideas. Doctrine was explicitly designed to drive all aspects of defense policy, from arms control to military strategy to expenditures. Control of doctrine meant control of men and materiel: control of doctrine meant power. Thus a concept designed to enforce harmony in Soviet politics itself became a resource for power in the Soviet system.

Finally, the existence of doctrine meant that national security debate in the USSR would be phrased in highly charged ideological terms. If defense policy was the result of the Party's Marxist-Leninist evaluation of the international situation, how could one then oppose or support it on grounds any less grandiose? If a certain weapons system or arms-negotiating position was described as an extension of military doctrine, as in theory all such matters were, then it was hardly a convincing rejoinder to argue the issue on grounds of cost, even if that might have been the real issue at hand. In other words, the creation of a formal military doctrine provided a rhetorical high ground to be seized in debating national security policy. To begin an argument with "military doctrine requires that . . ." was another way of saying that the position to be defended was unassailably scientific; moreover, it implied the weight of the wisdom of the Party, and that to challenge the issue was to challenge the Party itself.

Needless to say, this outcome was not the intention of the framers of Soviet military doctrine. In theory, military doctrine might well have served to "militarize the military," in the Huntingtonian sense, and to reinforce the rational division of labor between soldiers and commissars. As will be seen, this was subverted first by Stalin, and later by Khrushchev and even Gorbachev.

Prologue: Trotsky, Frunze, and a "Unified Doctrine"

Several defense-related questions were included in the more general theoretical debates of the 1920s. In 1921, Frunze and fellow Red Army hero S. I. Gusev submitted twenty-two theses to the Tenth Party Congress on military matters; Frunze's contributions were numbers seventeen to twenty-two.[4] These last, and most substantive, six propositions called for providing the Red Army with a unified military doctrine and a broadening of the General Staff into the "military-theoretical staff of the proletarian state."[5] The Congress, of course, was concerned with more pressing matters, particularly the uprising in Kronstadt, Lenin's call to ban factions within the Party, and the move to end the worst elements of War Communism. Besides, the theses calling for a unified doctrine were rather unclear, and in the end the Gusev-Frunze document was rejected.

That did not end the debate on a unified doctrine, however. In June 1921, Frunze laid out the theory behind a unified doctrine in a watershed article in *Armiia i Revoliutsiia*. The importance of Frunze's article does not lie in detailed suggestions; he made few, admitting that the

---

[4] For the life of Gusev, see V. Erashov, *Kak molniia v nochi* (Moscow: Politizdat, 1988).
[5] M. Gareev, ed., *M. V. Frunze: Izbrannye proizvedeniia* (Moscow: Voenizdat, 1984), pp. 29–30.

"crystallization" of actual military doctrine is something that would require "further practical and theoretical work."[6] Rather, the article is crucial because it makes the case for the very existence of something called "military doctrine," on both empirical and normative grounds.

Using the examples of England, Germany, and France, Frunze made the orthodox Marxist argument that the methods by which states wage war is an expression of their class situation.[7] The Soviet Union could be no different, and Frunze claimed that a proletarian state can and should create a distinct "military doctrine," namely, "a teaching accepted in the army of a given state which establishes the character of the building of the armed forces of the nation, the methods of combat preparation of the troops and their leadership on the basis of the views of those ruling in the state on the character of the military problems facing them, and means of their solution, which arise from the class essence of the state and [are] determined by the development of the forces of production of the nation."[8] Frunze went on to assert that a nascent "military doctrine" already existed in the USSR and should be developed as a form of military guidance. In a proletarian state, he said, military doctrine is founded upon the guidance of Marxism-Leninism, and therefore the responsibility for formulating military doctrine rests with the Party. Indeed, Frunze even went so far as to assert that the "concrete social-political content of this part of our future doctrine has been given to us as a whole, ready-made, in the ideology of the working class—in the Program of the [Party]."[9]

This last assertion about Party dominance is important. The theoretical point has roots in both Marx and Karl von Clausewitz, two teachers well known to Frunze.[10] From a Marxist perspective, the Party must be the final source of military doctrine: if doctrine is an expression of class interests, and the Party is the vanguard of the proletariat, then only the Party can properly express the proletariat's class interest in military doctrine. From a Clausewitzian perspective, Party dominance of military doctrine corresponds to Clausewitz's belief that the military is a tool of the state, used by political leaders for political ends.

---

[6] Ibid., p. 35.
[7] Ibid., pp. 35–41.
[8] Ibid., pp. 34–35.
[9] Ibid., p. 44.

[10] Frunze learned much of his military theory from a senior tsarist officer, which influenced much of his thinking on civilian dominance of the military instrument. I am indebted to William Fuller for these insights into Frunze's early training.

Trotsky responded quickly, for it was evident that Frunze's attack was aimed at him as the figure instrumental in defeating the Frunze-Gusev theses at the Tenth Party Congress.[11] Trotsky countered by rejecting the idea that there was a distinct proletarian form of war, any more than there was a distinct proletarian form of pottery or any other trade. For Trotsky, war was a skill to be learned, and there was nothing compelling about the idea of a "military doctrine" in Soviet Russia or anywhere else. As he put it, "There is for us but one single 'doctrine': *be on guard and keep both eyes peeled!*"[12]

This dispute implied political consequences for its protagonists, and it carried over to the Eleventh Party Congress in March 1922. In his concluding statement to the military delegates at the Congress, Trotsky deconstructed Frunze's suggestions one by one with characteristic wit and incisiveness. Concerning Frunze's thesis, for example, that the Red Army in future revolutionary wars would attack or defend alongside the proletariat of other nations, Trotsky said: "Well, now, how do you tell a Saratov peasant: either we shall send you to Belgium to overthrow the bourgeoisie or you will defend the Saratov province from an Anglo-French landing in Odessa or Arkhangel'sk?"[13] Likewise, he lampooned Frunze's belief that the offensive was always superior to defense, an argument that Frunze had foolishly supported by citing foreign regulations. Trotsky actually got laughs from the delegates when he parodied Frunze: "You see— strategy must be offensive, because, in the first place, it flows from the class nature of the proletariat and, in the second place, because this coincides with the French Field Service regulations of 1921." (Among those not amused was a Stalin crony and future defense minister, Kliment Voroshilov, who sulked "There's nothing funny here.")[14]

By the end of the Eleventh Congress, Trotsky had rhetorically eviscerated most of Frunze's theses on military policy.[15] Although the

[11] Trotsky's original article, "Military Doctrine or Pseudo-military Doctrinairism?" appeared in the November-December 1921 issue of *Voennaia nauka i revoliutsiia*, and is reprinted in L. Trotsky, *Kak vooruzhalas' revoliutsiia* (Moscow: Vysshii voennyi redaktsionnyi sovet, 1925).

[12] Trotsky, "Voennaia doktrina ili mnimo-voennoe doktrinerstvo?" in *Kak vooruzhalas' revoliutsiia*, bk. 5, p. 218, Trotsky's emphasis.

[13] Ibid., p. 248.

[14] Ibid., p. 254.

[15] In 1928, for example, A. S. Bubnov did not even refer to the Frunze-Gusev theses in his review of military developments at party congresses after the Civil War. Bubnov, *Grazhdanskaia voina, partiia i voennoe delo, Sbornik stat'ei* (Moscow: Izdatel'stvo "Voennyi vestnik," 1928), p. 67.

issue never came to an actual vote, time proved Frunze the victor, for several reasons. For one, Frunze forced a retreat by Trotsky on the idea of a "military doctrine" by arguing that the concept could be derived from Engels. Frunze's resort to Engels is significant, for it cornered Trotsky into defending the "classical" military thinking of the tsarist military officers still present in—and viewed with suspicion by—the new Red Army. Further weakening Trotsky's arguments was his shortsighted treatment of the debate as somehow trivial. Not only did Trotsky's rebuke to Frunze seem arrogant, but Trotsky himself offered little in the way of an alternative. Whatever the merits of Trotsky's position (and there were many), his often flip and patronizing attitude failed to win him supporters. One of Frunze's biographers put it succinctly: "Trotsky missed the fact that the Military Communists understood so well. This was a battle to the death."[16] In his failure to comprehend the deadly seriousness of this debate, and by his condescension to his opponents, Trotsky ensured his long-term loss to Frunze, despite short-term rhetorical gains at the Eleventh Congress.

Finally, Frunze's position gained strength through Lenin's growing weakness, despite Lenin's acknowledged opposition. Frunze admitted in 1925 (in a recollection long since deleted from all later versions of Frunze's works) that Lenin had disagreed with him even before the debate with Trotsky. Lenin told Frunze:

> You [military Communists] are not correct here. Your approach is of course correct from the point of view of perspective. . . . Perhaps you can study and advance a new force, but if you come forth now with a theory of proletarian art, you fall into the danger of communist swaggering. It seems to me that our military Communists are still insufficiently mature to pretend to the leadership of all military affairs.[17]

Trotsky recognized his advantage with Lenin; as Frunze later recalled, "During Vladimir Il'ich's speech at the congress, at every point where Vladimir Il'ich spoke about 'communist swaggering' [*komchvanstve*], Trotsky said to me: 'Vladimir Il'ich's entire speech lashes you.'"[18]

[16] Walter Jacobs, *Frunze: The Soviet Clausewitz 1885–1925* (The Hague: Martinus Nijhoff, 1969), p. 74.

[17] This comment is reproduced in ibid., p. 92, but does not appear in any Frunze anthology since 1927. Jacobs claims it is missing from the 1957 collection of Frunze's works, and it is in fact missing from the 1936, 1977, and 1984 collections. Fedotov-White attributes a similar recollection (nearly word for word) of Lenin's position to A. S. Bubnov; see D. Fedotov-White, *The Growth of the Red Army* (Princeton: Princeton University Press, 1944), p. 161.

[18] M. V. Frunze, *Stat'i i rechi* (Moscow: Gosvoenizdat, 1936), p. 109.

Lenin's increasing debilitation ensured that this criticism did not reemerge more forcefully, but in any case Trotsky had overplayed his hand. From his position as Trotsky's deputy, Frunze managed to prevail, eventually taking over as war commissar. By 1925, many of Frunze's concepts were officially accepted, all resting on the foundation provided by the acknowledgment of the existence of "military doctrine."

ENTER STALIN

Frunze, not surprisingly, was supported in his efforts by Stalin. As Frunze ascended, Trotsky descended. This change of status is important both because of the degree to which Trotsky was weakened, and the subject on which he had been defeated. The Trotsky-Frunze debate foreshadowed the combat yet to come between Trotsky and Stalin. Trotsky lost control of an important post by 1925, in part by taking a position that made him suspect in the eyes of many fellow Bolsheviks, especially the military Communists. The "Socialism in One Country" debate repeated the structure of the "unified doctrine" debate: Trotsky was probably correct in theory and powerful in speech, but it was Stalin who spoke to the interests of his audience, in terms they supported and understood. Trotsky was again felled by a victory of visceral appeal over intellectual virtue.

Within a year of Frunze's ostensible defeat at the Tenth Party Congress (and months after Trotsky's counterattack at the Eleventh), the USSR signed the Treaty of Rapallo and secured both German recognition and economic cooperation. Although this general improvement in European security might have seemed to further weaken Frunze, it was Trotsky who would suffer more from the Soviet-German rapprochement. Indeed, Stalin saw to it, undermining Trotsky's alarmism by joining the sanguine majority view of the international political situation at the Fourteenth Congress in late 1925 while *simultaneously* warning of world war and supporting Frunze's call for increased arms in secret before the January Plenum of the Central Committee that same year.[19]

In October 1925, Frunze underwent, at Stalin's insistence, surgery for an ulcer. Although the surgeons found the ulcer already healed and scarred over, the political surgery was more successful, for Frunze died on the table (technically of a chloroform overdose) under suspicious circumstances. Kliment Voroshilov—accurately described

[19] Robert Tucker, *Stalin in Power* (New York: Norton, 1990), p. 48.

by Timothy Colton as a "military ignoramus and fawning Stalin supporter"—replaced Frunze as war commissar.[20] At Frunze's funeral, Stalin spoke prophetically. "Perhaps," he said, "this is the way, just this simply and easily, that all the old comrades should be lowered into their graves."[21] Trotsky was almost vanquished. Frunze was dead. The Stalinization of Soviet military doctrine, and Stalin's rise to absolute power, were both under way.

The Attack on the Professionals

Soviet military thought did not die with Frunze on that autumn day in 1925. Several military theorists continued to debate the means and goals of a future war, including such luminaries as M. N. Tukhachevskii, A. A. Svechin, and V. K. Triandafillov. In effect, between 1925 and 1935 the future of military doctrine and Soviet foreign policy was controlled by the professional military.[22]

There was plenty to debate. Unresolved questions included the likelihood of war, the German threat, the problem of positioned versus maneuver warfare, the role of armor, and the merits of cadre and militia militaries. The history of these debates is extensive, and will not be reproduced here.[23] The point is that several bright and able men stood between Stalin and the legitimate control of military doctrine, in that they had greater claim to it through expertise, experience, and prestige. Into the early 1930s, these were the men who controlled critical aspects of Soviet defense policy, while Stalin's power grew elsewhere in the political structure. Just as Stalin could not tolerate being intellectually eclipsed by a Trotsky or a Bukharin, he would allow no possibility of being overshadowed by a Tukhachevskii or a Svechin. The eventual answer would be violence, and even in the 1920s and early 1930s Stalin's desire to eliminate his rivals for mastery of military issues was evident.

---

[20] See Timothy Colton's introduction in Colton and Thane Gustafson, eds., *Soldiers and the Soviet State* (Princeton: Princeton University Press, 1990), pp. 18–19.

[21] Cited in Mikhail Heller and Aleksandr Nekrich, *Utopia in Power* (New York: Summit Books, 1982), p. 190.

[22] For a modern Soviet testimonial to the role played by the military experts in Soviet defense policy in this period, see R. Savushkin, "Zarozhdenie i razvitie sovetskoi voennoi doktrine," *Voenno-Istoricheskii Zhurnal* (February 1988).

[23] For a good (even by pre-*glasnost'* standards) Soviet account of this period, see I. A. Korotkov, *Istoriia sovetskoi voennoi mysli* (Moscow: Nauka, 1980), and P. A. Zhilin, *Problemy voennoi istorii* (Moscow: Voenizdat, 1975), esp. pp. 100–153. See also Condoleeza Rice's contribution to Peter Paret, ed., *Makers of Modern Strategy* (Princeton: Princeton University Press, 1986).

One revealing episode was the sacking of Marshal Tukhachevksii as chief of the Red Army Staff. In 1928, Tukhachevskii proposed enlarging the functions of the staff; the result, in the words of historian Phillip Bayer, would have been to give the Red Army Staff "total control over the planning and organization of defense."[24] A group of Stalin's allies in the military (including Budennyi, Unshlikht, and Egorov), then wrote to Voroshilov to oppose Tukhachevskii's plans, after which Tukhachevskii resigned, complaining (according to one Soviet account) that "against his will and over his head" the Staff had been made into a "purely technical apparatus."[25]

To this end, Stalin replaced Tukhachevskii as chief of the Red Army Staff with B. M. Shaposhnikov, a man whose political views and approach to his job were much more acceptable to Stalin, despite Shaposhnikov's reputation as a military intellectual. A careful, cautious, and generally neutral follower of the Party line, Shaposhnikov gladly undertook the job Tukhachevskii rejected: the creation of a staff concerned purely with internal military matters. Bayer explains that Shaposhnikov's "views on the nature of modern military leadership probably found favor with the Soviet political authorities because he rejected the notion that the high command and general staff should be responsible for all aspects of military and defense policy." Moreover, Shaposhnikov "believed that the general staff should not play a major role in politics or society."[26] His appointment under Stalin, and his subsequent survival of the purges, should be no surprise. In Shaposhnikov, Stalin had found an invaluable asset, and his appointment as Chief helped to smooth the way for the civil takeover of military affairs and the political subordination of the armed forces.

This was a canny move, allowing Stalin to extend control over strictly military issues through a respected but compliant subordinate in a key military position. There is an interesting historical parallel here with Hitler, who made a similar appointment in 1938 in order to finalize his own takeover of German military matters. After removing

[24] Phillip Bayer, *The Evolution of the Soviet General Staff 1917–1941* (New York: Garland Publishing, 1987), p. 111. I am indebted to Bayer for several enlightening conversations on this subject.

[25] G. Isserson, "Zapiski sovremennik o M. N. Tukhachevskom," *Voenno-Istoricheskii Zhurnal* (April 1963), p. 66; see also Bayer, *Evolution*, pp. 111–112. Isserson was writing during a time of sanctioned criticism of Stalin, so this may not be an entirely honest portrait of Tukhachevskii. In his introduction to *High Treason* (originally a *samizdat* publication), Vladimir Treml points out that the Soviet authors present Tukhachevskii as "very egocentric." See *High Treason: Essays on the History of the Red Army, 1918–1938*, Vitaly Rapoport and Yuri Alexeev, eds. (Durham: Duke University Press, 1985), p. xv.

[26] Bayer, *Evolution*, p. 153, 155.

the more headstrong Werner von Fritsch as Staff chief on a Gestapo-manufactured charge of homosexuality, Hitler placed Field-Marshal Walther Brauchitsch at the head of the German General Staff. Brauchitsch, like Shaposhnikov, was an honorable and generally able officer; but he lacked, in Brian Bond's words, "the strength of character and moral commitment" to oppose Hitler in any but the most "vacillating and ineffectual" way.[27] Much the same could be said of Shaposhnikov, and it is understandable that both the Soviet and German officer corps suffered the same sort of political downfall as a result.

Stalin's control of military issues accelerated in the late 1920s. He had eliminated his main rivals in the military sphere and placed his own men (who were hardly of command caliber) in key military posts. This, of course, ran parallel to, and intersected with, his political efforts. A review of events reveals the growth of Stalin's political and military powers: in 1921–22, he sided with Frunze in the battle against Trotsky. In 1925, he replaced Trotsky, and then (allegedly) liquidated Trotsky's successor, thereby gaining control of the War Commissariat; a year later he joined battle against a united Trotsky-Zinoviev opposition. Through Voroshilov and other henchmen, Stalin managed the resignation of Tukhachevskii in 1928, and replaced him with an obedient surrogate, a move that came on the heels of the similarly structured crushing of Trotsky, Grigorii Zinoviev, Lev Kamenev, and others.

The orgy of glorification that surrounded Stalin's fiftieth birthday marked the beginning of his cult, and the beginning of the end of the old Bolsheviks. By 1930, Stalin enjoyed near-total political control. A final barrier remained in military matters, however: the persistence of scores of so-called military specialists (i.e., former tsarist soldiers), as well as a number of genuine war heroes of undeniable stature. Although the groundwork had been laid in the 1920s for Stalin's growing control of military policy, Tukhachevskii and the others still lived, a dilemma for which Stalinist logic provided only one answer.

A sign of the future came in one of Stalin's first official steps into the military limelight, Voroshilov's 1929 *Pravda* article (in honor of the *vozhd*'s birthday), "Stalin and the Red Army." Suddenly, Stalin was a brilliant military theorist: "The importance of comrade Stalin," Voroshilov wrote, "one of the chief architects of victory in the Civil War, has been pushed somewhat to the background [because of re-

---

[27] Brian Bond, "Brauchitsch," in Corelli Barnett, ed., *Hitler's Generals* (New York: Grove Wiedenfeld, 1990), p. 75.

cent political struggles] and he has not received the credit he is due."[28] What Voroshilov was actually referring to was a longstanding feud between Stalin and the military over the defeat in the Battle of Warsaw in the Polish war of 1920, in which Tukhachevskii's attack on the city was weakened by the refusal of Stalin and Voroshilov to commit their forces to support Tukhachevskii's position. Stalin chose instead to order Budennyi to drive on Lvov, with disastrous results in both campaigns.[29] As Robert Conquest notes, "The whole [Lvov] incident rankled bitterly with Stalin, and when he gained full control of the history books the whole episode was represented as a strategically sound drive on Lvov, sabotaged for motives of treason by Tukhachevskii and Trotsky."[30]

Stalin maintained his own blamelessness by alternating between the roles of military figure and political leader as it suited him: as a commissar in the field, he claimed that the whole campaign was flawed, but as a political figure he was able to point the finger at the military leadership for "criminal" incompetence. "It never occurred to him," Volkogonov writes, "that as a member of the Military *soviet* he bore full responsibility for the failures as well as the successes of the troops at the front."[31] The Voroshilov article of 1929 and the revision of the Polish disaster quickly became part of official Soviet military historiography. It was, as one modern *samizdat* account describes it, "a spit in the face" of the Red Army, a "warning [that] all your honors count for nothing."[32]

Purging the Military

A year after Voroshilov's article, Stalin opened his political offensive. In 1930, the purges of engineers and industrial figures were accompanied by widespread arrests of the "military specialists," including officers of stature such as Svechin. Sent to camps near Leningrad, many who survived were released in 1932. "Despite their subsequent liberation," according to the *samizdat* account, "the blow

[28] Voroshilov's article is reproduced in Rapoport and Alexeev, *High Treason*, p. 139.

[29] W. Bruce Lincoln makes it clear that there were military reasons to be concerned about Tukhachevskii's drive on Warsaw, but Stalin had nonetheless been ordered by the Red Army high command to support Tukhachevskii's operation, and his refusal, according to Lincoln, was "outright insubordination." Lincoln, *Red Victory* (New York: Touchstone, 1989), p. 416.

[30] Robert Conquest, *The Great Terror: A Reassessment* (New York: Oxford, 1990), pp. 184–185.

[31] Volkogonov, *Triumf i tragediia*, vol. 1, book 1, p. 103.

[32] Rapoport and Alexeev, *High Treason*, p. 145.

to the Army was serious."[33] These incidents, perhaps understandable in the greater context of the campaign against the specialists and the Shakhty affair (in which several engineers were falsely accused of sabotage), were followed by a brief period of relative stability that was in fact only the calm before the storm.

For a temporary period (1930 through 1934), the positions of other prominent military leaders did not seem threatened. In 1931, for example, Tukhachevskii became chief of armaments for the Red Army. The General Staff Academy was expanded and improved that same year.[34] Production of newer weapons, such as tanks, increased and discussion of their uses continued. Despite such occasions as Tukhachevskii's ordered savaging of former tsarist officer Svechin, various military debates continued well into 1935. Nonetheless, Stalin had made it clear that the Red Army would not remain beyond his control.

Tukhachevskii was a source of special envy. Volkogonov claims that "Stalin could not accept that Tukhachevskii's intellectual level" and "his theoretical background, and the originality of his thinking were significantly superior to that of his chief. But of course, that was often the case. The chief . . . the '*vozhd*' believed, was not required to be smarter than his deputies. It was important to carry out the 'line.' Voroshilov knew how to do that. But Tukhachevskii . . . "[35] Tukhachevskii was made a candidate member of the Central Committee in 1934, and promoted to Marshal of the Soviet Union a year later. "All the same," according to a 1988 Soviet account, "he did not feel that Stalin fully trusted him."[36]

Tukhachevskii's instincts were sharp; Stalin renewed his attack on the military in 1936, when the dictator settled scores with a certain Shmidt, a hero of the Civil War who had later sided with Trotsky. Shmidt was a natural choice for elimination, since he was a not only a war hero but he had also managed to humiliate Stalin in public some years before when, after being informed of Trotsky's expulsion from the Party, he confronted Stalin and yelled, "Watch out, Koba. I'll cut your ears off!"[37] The case built against Shmidt in late 1936 generated more accusations, and in 1937, a year after the arrests of other Old Bolsheviks, the military leadership fell to the Great Purge.

[33] Ibid., p. 171.

[34] *Akademiia General'nogo Shtaba* (Moscow: Voenizdat, 1987), p. 6.

[35] Volkogonov, *Triumf i tragediia*, I/ii, p. 263.

[36] "Marshal Tukhachevskii," *Krasnaia Zvezda*, June 4, 1988, p. 3.

[37] "Koba" was Stalin's revolutionary *nom de guerre*, derived from one of his childhood Georgian folk heroes. Rapoport and Alexeev, *High Treason*, p. 237.

The purge decimated the ranks of the Soviet military, and served the crucial purpose of eliminating anyone with claims to military expertise greater than Stalin's. "The accused," as Conquest points out, "were all leaders of the group around Tukhachevskii which had pioneered military rethinking through the 1930s. They had developed the ideas and to some degree the organization of an efficient, modern army."[38] This marked them for death: Conquest notes that "far from their fine records being of any service to the generals, the contrary seems to apply." Actually, the forceful personalities of many of the doomed men had led them to be accused of being part of an "intra-army opposition group" dating from 1928 (and supposedly centered around a "Belorussian-Tolmachev Academy" axis); in reality the "axis" was nothing more than an loosely affiliated group of officers interested in issues of military reform. In 1938, however, then-MPA chief and Stalin crony L. Z. Mekhlis resurrected the "axis" charges, accusing the senior men in the dock of "Trotskyism, right deviationism, antiparty, anticommunist, and counterrevolutionary factional activity," as well as the now-standard charges of treason and espionage.[39] Their true crimes had been initiative and professionalism. An official 1991 Soviet investigation into the matter concluded,

> A thoroughgoing analysis of the so-called "intra-army opposition of 1928" shows that the entire "guilt" of the [accused officers] consisted only in that they stood out as initiators of sober discussion, that they allowed critical statements to be directed at the leadership of the Red Army, and that they advanced a series of propositions aimed at widening the democratic beginnings in military construction.[40]

The charges in all cases, the report added, were fabricated and the subsequent action against the accused unlawful.

The most senior men arrested in June 1937 included Tukhachevskii, *komandarm* Yakir of the Kiev Military District, and General Staff Academy head A. I. Kork.[41] (Jan Gamarnik, the head of the army's political directorate, was also to be arrested but committed suicide.) According to Soviet counts, the Great Purge claimed nearly half the regimental

---

[38] Conquest, *The Great Terror*, p. 183.

[39] "O tak nazyvaemoi 'vnutriarmeiskoi oppozitsii' 1928 goda," *Izvestiia TsK KPSS*, March 1991, p. 85.

[40] Ibid., p. 85. The article was prepared by members both of the Main Political Administration and the Central Committee CPSU Institute of Marxism-Leninism.

[41] Almost all have been rehabilitated. Since 1987, *Krasnaia Zvezda* has been publishing several articles on the careers of the men killed in 1937 including Yakir, Tukhachevskii, Uborevich, and others.

commanders, nearly all brigade commanders, all corps commanders and district commanders, and the majority of political commissars at almost all levels.[42] More than 40,000 commanders were murdered or imprisoned, and by 1938, the military purge had taken such a toll that the year's military students, some 10,000 new officers, were graduated early.[43] By 1941, only 7.1 percent of the Red Army's commanders had completed their higher military education (more than 12 percent had no military education at all), meaning that junior officers who had been spared were forced to undertake huge responsibilities for which they were scarcely prepared.[44]

Many of Stalin's fears were probably buried with Tukhachevskii and the others. His victory over both the military and society was complete. By 1938, there was no one who could even begin to challenge Stalin's military authority on any grounds, nor anyone, of course, who was foolish enough to try. The military was decapitated, intellectually and numerically.

It was perhaps a sign of Stalin's insecurity that he chose, even after obliterating the Soviet armed forces, to dress in a martial fashion for so many years (according to his Soviet biographer, he loved to stare at his reflection in uniform), and that he adopted at least the semblance of a military bearing.[45] Although he had destroyed the Soviet military in mind and body and placed himself at the head of its remnants, he probably understood that he, the Statesman, never truly succeeded in becoming the General.

Stalin's control of national security matters was a prerogative that he guarded with fanatical jealousy once it was gained. As Marshal N. N. Voronov attested, Stalin "could not tolerate the decision of even secondary [military] matters without his knowledge," and Khrushchev himself described Stalin as an outright paranoid about military policy: "He refused to discuss military matters with us; he gave us no training in the management of the army. Defense was his exclusive concern, and he guarded it fiercely."[46] One of the most intrusive

---

[42] Heller and Nekrich, *Utopia in Power*, pp. 304–305. See also Table 20.2 in Rapoport and Alexeev, *High Treason*, p. 276.

[43] Yazov gave this figure on Soviet television, May 9, 1990, but his source was almost certainly Volkogonov's biography of Stalin, in which the same figures appear. See Volkogonov, *Triumf i tragediia*, II/i, pp. 52–54, and "Yazov Congratulates Soviet People on Anniversary," FBIS-SOV-90–091, May 10, 1990, p. 58

[44] Volkogonov, *Triumf i tragediia*, II/i, p. 54.

[45] Ibid., p. 254.

[46] N. N. Voronov, "The Vexations of Centralization," in Seweryn Bialer, ed., *Stalin and His Generals* (Boulder, Colo.: Westview, 1984), p. 367, and Nikita Khrushchev, *Khrushchev Remembers: The Last Testament*, trans. Strobe Talbott (Boston: Little, Brown, 1974), p. 12.

methods of Stalinist control consisted of naming himself to posts, including chairman of the Council of People's Commissars, head of the State Defense Committee, and later, Generalissimus of the Soviet Union, all in addition to his Party post. He also, as Admiral N. G. Kuznetsov pointed out after the war, supervised the People's Commissariat of Defense, "without delegating any of his authority" elsewhere.[47] Later Soviet leaders—especially "Marshal" Brezhnev—emulated this pattern, and the interplay of political power and military control is evident, with the goal, as always, to dilute the power of the military, and to concentrate the power of the general secretary.

Stalin's control of military matters quickly merged with the "cult of personality." As Stalin's stature grew, his decisions were respected even in the face of military expertise greater than his own. Marshal Georgii Zhukov for example, said in 1971, "I did not feel then [in 1941] . . . that I was wiser and more far-seeing that Stalin, that I could appraise the situation better, or that I knew more than him." He and his fellow generals were, as Colton has noted, "as captivated as civilian politicians . . . by the myth of Stalin's omniscience."[48]

The consequences of the Stalinist system of subjective control became painfully evident during the Nazi invasion of 1941. Consider this excerpt from a previously censored section of Admiral Kuznetsov's memoirs, which captures both the vagueness of Stalin's defense policy and his breadth of control:

> We did not have [on the eve of the Nazi invasion] a single view of a doctrine of the conduct of war. And of course, this is very important for a common understanding of defense questions. Doctrine was something intangible for us, "hidden away" in Stalin's head, and he only reluctantly shared his thoughts and intentions. . . .
>
> In a word, on the eve of war we did not have a precise military doctrine, and therefore precise tasks for the Navy could not be formulated as well, nor had its role in the system of the Armed Forces been defined.[49]

The disasters of 1941 would not be forgotten when Stalin was gone; they resulted in strong pressures to return a great deal of control over

---

[47] N. G. Kuznetsov, "Command in Transition," in Bialer, *Stalin and His Generals*, p. 348. A Soviet diplomat who defected during the Great Purge claims that Stalin's assumption of the title of premier was a lesson learned from Hitler: "Stalin . . . seeing the greater simplicity of Hitler's position as Reichschancellor as well as Party *Fuhrer*, decided to dispense with . . . cumbersome fictions and make himself Premier." See Alexander Barmine, *One Who Survived* (New York: G. P. Putnam's Sons, 1945), p. 218.

[48] Colton, "Perspectives on Civil-Military Relations in the Soviet Union," p. 19.

[49] "Chemu uchila voina," *Krasnaia Zvezda*, July 29, 1988, p. 4.

military and security issues to the military professionals, thereby setting the stage for later conflict between the leadership and the armed
forces.

Stalin and the Power of Doctrine

Although logic may have mandated reintegrating the military into
the national security process, Stalin's successors had good reason to
be reluctant to return military doctrine to the General Staff. Due to the
theoretical structure of military doctrine as well as to Stalin's control
of military issues, doctrine and resource control had become inex-
tricably linked to the general secretary, and this link, as will be seen in
the next chapter, outlived Stalin himself.

Stalin was a good tutor, providing object lessons in melding personal prerogatives to his own authority in military affairs. This authority, gained in the systematic destruction of the military and the subsequent capture of military doctrine, allowed Stalin to use both
authority and intimidation in directing the development of Soviet
defense. His involvement went beyond approving or quashing the
production of this or that weapons system; he also arrogated to himself judgments about the future directions of military strategy and
force structure. These decisions, linked to the powers of the general
secretary, resulted in the ability to make massive shifts in resources
and war planning. Consider, for example, the efforts aimed at satisfy-
ing Stalin's obsession with acquiring strategic airpower. Khrushchev
reports that Stalin personally asked A. N. Tupolev to design a bomber
capable of reaching the United States. Tupolev refused, on the
grounds that "the limits of contemporary [c. 1950] technology made
such a task simply impossible to fulfill . . . and [Tupolev] told Stalin
so."[50] Stalin then turned to designer V. M. Miasishchev, and made the
creation of such a bomber a high priority. Miasishchev's biographer
confirms that this bomber project (the result of which would be the
mediocre Mya-4 *Bison*) was created by Stalin's direct order.[51]

[50] Khrushchev, *The Last Testament*, p. 39

[51] David I. Gai, *Nebesnoe Pritiiazhenie* (Moscow: Moskovskii Rabochii, 1984), pp. 123–
124. Tupolev, apparently, is a figure about which the Soviets have yet to make any clear
determination (unlike the near-canonization of S. P. Korolev in recent years). Gai and
others have depicted Tupolev as simply too conservative for the "daring" work of the
early jet age. See, for example, ibid., p. 127. Although Khrushchev speaks in his
memoirs of his great respect for Tupolev (*The Last Testament*, p. 42), M. S. Arlazorov
claims that Tupolev had to turn for help to Artem Mikoian when faced with the daunting task of building the Soviet supersonic transport. See Arlazorov, *Vint i Krylo*
(Moscow: Znanie, 1980), p. 155.

Miasishchev was given wide authority to draw upon the best talent for the project, even at the expense of other bureaus.[52]

Marshal E. Savitskii points out that real doubts about the reliability of jets among both pilots, and even some representatives of "engineering-design circles," did not deter Stalin from pressing ahead with the modernization of the Soviet Air Defense Forces (*Protivo-vozdushnaia Oborona*, or PVO) as whole.[53] As a result of Stalin's decisions, Savitskii says, huge human and material resources were thrown into the effort to create a viable air defense, the reservations of the defense establishment notwithstanding, and Savitskii himself was chosen to lead the Air Defense Forces because, as Stalin told him personally, "We need a man there who himself has mastered this [jet] equipment and believes in its possibilities."[54] Similar incidents occurred throughout the 1950s and 1960s; Stalin's lieutenants, above all Khrushchev, had learned their lessons well. Without the threat of force to underpin their policies, they would choose instead to exercise control by exploiting military obedience to the concept of doctrine.

After Stalin: The Military Reawakens

The military obedience to doctrine, however, did not automatically translate into obedience to the new leaders. Indeed, as it turns out, it did not even mean obedience to the doctrines created by Stalin himself once the dictator was dead. The first warnings that the civilians were to be disappointed in their attempts to exercise complete control

---

[52] At one point, a famous (although unnamed) designer called Miasishchev to complain about the raiding of personnel. He asked Miasishchev what his military rank was. "Major General," answered Miasishchev. "Then you should respect the request of a Colonel General," the other retorted, "and not take away from me . . ." and a series of names followed. Miasishchev, according to this account, answered by agreeing that military subordination naturally required compliance with an order, but that the colonel general should understand that Miasishchev was working under a Marshal of the Soviet Union (which one is not clear), whom Stalin had personally assigned to oversee the new project. That ended the problem. Gai, *Nebesnoe Pritiiazhenie*, pp. 120–121. Miasishchev joined the Party in 1953, a year described, in a sly joke by the biographer, as one of the happiest in Miasishchev's career. Ibid., pp. 136, 142.

[53] E. Savitskii, "Polveka s nebom," *Oktiabr'* 7 (1987), p. 16. Other designers ran into similar stubbornness on a variety of issues, especially after Stalin's death. Ministry of Aviation Industry specialists, for example, ridiculed Pavel Sukhoi's plans for a swept-wing jet in 1953. Sukhoi got the last laugh: the Su-7 netted him the Order of Lenin. See L. Kuzmina, *General'nyi konstruktor Pavel Sukhoi* (Moscow: Molodaia Gvardia, 1983), p. 127.

[54] Savitskii, "Polveka s nebom," pp. 25–35.

of doctrine became evident in the "permanent factors" debate after Stalin's death.

After the war, Stalin laid down a set of theoretical musings about war that came to be known as "the permanent factors." He opined that certain factors—such as the stability of the rear, military morale, quantity and quality of divisions, equipment, and officer talent— were "decisive" in war, while others, such as surprise, were merely "transitory."[55] The permanent factors were hardly insightful; most of them, as Marshal Rotmistrov later pointed out, simply reflected common sense.[56] Of course, Stalin was no more a brilliant military theoretician than Trofim Lysenko was a brilliant geneticist, and the permanent factors became the first targets for military revision almost as soon as Stalin was entombed.

The reconsideration of the permanent factors was a brief but important period in the history of Soviet doctrinal politics, a small event with large implications. For the first time in years, the military (or at least the young cohort that survived the purges of 1936–1938) was able to consider a military-theoretical problem in the light, out from under the shadow of Stalin. This would soon merge into military research on the military and political implications of the coming generation of nuclear weapons, and the stage would be set for the clash between Khrushchev and the armed forces.

The first reconsideration of the permanent factors by the military came not, as might be expected, in 1956, but rather in 1953, barely six months after Stalin's death, in the pages of the Soviet military-theoretical journal *Voennaia Mysl'* (Military Thought). In a watershed article, Gen. Nikolai Talenskii carefully questioned the wisdom of the "permanent factors." As Herbert Dinerstein noted:

> Talenskii's first article seems to have been an awkward attempt to dignify the pragmatic [i.e., non-Stalinist] approach, at the expense of the dogmatic. . . . Moreover, he had to perform this *volte face* without appearing to move. Hence he found himself postulating the existence of basic laws, the knowledge of which was essential to victory, and simultaneously suggesting that a little human ingenuity could readily evade those laws.[57]

---

[55] Much of this discussion is taken from Herbert Dinerstein's classic, *War and the Soviet Union* (New York: Praeger, 1962), pp. 28–63.

[56] While many of the "permanent factors" were beyond the control of a field commander (such as the stability of the rear), Rotmistrov asked if there had ever been a competent general who *didn't* at least try to take such things into account. See ibid., p. 50.

[57] Ibid., pp. 41–42.

There were, of course, early defenses of Stalin's thinking by some officers. These were few, and most officers quickly joined in the rejection of the Stalinist axioms. By 1956, the "permanent factors" had been largely discarded, and a Rubicon of sorts had been crossed.

The "permanent factors" revision indicated not only dissatisfaction with the Stalinist interference in military affairs, but also a willingness among the military intellectuals to take matters into their own hands. (Later, civilian leaders would try to harness these intellectual energies, to little avail.) The military had finally managed to jettison the mainstays of Stalinist military theory, and it was only a matter of time before they tried to shake off Stalinist military controls as well.

After the burial of the "permanent factors," the military moved to other issues. Stalin had thoroughly repressed consideration of the nuclear question during his lifetime, and it reemerged quickly in his absence as the military intellegentsia began to reexamine Soviet doctrine quickly and efficiently. Although the Soviet history of the General Staff Academy dates most of the academy's theoretical research on nuclear weapons after 1956, there are signs that work was begun earlier. To take but one example, a military-historical faculty was being formed at the General Staff Academy in 1953 as part of a restructuring of academy work aimed at creating a more realistic curriculum, even as Talenskii's opening shot was being fired in *Voennaia Mysl'*. In 1954, Lt. Gen. N. A. Lomov (later a prolific contributor to the military literature) was named a deputy head of the academy for scientific research, apparently in response to "new tasks" arising in strategy and operational art in the nuclear era.[58] Work on fulfillment of these "new tasks" under "new conditions" is described as ongoing from 1954 onward, with ten pedagogical works on these new questions, and their relation to questions of strategy, produced between 1954 and 1956 alone.[59]

Clearly, the General Staff Academy was looking ahead, delving into questions that the civilians were not to take up for at least three more years. Although military theoreticians were officially in step with civilian interests after 1957, it is apparent that they did not wait for civilian approval to begin the sort of deliberations (within the safety of academy walls) that would have been impossible under Stalin. This was the first taste of autonomy in military-theoretical work, and it was seized upon by military thinkers concerned about the damage done

[58] The new curriculum was introduced in 1959. *Akademiia General'nogo Shtaba* (Moscow: Voenizdat, 1987), pp. 113–114.
[59] Ibid., p. 122.

during the years of Stalinist stagnation. Among the graduates of the academy in this 1954–61 doctrinal interregnum were men who became senior officers of long tenure: Marshals V. Kulikov, S. Kurkotkin, and N. Ogarkov; Marshal of Aviation A. Koldunov; Ground Forces Commander in Chief (CINC) Gen. Ivanovskii, as well as Generals I. Tret'iak and Shkadov and others.[60]

This periodization of Soviet military thinking is supported by other Soviet materials.[61] Marshal V. Sokolovskii and M. Cherednichenko date consideration of the nuclear question in earnest from 1954, although they predictably genuflect to the military importance of the XX Party Congress of 1956. The first period in Soviet military development, for these authors, is 1945–53, for obvious reasons. The second is 1954–58, when the ramifications of nuclear arms were considered, and the third, 1959–65, encompassed the actual changes in the Soviet Armed Forces to meet the challenges of the nuclear age.[62] Again, it is evident that the Soviet military began serious consideration of the nuclear question long before the leadership did, perhaps because of what we now know to be the political disarray inside the Kremlin between 1953 and 1957. After 1957, the leadership question was largely settled (for the time being), and the victor, Khrushchev, began the herculean tasks of reorganizing national defense and of reasserting the supremacy of the civilian leadership in that momentous work.

CONCLUSION: THE STALINIST LEGACY

The Stalinist era brought to a quick end any possibility of creating an autonomous, professionalized military in the USSR. Indeed, officers such as Tukhachevskii who sought to create a "militarized military" were specific targets of Stalinist repression. But the purges and the cronyist appointments that followed did more damage to the civil-military relationship than merely creating an atmosphere of fear and

---

[60] Ibid., pp. 120–121.
[61] See A. A. Babakov, *Vooruzhennye Sily SSSR posle voiny (1945–1986 gg.): Istoriia stroitel'stva* (Moscow: Voenizdat, 1987). At least one military theorist in the Gorbachev era has criticized the 1954–1961 periodization; see the review of Babakov's book by Lt. Gen. V. Reznichenko in *Kommunist Vooruzhennykh Sil* 1 (January 1988), pp. 86–88. Reznichenko argues that the 1954–61 periodization is not informative, and asks Babakov to explain why he chose it—a strange criticism to say the least, given the overwhelming prevalence of this time scale in Soviet military literature.
[62] V. Sokolovskii and M. Cherednichenko, "Nekotorye voprosy voennogo stroitel'stva v poslevoennoi period," *Voenno-Istoricheskii Zhurnal* (March 1965), pp. 6–11.

intimidation (although this effect should not be underestimated). They also served to create an officer corps that had no sense of self-confidence, kept in check both by coercion and by institutionalized myths that melded the Russian version of the *Fuhrerprinzip* to the catechism of Party omniscience. In short, Stalin's legacy was the creation of an unstable system of subjective control of the military.

Worse yet, the military would draw the lesson from the Stalinist experience that serving the interests of the *Party* and serving the interests of the Party *leadership* may not mean the same thing. This was the beginning of the persistent habit of Orwellian doublethink among senior officers, who henceforth would be committed Marxists but would nonetheless keep a watchful eye on the Party leadership (rather than vice versa).

Meanwhile, the CPSU found itself ever more reluctant to enforce the system of loyalty to a single leader that had been imposed upon Soviet society. The leadership, however, did not intend to grant equality to their military comrades, thereby placing the officer corps in a political limbo unsatisfactory, in the end, to civilians and soldiers alike. Thus, the uneasy cohabitation between the newly emancipated soldiers and the newly regnant civilians was, inevitably, short-lived.

This was the beginning of the dilemma posed by a Marxist military. On the one hand, the Soviet Armed Forces were intentionally created, as even Frunze and Trotsky would have agreed, as an organic arm of the Party, believers in both the Marxist mission of class revolution and Leninist obedience to the vanguard, the Party leadership. But the betrayal of the Party by its own leader, and the subsequent ascension of a cadre of mediocrities, meant that the military was left with a firm faith in ideology, but a tenuous confidence in the political stewards of that ideology. In a sense, Stalin began the process that would culminate, by 1991, in the Soviet officer corps believing that the stewardship of the Revolution had in fact passed to them—and that they were allowed to accept it.

Enter Khrushchev

Khrushchev stepped in and tried, with limited success, to pull the sword from the stone and assume Stalin's mantle in military affairs, despite his otherwise Leninist rhetoric. With both international and domestic interests in mind, Khrushchev hoped to capitalize on the Stalinist pattern of subjective control. This attempt altered both the nature of the nation's defense policy (perhaps more due to the later backlash against his efforts), as well as the future course of Soviet military politics. By the time Khrushchev tried to institute his own defense plans after 1957—using the doctrinal weapon forged under Stalin—the military had been free too long, and Khrushchev would never regain the control Stalin had enjoyed. The military genie was finally and irreversibly out of the bottle.

[3]

Khrushchev's Revolution: Stalinism without Stalin?

The entire Army is in a state of turmoil; everyone in the Army recalls Stalin and says that under Stalin things were better, that is, Stalin never insulted the Army, but this scoundrel [Khrushchev] has dismissed good officers from the Army. And now this same scoundrel lifts his goblet high and drinks a toast, saying, "I love our Army." His control of the Army is strong, however. As a General Staff colonel, I hate to write this.

—Oleg Penkovskii, 1961

KHRUSHCHEV AND THE STALINIST TRADITION

Although Nikita Khrushchev came to power in the 1950s promising a return to Leninist codes of conduct in a shattered and fearful Party, he had no such plans for restoring relations with the military. In a sense, Khrushchev tried to retain the Stalinist tradition in the making of defense policy, to preserve the unarguable prerogative of the general secretary established by Stalin—in other words, to preserve and exploit the system of subjective control. It is not surprising that it was this era that generated the first major study of modern Soviet military politics, Kolkowicz's *Soviet Military and the Communist Party*, with its alarming picture of a military chafing under the intrusive meddling of the Party. In many ways, Gorbachev's efforts to redefine the Soviet civil-military relationship in the late 1980s resembled a kind of "new Khrushchevism," in both style and substance, and it is important to understand what Khrushchev wanted to accomplish in the civil-military relationship.

The most striking aspect of Khrushchev's control of military affairs was its paradoxical nature. Even as political reform was lifting fear from Party cadres and the society at large, military issues were frozen in the totalitarian pattern, with Khrushchev hijacking defense policy, and demoting or dismissing officers who dared disagree with him. But this imperious style ran at cross-purposes with the need to open defense questions to study by Party leaders and military experts. The idea of including many in debate and few in decision was not new to democratic centralism, but the increasingly complex and technical nature of military doctrine mandated the inclusion of the Soviet high command, whether Khrushchev liked it or not.

Moreover, there was a sense that the military, as members of the Party, had a right to return to the political arena. As Georgii Arbatov has noted, "after Stalin's death, military men took part in those kinds of internal [political] matters, as is right."[1] Khrushchev may have wanted to gain Stalin's powers over the military, but neither he nor his colleagues were willing to use Stalin's methods; the senior military leaders were, after all, Party members if nothing else. Thus the stage was set for chronic civil-military conflict over both the content of national security policy and the proper role of the soldier in Soviet politics.

This use of the dictatorial approach led to a quick loss of Khrushchev's control both of the military agenda and of the military as an institution. Khrushchev was not Stalin, the nation was not at war, and nobody was going to get shot (as Marshal Georgii Zhukov could attest) for holding an opposing viewpoint. Soon, the military began to compete with the premier by presenting alternatives to his policies and defending themselves against his open attacks on their prestige. This successful counterattack gained the military a right to legitimate opposition over the course of the clashes with Khrushchev, a right that remained unchallenged by Brezhnev. This newfound right was perhaps the most trying part of Khrushchev's legacy that Gorbachev was to face in the 1980s.

The Nuclear Revolution and Soviet Civil-Military Affairs

The development of nuclear missile technology provided the substance of the civil-military rupture that took place in the late 1950s. The creation of a missile force was the source of controversy, and eventual enmity, between Khrushchev and the military. Rather than working cooperatively with the military, Khrushchev seized upon

---

[1] Georgii Arbatov, *Zatianuvsheesiia vyzdorovlenie (1953–1986 gg.)* (Moscow: "Mezhdunarodnye otnosheniia," 1990), p. 107.

ICBMs as a means to gain control of the military agenda more broadly, thereby subverting the possibility of objective control over the Soviet Armed Forces. This civil intrusion into military matters was complemented by a general attack on military prestige, a combination that would be seen again in the Gorbachev era. This addition of insult to injury actually served, in the long run, to strengthen the armed forces, solidifying both their corporate identity and their position as coequals in the creation of national policy.

The Revolution Defined: The Impact of ICBMs

Nuclear missiles, even more than the atom bomb itself, shook the politics of war at their foundations. The Soviets quickly grasped the fact that "the turning point in the development of new weapons was the uniting of nuclear charges with rockets," a position that emerged in the late 1950s and remained unchanged thereafter.[2] Despite the destructive power of nuclear bombs, the Soviet definition of "the turning point" is understandable. Before long-range missiles were developed, the ability to destroy enemy cities and economic assets was still a matter, as in World War II, of getting a manned bomber close enough to a target to destroy it, and the Soviets did not have a bomber that had both the range and survivability to challenge the American nuclear threat emanating from European air bases.[3]

Soviet military and civilian leaders both agreed that the development of nuclear missiles constituted a "revolution in military affairs." Disagreements, however, quickly surfaced over the nature of that revolution and the proper response to it. Khrushchev's approach was to break with the military past and to prepare only for a short, global ICBM duel, rather than a large-scale, protracted ground war. The Soviet military, by contrast, argued that it was necessary to be ready for more contingencies than the Apocalypse. Each approach was based on different interpretations of the threat, although by strict doctrinal definition it was the Party's view that should have prevailed without opposition. The first civil-military Rubicon of the post-Stalin era would be crossed when these two very different views of the world entered into direct conflict.

[2] *Programma KPSS o zaschite sotsialisticheskogo otechestva*, 2d ed. (Moscow: Voenizdat, 1965), p. 87.

[3] General Nikolai Chervov recently described the early 1960s: "I used to take a pencil and compute the number of atomic shells, atomic bombs and launchers on the American side. And the sad fact was that the U.S. nuclear superiority was absolute. Apart from that, U.S. territory was at that time invulnerable." See John Newhouse, *War and Peace in the Nuclear Age* (New York: Knopf, 1989), p. 109.

At first, there seemed to be little reason for disagreement about the nature of the new threat to Soviet security. "Massive Retaliation," the official U.S. policy from 1954 to 1960, was, at least as far as the Soviets could tell, hardly a complex or nuanced approach to deterrence. The message of Massive Retaliation, that the United States would respond to Soviet aggression anywhere in the world with nuclear retaliation "instantly, by means and at places" of America's choosing, seemed unambiguous, and it was taken seriously and literally by the Soviets (and by many American critics of the Eisenhower administration as well).[4] The Khrushchevian strategy, enunciated in 1959, five years after Secretary of State John Foster Dulles described Massive Retaliation, indicated preparation for the escalation to global war that "retaliation" necessarily entailed, despite Dulles' subsequent denial in April 1954 that Massive Retaliation meant "turning every local war into a world war."[5] In some respects, Khrushchev's later thinking on nuclear war represented a political isomer of Massive Retaliation, and Soviet historians are in wide agreement that the development of the Soviet missile-centric doctrine had direct roots in the Eisenhower-Dulles strategy.[6]

Initially, the civilians encouraged the military to take the lead in bringing Soviet defense policy into the nuclear age. The revolution had been identified; it had yet to be defined. After the years of Stalinist stagnation in military thought and the exclusion of even the Politburo from defense matters, both the leadership and the marshals were in need of education. In 1957, the Ministry of Defense (apparently at the direction of the Politburo) formed a study group to examine the impact of nuclear arms on modern warfare, in what was at first intended as a "controlled debate, directed from the highest level."[7]

This debate was apparently inconclusive, in part because there was

---

[4] James Reston of the *New York Times* wrote that this was in effect serving notice that any "bushfire" war might well bring nuclear retaliation upon the USSR or Red China, one of the many criticisms prompting Dulles's backpedaling "clarification" in *Foreign Affairs* in April 1954. See Lawrence Freedman, *The Evolution of Nuclear Strategy* (New York: St. Martin's, 1983), pp. 86–88.

[5] J. F. Dulles, "Policy for Security and Peace," *Foreign Affairs* (April 1954), p. 363; see also Newhouse, *War and Peace in the Nuclear Age*, p. 96.

[6] See: A. A. Babakov, *Vooruzhennye Sily SSSR posle voiny* (Moscow: Voenizdat, 1987), pp. 81–83; R. G. Simonian, *Real'naia Opasnost': Voennye bloki imperializma* (Moscow: Voenizdat, 1985), pp. 57–58; Daniel Proektor, *Mirovye Voiny i sud'by chelovechestva* (Moscow: Mysl', 1986), pp. 156–158; Iu. M. Mel'nikov, *Sila i Bessilie: Vneshniaia politika Vashingtona* (Moscow: Politicheskoi literatury, 1983), pp. 87–105. There are, of course, many other similar accounts.

[7] Harriet Scott and William Scott, *Soviet Art of War* (Boulder, Colo.: Westview Press, 1982), p. 125. This conference is mentioned in *Akademiia General'nogo Shtaba*, p. 121, and

disagreement within the military about the applicability of previous military experience to the future. Initially, there was general agreement within the military was the recognition that nuclear weapons should join, but not displace, other means of combat. In 1956 Zhukov himself told the XX Party Congress, "We proceed from the fact that the newest weapons, including even the means of mass destruction, do not lessen the decisive significance of the ground forces, the navy, and aviation. Without strong ground forces, without strategic, long-range, and frontal aviation, without a modern navy, and without good organization of their cooperation, it is impossible to conduct modern war."[8] This was more than talk: records of the General Staff Academy indicate that the bulk of the problems studied between 1954 and 1957 were at the level of operational art, suggesting continued focus on a large-scale European ground war.[9] Dissertations defended during the 1955–58 period by such prominent figures as P. A. Zhilin, P. A. Rotmistrov, M. A. Gareev, and others did not concern nuclear issues, and these officers would later be vocal critics of Khrushchev's missile-dominant strategy.[10] Public pronouncements by both civilian and military leaders alike, especially in the wake of the XX Party Congress, were at times confusing in their emphasis, pointing both to the revolutionary impact of nuclear arms as well as to the importance of traditional means of combat.[11]

Khrushchev himself understood well the brewing opposition within the academy, and he reacted with repeated attempts to keep the military intellectuals off balance. New academy heads were appointed in 1956, 1958, 1961, and 1963, the last being the deposed chief of the General Staff, Marshal M. Zakharov. In comparison, the less illustrious and less contentious Frunze Academy had one chief from 1954 to 1968, probably due to Khrushchev's later scheme to eviscerate the General Staff Academy and reassign its staff to the Frunze Academy.

Babakov, *Vooruzhennye Sily SSSR posle voiny*, p. 116. Other evidence of a study group (whose works were termed the "special collections") may be found in Oleg Penkovskii, *The Penkovskii Papers* (New York: Doubleday, 1965), pp. 251–260. Penkovskii's papers were published after he was caught and executed.

[8] See I. N. Levadov, B. A. Belyi, and A. P. Novoselov, eds., *Marksizm-leninizm o voine i armii* (Moscow: Voenizdat, 1957), p. 206.

[9] Other issues studied in this period were largely pedagogical. Although it could be argued that subjects beyond operational art might have been considered (especially so soon after Stalin's death) outside the intellectual and political jurisdiction of the General Staff Academy, the fact remains that the academy concerned itself with strategy and doctrine then, as it does today. *Akademiia General'nogo Shtaba*, p. 122.

[10] Ibid., p. 126.

[11] See Yosef Avidar, *The Party and the Army in the Soviet Union* (Jerusalem: Magnes Press, 1983), pp. 241–249.

This and other evidence suggests that the outlines of Khrushchev's 1959 decision were recognized by several military leaders as early as 1955, and internal opposition began to form at least that early. While many recognized the importance of nuclear weapons early on, no one was prepared to participate in Khrushchev's exclusive, one-war variant and the consequent gutting of the Soviet Ground Forces, Navy, and Air Force that it implied. Khrushchev's thinking was also firming up very early, and he set out quickly to rid himself of the military impediments to his plans. In the process, he sought to make a political double play, simultaneously capturing defense policy and fracturing—thereby taming—a military that was still struggling to overcome the fallout of Stalin's interference in defense matters.

The Revolution Interpreted: Khrushchev's Doctrine

Khrushchev ended any speculation that defense policy was still an open question in late 1959, when he officially brought his new concept before the Central Committee in December. Khrushchev had been moving toward a missile-heavy force structure for some time, and it is obvious that the Central Committee knew well what to expect. Nuclear weapons, ICBMs in particular, were enshrined at the center of this new doctrine. As articulated in later months by senior figures such as Minister of Defense Rodion Malinovskii (Zhukov's replacement after the removal of the anti-Party group in 1957), the new vision of war involved immediate and massive use of intercontinental weapons in a short, brutal, and decisive war. Accordingly, a new organization was created in the wake of the December 1959 meeting: the Strategic Rocket Forces, until the late 1980s the premier Soviet service branch.

Khrushchev's January 1960 speech to the Supreme Soviet represented a turnaround on the issue of nuclear war. He had, after all, been part of the group that had politically castigated Malenkov after the latter's 1954 statement that a new global war would mean "the end of world civilization."[12] Two years later, at the XX Party Congress, Khrushchev himself retired Stalin's thesis that world war was somehow inevitable, thus outflanking his critics on the right after outflanking Malenkov on the left.[13]

Before the Supreme Soviet, Khrushchev declared that the very na-

[12] See Raymond Garthoff, *Soviet Strategy in the Nuclear Age* (New York: Praeger, 1962), pp. 22–25.

[13] Stalin had reaffirmed that thesis in his 1952 pamphlet, *Economic Problems of Socialism* (Moscow: Foreign Languages Publishing House, 1952).

ture of war had changed, and that the experience of past wars could not predict the intensity of the violence that would occur in a new war.

> Now if war begins, military operations would proceed differently, since states will have the means to deliver weapons over thousands of kilometers. War would begin in the heart of the warring countries; moreover there would not be a single capital, not a single major industrial or administrative center, not a single strategic area which would not be subjected to attack, not only during the first days, but during the first minutes of the war.[14]

He followed this description with a discussion of his plans for troop cuts, and with a defense of his efforts at arms control in the United Nations.

The new Khrushchev doctrine represented a Soviet version of Massive Retaliation. (Indeed, a month after the Supreme Soviet speech, the *New York Times* called the new doctrine "the sincerest form of flattery," and claimed that "Khrushchev has been compelled by fundamental logic to embrace NATO concepts.")[15] Ironically, Khrushchev was coming to this position at roughly the time the Americans were abandoning it; Eisenhower had never fully agreed with Dulles's vision of Massive Retaliation (as the second Quemoy crisis in 1958 showed), and John F. Kennedy would outright abandon it once in office.[16] Indeed, no US president wanted to be left with the two-option strategy Khrushchev was now pursuing: surrender or global *Götterdammerung*. Moreover, Khrushchev did not seem to share, at least publicly, Kennedy or Eisenhower's doubts about the outcome of a nuclear war; the Soviet Union, he argued, although crippled, would emerge from this war to act as capitalism's pallbearer and successor. "Should the aggressors unleash a new war," Khrushchev told the Supreme Soviet, "not only would it be their last war, but it would be the death of capitalism."[17]

Khrushchev's line on deterrence, however, was somewhat more sophisticated. The Khrushchevian view was that deterrence, for better or worse, existed as a fact, in that the imperialists were aggressive,

---

[14] *Pravda*, January 16, 1960, p. 2.

[15] "Khrushchev Adopts NATO Strategy," *New York Times*, February 6, 1960, p. 18.

[16] Newhouse quotes Ike as saying in 1958, "You just can't have this kind of war. There aren't enough bulldozers to scrape the bodies off the streets." Newhouse, *War and Peace in the Nuclear Age*, pp. 121–126.

[17] *Pravda*, January 16, 1960, p. 2.

but they were neither stupid nor insane.[18] Here, at least, Khrushchev and the military agreed to reject the emerging Western view of nuclear war as mutually "suicidal." Victory would be to the USSR, at an admittedly high cost.

The new doctrine carried implications for all areas of Soviet defense policy. Since the nature of the ensuing war would be a short one, perhaps only a matter of hours, there was therefore little point in structuring the economy for a quick mobilization for a protracted war. Industrial priorities, too, would change, since traditional roles of nonnuclear military forces were to change, and in some cases, cease to exist. The Soviet "New Look" brought about key changes in force levels and composition, as well as in strategy. A detailed analysis of some these changes will help to frame the opposition that arose in the wake of the 1960 speech.

THE CONVENTIONAL DEEMPHASIS

It is axiomatic that people are the most expensive component of military budgets. In line with a conceptual shift from a European land war to a thermonuclear war, Khrushchev's January 1960 announcement included a plan to cut Soviet standing forces by 1,200,000 men.[19] The actual implementation of these reductions was suspended at the halfway mark due to the 1961 Berlin crisis and never resumed, although Khrushchev did publicly call for resumption of the cuts in late 1963.[20]

The logic of Khrushchev's deemphasis on conventional forces was in his refusal to disaggregate nuclear and conventional might:

> You, comrades deputies, will probably agree that one cannot now approach the problem of the numerical strength of the army as one did just a few years ago. . . . In our time the defense potential of the country is not determined by the number of our soldiers under arms, by the num-

[18] According to the most recent installment of his memoirs, Khrushchev claims that Fidel Castro never understood that the purpose of the Cuban missiles was to deter, rather than to destroy, the United States, and that he even told the Soviets that they should preempt U.S. retaliation and inflict a nuclear first strike on the Americans, a policy Khrushchev thought reckless. See N. Khrushchev, *Khrushchev Remembers: The Glasnost Tapes*, trans. Strobe Talbott (Boston: Little, Brown, 1990), pp. 177–178.

[19] *Izvestiia*, January 15, 1960, p. 1.

[20] The cuts never resumed. See Thomas Wolfe, *Soviet Power and Europe 1945–1970* (Baltimore: Johns Hopkins University Press, 1970), p. 165; see also Robert Slusser's account of this period in *The Berlin Crisis of 1961* (New York: Praeger, 1973).

ber of persons in naval uniform . . . the defense potential of the country, to a decisive extent, depends on the total firepower and the means of delivery available to the given side.[21]

One argument that Khrushchev did not make, but of which he was no doubt aware, concerned the problem of finding enough men to staff the army, even if a way could be found to pay for them. The deaths of so many men in World War II produced a massive shortfall of expected births, with the number of males reaching age nineteen falling from 2,300,000 in 1960 to 960,000 in 1963.[22]

If the military as whole found the troop cuts galling, the Soviet Ground Forces had an even bigger surprise in store for them. Between 1960 and 1964, there was a continual downgrading of the Ground Forces, the very core of the Soviet military. Khrushchev even eliminated the Ground Forces' high command structure in August 1964, a slap in the face that would not be rectified until late 1967.[23]

The Ground Forces were not to suffer without companionship. The Soviet Navy, never a privileged service branch, was not to be expanded. The new naval emphasis was on submarines, and the rest of the Soviet Navy was left, so to speak, high and dry. This situation persisted until after Khrushchev's departure, despite a painful lesson in the utility of naval forces during the Cuban missile crisis. Although there would be an increase in submarine and anti-submarine warfare (ASW) forces, the surface navy was considered obsolete and was treated accordingly.[24]

The Creation of the Strategic Rocket Forces

The new doctrine led to creation of the Strategic Rocket Forces (SRF) as a separate service branch, reflecting the time-honored bureaucratic maxim that the best way to protect a new idea is to create another organization.[25] Soviet authors always list the SRF first in their

---

[21] *Pravda*, January 16, 1960, p. 1.

[22] Scott and Scott, *Soviet Art of War*, p. 158.

[23] See Edward Warner, *The Military in Contemporary Soviet Politics* (New York: Praeger, 1977), p. 30.

[24] Khrushchev believed that carriers, as impressive as they were, would be vulnerable to submarines. For this and other aspects of his naval policy, see Khrushchev, *The Glasnost Tapes*, pp. 28–32, and Thomas Wolfe, *Soviet Strategy at the Crossroads* (Cambridge-Harvard University Press, 1964), pp. 183–187.

[25] The creation of the Strategic Defense Initiative Organization in the 1980s is good modern parallel. See Sanford Lakoff and Herbert York, *A Shield in Space? Technology, Politics and the Strategic Defense Initiative* (Berkeley: University of California Press, 1989).

discussions of the services, and this genuflection is evidence of the avowed institutional supremacy of the SRF, a hierarchy unchallenged until the 1980s in the USSR.[26] The blow to interservice prestige was lessened somewhat by rhetorical adherence to the "combined arms" concept, in which *final* victory was achievable only through interservice efforts. Even this compromise was the result of sustained military opposition and reflected a retreat by Khrushchev, but it remained nonetheless clear that the SRF was, at the very least, *primus inter pares*. Accompanying the SRF at the military pinnacle was the organization devoted to defeating enemy strategic forces, the Air Defense Forces (PVO). Marshal Malinovskii affirmed in 1960 that the SRF was "unquestionably the main service of the Armed Forces," although the true organizational standing of the SRF and the Air Defense Forces were probably better revealed in the shoddy treatment of the Navy and the Ground Forces.[27]

The size of the resources devoted to the creation of the SRF and the speed with which they were marshaled are testimony to the general secretary's influence on military matters. Once the decision was made (there were some disagreements, as will be seen), things moved quickly. The establishment of the SRF involved the energies of most major Soviet institutions: the Central Committee, the Council of Ministers, the Defense Ministry, and the MPA. All of the other services were raided for their best officers, some of whom had to be practically ordered to accept their new assignments. Marshal M. I. Nedelin, a forefather of the Soviet ICBM industry, was named service chief, although his death soon after led to the naming of Marshal K. S. Moskalenko, initially a Khrushchev client and former commander of the prestigious Moscow Military District, as his successor. By June 1960, the *voennyi sovet*, or military council, of the SRF had been created, indicating that the "period of the organizational establishment of [the SRF] was basically completed."[28]

This reorganization was accompanied by a much needed modern-

[26] There was a certain amount of controversy in the West about the possibility that the Soviets were aggregating their nuclear forces in the late 1980s, and that the SRF became part of the Strategic Nuclear Forces (SNF). Evidence usually cited includes Minister of Defense Sergei Sokolov's reference to the "strategicheskye iadernye sily" [the SRF plus Air Force and Navy strategic weapons] as the "basis of fighting power of the armed forces of the Soviet state" in *Krasnaia Zvezda*, March 2, 1986, p. 1. However, there is no evidence to support this purely Kremlinological conjecture; in any case, whatever the terminology, strategic forces were always listed first in Soviet writings from the 1960s on.

[27] Quoted in Scott and Scott, *Soviet Art of War*, p. 157.

[28] Babakov, *Vooruzhennye Sily SSSR posle voiny*, p. 98.

ization program in the armed forces. The conventional wisdom, that Khrushchev gutted the military budget in absolute terms, is mistaken. Khrushchev's policies resulted in a shift of resources *within* the military, but not an overall diversion of resources away from defense-related activities.[29] Between 1955 and 1961, Soviet forces in the field received new weapons, such as the T-54 tank and the MiG-17 (and later, the MiG-21) fighter, and officer expertise (at least as reflected by educational achievement) rose dramatically.[30] Many of these weapons systems were planned long before the 1959 speech, of course, and in later years this modernization program would slow as emphases were shifted from theater to strategic systems.

Industrial Reorganization

The dictates of doctrine and the authority of the Party combined to allow Khrushchev to reorient resources as Stalin once had. The speed with which Khrushchev overturned Soviet defense policy in 1959 initially translated into a massive reorganization of the defense industry, with the creation of new programs and the canceling of others. Although short-lived, the power Khrushchev gained over the Soviet military-industrial complex in 1959 was considerable.

One of the clearest examples of the link between leadership and design priorities was revealed in a argument between fighter designer Artem Mikoian and his brother, Politburo member Anastas Mikoian. The designer, upset over the fate of the aviation industry under the new missile doctrine, called his brother to lodge a protest. As Anastas related the episode, Artem

> spoke with anxiety about the fate of aviation. This was when we had taken a line sharply in favor of rockets. America had surpassed us in quality of strategic rockets, and this was dangerous for us, and so we made a drastic turn in favor of rockets. . . .
>
> [Artem then disagreed:] "That's right, of course, but aviation will still play its part, even in a large rocket war!

Anastas did not wish to argue with his brother, and so terminated the argument: "Temporarily, we must put our efforts into rocketry. There isn't enough to do everything!"[31]

[29] Thomas Wolfe, "Impact of Khrushchev's Downfall on Soviet Military Policy and Detente," RAND P-3010, November 1964, p. 2n.
[30] Ibid., pp. 2–3.
[31] M. S. Arlazorov, *Vint i Krylo* (Moscow: Znanie, 1980), p. 148.

The aviation designers had good reason to be upset, for they were directly and immediately affected by the change in military doctrine. Pavel Sukhoi's biographer notes that, even as Khrushchev's new doctrine was being presented, a directive arrived at Sukhoi's design bureau ordering that further research on fighter design be halted, and that attention be switched over to missiles.[32] Sukhoi was in the middle of an experimental fighter project involving titanium alloys when the change was ordered, and the abandonment of the project apparently depressed him. Upset as Sukhoi might have been, he was apparently powerless to do anything, and during a 1960 meeting of his workers at which he announced the new missile orders, he sadly referred to the stymied project as "aviation's swan song."[33]

Khrushchev himself has attested to the power of the civilian center to influence military decisions in other anecdotes. Once Khrushchev was certain, for example, that the United States was putting ICBMs into underground silos, he was furious at the engineers who he claims had talked him out of the idea:

> I'd been careful not to push [the engineers] around; I'd simply proposed the [silo] plan as part of a free exchange of opinions. But now I felt justified in giving some orders.
>
> I summoned the people responsible and said, "Now look what's happened! The Americans have begun to dig the ballistic missile shafts I proposed a long time ago. Let's get started on this program right away."[34]

And so they did. Former SRF CINC Marshal N. I. Krylov's biographer proudly writes that the process of silo-basing was completed "in a short period," in about 1963.[35] This may have been the reason that future Marshal of Engineering A. V. Gelovani was pulled from naval duty and reassigned to the SRF in 1962. In a 1987 account, Gelovani's biographer noted that "during the building of the rocket complexes, many questions arose which our builders had not encountered before."[36] The author does not specify those problems, but they were

---

[32] Kuzmina, *General'nyi konstruktor Pavel Sukhoi* (Moscow: Molodaia Gvardia, 1983), p. 195. The chronology of Kuzmina's book is at times somewhat Heisenbergian, but it is clear that this *direktiv* arrived in late 1959 or early 1960.

[33] Ibid., p. 196. Here, the date was given explicitly.

[34] Khrushchev, *The Glasnost Tapes*, p. 49.

[35] I. G. Dragan, *Marshal N. I. Krylov* (Moscow: Voenizdat, 1987), p. 226.

[36] Il'ia Tatishvili, *Marshal Inzhenernykh Voisk A. V. Gelovani* (Tbilisi: Merani, 1987), p. 42.

important enough for the SRF CINC, Marshal Biriuzov, to call in Gelovani and practically order him personally to help out in the SRF.[37]

Changes in Strategy

Soviet military exercises in the early 1960s indicate that attempts were being made to translate Khrushchev's concepts in the field. Khrushchev's doctrine was not exactly intricate in its implications for scenario planning: until 1967 all major Warsaw Pact exercises were conducted under the assumption of a war begun with massive missile strikes.[38] By 1961, the arming of USSR-based ground and aviation units with medium-range missiles was complete, two years after the creation of the Strategic Rocket Forces.[39] Even in the field, it was believed that the "basic force" of the ground troops would be operational-tactical and tactical nuclear weapons.[40] The belief that escalation was inevitable became self-fulfilling, as Soviet forces by 1961 were structured and trained at every level primarily to fight a nuclear war.

Another question of strategy posed by the Khrushchev program involved the role of surprise and preemption. Nuclear missiles of the late 1950s and early 1960s were exposed, vulnerable weapons, and this, combined with traumatic Soviet losses in World War II, led the Soviets to a strategy of nuclear preemption, although under which circumstances is unclear. Marshal V. D. Sokolovskii in particular, in his 1962 classic *Voennaia strategiia* (*Military Strategy*), argued that Western doctrine left the USSR with no other choice:

> The imperialists are preparing an offensive war against our country, a war of total destruction and annihilation of the population with nuclear weapons. Consequently, they must be countered by the determined and active operations of our Armed Forces, and primarily by devastating nuclear strikes. . . . Under present conditions, strategic defense and

[37] When Gelovani modestly agreed, Biriuzov then apparently suggested Gelovani to the Defense Ministry as his own pick for the job. The exact duties associated with Biriuzov's request are left unspecified in this account. Ibid., pp. 40–41.

[38] Desmond Ball, "Can Nuclear War Be Controlled?" *Adelphi Paper*, no. 169 (1981), p. 34.

[39] The deployment of medium-range weapons began in 1959. Babakov, *Vooruzhennye Sily SSSR posle voiny*, p. 93.

[40] N. A. Sbitov, "Revoliutsiia v voennom dele i ee resultaty," in *Problemy revoliutsii v voennom dele* (Moscow: Voenizdat, 1965), p. 93.

[69]

subsequent counterattack cannot guarantee that the aims of the war will be completely accomplished.[41]

Other Soviet sources in this period and thereafter continued to indicate a strategy of preemption, reflecting a preoccupation with seizing the initiative and striking first, an idea that predated and then outlived Khrushchev. There are no definitive statements on this issue from the political leadership, then or now, for obvious reasons.[42]

Changes in Soviet strategy and training did not mean that the military had overcome its reservations about the Khrushchev scenario. To the contrary, the high command found training for a single variant of war a disturbing and short-sighted policy. In the end, the military attacked the feasibility of the new doctrine not because it was all wrong, but because it was only half-right. Why assume that a Soviet-American conflict would begin with ICBM strikes? If deterrence was part of the raison d'être of the SRF, why assume that only the West was deterred? Are all conflicts worth threatening global destruction? In any event, why risk being prepared for only one contingency, especially an unlikely one? These criticisms were especially relevant in light of the U-2 affair in 1960 and the Berlin crisis a year later.

The military issue might have been settled more cooperatively had there not been so obvious a political motive behind the new doctrine. What right, military leaders no doubt asked, did Khrushchev have to use this new conception of warfare as a means of attacking the rights and privileges of the Soviet Armed Forces, only so recently the victors of the Great Patriotic War? And how could a premier with little command experience and even less experience in foreign affairs, properly evaluate the nature of the threat to the USSR—especially after a most un-Marxist flip-flopping on the war issue in the dispute with Malenkov?

This military dissatisfaction might have been contained had Khrushchev retained all of the Stalinist rules of the political game. Khrushchev's express avowal that he was not a new Stalin, however, meant that defense policy was no longer safe under a Stalinist shield of capricious absolutism and implied or explicit violence. Although the military supported the basic idea of the revolution in military

---

[41] V. D. Sokolovskii, *Military Strategy* (Englewood Cliffs, N.J.: Prentice-Hall, 1963), p. 403.

[42] The Americans have never revealed their plans on this subject, either, precisely because uncertainty on this point is deemed crucial to deterrence. Some Soviet officers resurrected the issue in the 1980s, as will be seen in chap. 6 and 7.

affairs, they objected to its Khrushchevian definition, and in short order their initial acquiescence turned to outright opposition.

THE REVOLUTION CHALLENGED

The military welcomed the overdue recognition of the importance of nuclear weapons, but their enthusiasm was quickly dampened by the implications of Khrushchev's program. Their opposition emerged on the question of the nature of war, as well as on more detailed issues of military organization. The professional military in the non-missile branches were openly critical of the deemphasizing of the traditional services, especially since they also questioned the prudence of relying so heavily on so large and blunt an instrument as the SRF. The blow to military prestige was compounded by their concern over losing a more traditional war, should the imperialists not oblige the new doctrine by immediately launching the expected global missile offensive.

Opposition to the new plans was led by the chief of the General Staff himself, Marshal Zakharov. One of his later successors, Gen. Mikhail Moiseev, lauded Zakharov in a 1989 account both for his general opposition to Khrushchev and more specifically for opposing a scheme to eviscerate the General Staff Academy:

> [Zakharov] was one of those who rose in opposition to the groundless decisions taken by N. S. Khrushchev in the early 1960s with regard to artillery, aviation and the navy. It demanded no small courage from M. V. Zakharov to speak out against the virtual liquidation of the Academy of the General Staff, of which he had been the head for some time and in the development of which he had played a leading role.[43]

Zakharov was fired in early 1963 and reinstated immediately after Khrushchev's removal in the fall of 1964. Moiseev's approval appears in Zakharov's history of the General Staff, which was not published until 1989 after being suppressed since its writing in 1969. Moiseev's timing is probably not accidental, and his defense of Zakharov's insubordination may have been a veiled warning to the Gorbachev leadership not to repeat Khrushchev's intrusive mistakes.

---

[43] The plan against the General Staff Academy was to cut its size by half and then subordinate the remainder under the Frunze Academy. See Moiseev's afterword in M. V. Zakharov, *General'nyi shtab v predvoennye gody* (Moscow: Voenizdat, 1989), p. 305.

Organizational Disagreements

It is hard to imagine that a million conscripts were saddened by the news that they would have to leave the glamorous life of Soviet military service. Probably less well received, however, was the news that the troop cuts included 250,000 officers, generals, and admirals. (By March 1960, 500 generals had been sacked.)[44] Military pride was stung, in part, over the poor arrangements made for transition to civilian life. During a January 1960 party *aktiv* meeting after Khrushchev's speech, Marshal Malinovskii—himself eventually to defect from supporting Khrushchev—used language strikingly similar to more recent Soviet pronouncements when he said, "Remember that we are patriots here . . . and that it does not befit a Soviet soldier to bear a grudge over the need to change his calling and to leave the military service before the end of the period needed to give him pension rights. I am sure that officers will prove their patriotism and comprehension as regards doing their duty."[45] To many officers, the changes were especially offensive in light of the new prestige being accorded the Strategic Rocket Forces and the Air Defense Forces. The problems of mid-level officers were in large part material ones, but the glorification of the SRF and the general deprecation of the Ground Forces and navy provided other good reasons for military indignation.

The troop cuts were not the only sources of practical disagreements. There was apparently some controversy over the nature of the SRF before its establishment. As Soviet military historian A. A. Babakov has explained, the advent of the missile age raised "many questions connected with the radical transformation of the USSR Armed Forces" in the Ministry of Defense, the Central Committee, and the Council of Ministers. These questions concerned the structure of the organization that would bear the responsibility for nuclear missiles. "From the beginning there were several different judgments and views," notes Babakov, "One, for example, proposed the proportional allocation of existing nuclear missile weapons among the branches of the Armed Forces—the Ground Forces, the Air Force, the Navy and the Air Defense Forces. Others considered it expedient to transfer nuclear missile weapons only to the air and naval forces."[46] A third group, the one that argued for an independent missile service,

---

[44] James Hansen, *Correlation of Forces: Four Decades of Soviet Military Development* (New York: Praeger, 1987), p. 67.
[45] Cited in Avidar, *The Party and the Army*, p. 261.
[46] Babakov, *Vooruzhennye Sily SSSR posle voiny*, pp. 96–97.

carried the day. Babakov does not say who represented which options.

Babakov's revelations support the idea that the creation of the SRF represented an end-run around the established services, who wanted a more comprehensive buildup, rather than a quick-fix missile solution to American military superiority. This is partly confirmed by defector Arkady Shevchenko's assertion that the Cuban Missile Crisis represented Khrushchev's attempts to gain a quick and easy missile advantage, an idea opposed by more thoughtful military leaders. "In the West," Shevchenko writes, "there has been a view that the Cuban operation was undertaken by Khrushchev at the instigation of the military. This is incorrect." He continues, "Khrushchev imposed an arbitrary decision on the political and military leaders. Although some of them supported his idea, most were not interested in 'quick fixes' and surrogate missile capability. They wanted solid, long-range programs to achieve parity with the United States, both in quantity and quality of strategic nuclear weaponry, and later to pursue superiority."[47] Shevchenko also believes that Khrushchev's blundering in Cuba had repercussions that lasted long beyond his tenure, for it served to strengthen the military's claims, particulary the clamor for a strong strategic buildup.[48]

A more striking source of criticism was Khrushchev's apparent belief that he had created the international conditions that allowed him to seize defense policy: "Claiming that 'the clouds of war have begun to disperse,' as a result of his 'historic' visit to the United States, [Khrushchev] initiated a significant reduction of the Soviet armed forces," according to Shevchenko.[49] This, of course, runs directly counter to the official Soviet view of the creation of the SRF and the circumstances of the Cuban fiasco.[50] The military, adhering to a world view driven by a Marxist class analysis that denied any but the most temporary respite in the tensions between the two camps, made it clear that they were not nearly as sanguine as Khrushchev about the prospects for Soviet security.[51]

[47] Arkady Shevchenko, *Breaking with Moscow* (New York: Knopf, 1985), p. 117.

[48] "In ensuing years," Shevchenko writes, "whenever opposition to [that] idea was voiced, someone would be sure to say, 'Remember what happened with Cuba?'" Ibid., p. 118.

[49] Ibid., p. 92.

[50] See, for example, V. Kobysh, "Uroki karibskogo krizisa," *Izvestiia*, October 23, 1987, p. 5, or A. Borisov, "U rokovoi cherty," *Krasnaia Zvezda*, October 21, 1987, p. 3, for typical examples of the Soviet explanation of the "missiles of October."

[51] One intriguing question suggested by Shevchenko's discussion is the possibility that Khrushchev's new doctrine created an informal alliance between the military and

In any event, it seems that rather than fight a unified military opposed to the emphasis on nuclear missiles, Khrushchev created a military institution whose survival was tied to the success of Khrushchev's doctrine. It is impossible to know if this was actually Khrushchev's explicit intention, but the possibility is especially plausible in light of similar American interservice debates; it has been argued, for example, that the U.S. Navy's rejection of the idea of the dominance of strategic air warfare in 1949 was largely motivated by its exclusion from the mission.[52] Similar attitudes may have motivated Khrushchev to avoid trying to weave nuclear weapons into established institutional attitudes.

Overall, this effort to divide the services failed, in part because the very nature of Khrushchev's attack served to bind the services in opposition. The Navy, in particular, was on the budgetary and theoretical defensive as early as 1955, when Khrushchev and his naval chief, Admiral Kuznetsov, exchanged words over the future of the Navy. "[Kuznetsov's] memorandum," according to Khrushchev, "contained proposals primarily for building cruisers and destroyers—in other words, the surface navy." (This follows Khrushchev's disparaging eyewitness account of the poor performance during exercises among the Soviet Pacific fleet.) The Presidium postponed action on Kuznetsov's proposals, and the admiral was livid. Khrushchev continues,

> Kuznetsov was waiting for me in the corridor. He started walking beside me. I could tell he was extremely agitated. Suddenly he turned on me very rudely and belligerently.
> "How long do I have to tolerate such an attitude toward my navy?" he shouted.[53]

The answer to Kuznetsov's question, in the end, turned out to be about ten years. The week after this incident, the Presidium met, and rejected his proposals; the following year, Kuznetsov was dismissed

---

Central Committee ideologists, who feared that the abandonment of power-projection abilities meant an abandonment of national liberation movements. Shevchenko, *Breaking with Moscow*, p. 93. Shevchenko does not say explicitly that such an alliance was formed, but the Soviet article on Kuznetsov (note 54) contains an account of a high-level meeting held after the October 1964 Plenum of the Central Committee, in which Mikhail Suslov and Malinovskii seemed to join in criticism of the single-war doctrine.

[52] Samuel Huntington, *The Common Defense* (New York: Columbia University Press, 1961), p. 412.

[53] Khrushchev, *The Glasnost Tapes*, pp. 25–26.

and demoted.[54] In the spring of 1960, as nearly completed Soviet warships were cut into scrap at the Leningrad dockyards, naval officers stood nearby and wept.[55]

That same year, 1955, Khrushchev was also served notice that long-range aviation supporters would be an obstacle. In a post-*glasnost'* profile of former long-range aviation chief Aleksandr Novikov, *Krasnaia Zvezda* reported this heretofore unknown scene:

> In February 1955, at a Central Committee meeting devoted to questions of raising the defense capability of the nation, Novikov gave a report on the state of long-range aviation.
>
> "We still have no strategic aviation," he said, quietly and directly. It means little to have a decision on paper. . . ."
>
> In response, they told him that there were new experimental forms of strategic jets. N. S. Khrushchev especially stressed ballistic missiles, for which there were no targets on earth that were unattainable, and never would be.
>
> Novikov firmly stuck to his position. "Having the prototypes does not mean having aviation."[56]

Apparently, Novikov stuck to his guns too resolutely. He, like Kuznetsov, was also removed, and he later found himself in charge of a civil air academy in Leningrad.

It is little wonder that there was confusion over which institution should be responsible for missile forces. Khrushchev's new doctrine, already foreseen by the premier in 1955, required the clearing away of impediments like Novikov and Kuznetsov; moreover, it showed the leadership that the missile emphasis of the new doctrine might not survive if "diluted" among the existing services, none of which would wish to accept it as it finally emerged in 1960. The creation of the SRF solved this problem.

The unintended side effect of Khrushchev's stubborn adherence to the SRF project and the rejection of any compromise was that it united the remainder of the Soviet military in their opposition. Rather than creating interservice tensions that he might later have exploited, Khrushchev instead gave the military a reason to put aside lesser institutional disagreements. It was a mistake—one that Gorbachev

---

[54] See also a Soviet account of Kuznetsov's friction with Khrushchev: "Narkom Kuznetsov," *Krasnaia Zvezda*, May 5, 1988, p. 4.

[55] Shevchenko, *Breaking with Moscow*, p. 93.

[56] "Svoia stroka," *Krasnaia Zvezda*, August 28, 1988, p. 4.

would repeat in 1987—to take on the entire military leadership at once, including, as will be seen, the intellectuals and theoreticians.

Theoretical and Conceptual Disagreements

Military opposition was rooted in deeper issues than organizational or institutional competition. Khrushchev's missile emphasis violated key tenets of Soviet military thought, and military criticism soon appeared in both open and restricted Soviet military writings. In 1958, for example, a book on Soviet military history reasserted the already outdated Stalinist line about lessons learned during World War II and the dangers of reliance on a single weapon: "The history of wars teaches that the most perfected military equipment in and of itself cannot decide the outcome of a battle or operation, [nor] can it bring victory."[57]

Other evidence suggests that there was direct civilian intervention in military-theoretical work as early as 1955. In 1960, a Soviet defector claimed that a 1955 article in the restricted journal *Voennaia Mysl'* by Marshal P. A. Rotmistrov, supporting Khrushchev's view of the importance of nuclear weapons (and even of striking first with them) did not reflect Rotmistrov's own thinking. "All officers," according to Capt. N. Artamonov, "were, of course, well aware that this article was not the result of Marshal Rotmistrov's own initiative, that he did not write it of his own free will."[58] Rotmistrov confirmed this in 1964, when he reversed himself during a period of pitched debate on Khrushchev's doctrine and stated that "calculations based on the anticipated results of using a single new type of weapon alone can lead to erroneous conclusions."[59]

Khrushchev's enforced orthodoxy quickly gave way to dissent. In 1961 and 1962 the military wrestled with the implications of the premier's seizure of defense policy, criticizing both as a matter of substance and of politics. *Kommunist Vooruzhennykh Sil* began 1961 with an article laying out the Khrushchev program in meticulous detail,

[57] *Boevoi put' Sovetskikh Vooruzhennykh Sil* (Moscow: Voenizdat, 1960), p. 553. Despite the 1960 publication date, the book was sent to press on September 3, 1958. A similar opinion was expressed in M. V. Smirnov, I. S. Baz', and P. A. Sidorov, *O Sovetskoi voennoi nauke* (Moscow: Voenizdat, 1960), pp. 239–250. This book was sent to press on August 18, 1959.

[58] U.S. House of Representatives, Committee on Un-American Activities, "Testimony of Nikolai Fedorovich Artamonov" (Washington, D.C.: USGPO, 1960), pp. 1916–1917.

[59] Quoted in Thomas Wolfe, "The Soviet Military Scene: Institutional and Defense Policy Considerations," RAND RM-4913-PR, June 1966, p. 61. The original statement appeared in *Krasnaia Zvezda* in April 1964.

including the rationale behind the troop cutbacks.[60] By the end of 1961, however, an unsigned editorial in *Voenno-Istoricheskii Zhurnal* found it necessary to defend the wisdom of the new doctrine. Indeed, by the end of 1961 there was little talk of the troop cuts; a *Voenno-Istoricheskii Zhurnal* editorial allowed (as would later authors) that "massive, multimillion-man" armies would still be essential to victory, even in the Third World War.[61]

The typical pattern among military writers, as in other areas of the Soviet media, was to begin with a Khrushchevian *pater noster* and then move on to substantial criticisms. Army General P. Kurochkin, for example, began a 1961 piece in *Voenno-Istoricheskii Zhurnal* by agreeing that the "third world war, should the imperialists unleash it, will above all be a rocket-nuclear war."[62] He then warns:

> However, it is impossible not to notice that under the influence of huge technological events, some comrades show a tendency to underestimate, or even to ignore, the experiences of past wars. . . .
>
> Nothing new, even the most revolutionary, appears by surprise, without links to the past.[63]

Kurochkin specifically absolved Marshal Malinovskii, claiming that the minister was well aware of the importance of the past, while quoting Khrushchev to much lesser effect. There could be no mistaking that Kurochkin was speaking to the ICBM strategists and their supporters.[64] This was significant criticism, for Kurochkin had been head of the Frunze Academy since 1954 (and managed to stay there throughout the early 1960s).[65]

Kurochkin's remark about the lessons of past wars, especially in light of his responsibilities as head of a combat academy, reflected military anxiety and offense at what appeared to them to be the

---

[60] S. Kozlov quotes Khrushchev's 1960 speech about the importance of firepower, and not men under arms, in reckoning state defense power. Kozlov, "O kharaktere voin sovremmnoi epokhi," *Kommunist Vooruzhennykh Sil* 2 (January 1961), p. 19.

[61] "Sovetskie Vooruzhennye Sily na strazhe stroitel'stva kommunizma," *Voenno-Istoricheskii Zhurnal* (December 1961), p. 5.

[62] P. Kurochkin, "Ob izuchenii istorii voennogo iskusstva v sovremmenykh usloviiakh," *Voenno-Istoricheskii Zhurnal* (August 1961), p. 3.

[63] Ibid., p. 4.

[64] Kurochkin actually quotes Malinovskii's direct comments on the subject of military history a few times, while Khrushchev is quoted once—in a reference that must be considered tangential to Kurochkin's point—in an excerpt taken from the premier's meeting with cosmonaut Yuri Gagarin. See Ibid., p. 4.

[65] Kurochkin served as academy head from 1954 to 1969. He died in 1989. See *Voennaia akademiia imeni M. V. Frunze* (Moscow: Voenizdat, 1988), pp. 187, 280–283.

unwarranted and disrespectful (and in the eyes of many veterans, outright stupid) dismissal of the lessons learned on the battlefield during the Great Patriotic War. Khrushchev's doctrine implied that military history had little applicability for the future, since the concept of a missile war does not encourage set-piece battles and year-long campaign plans. The issue was initially divisive even within the military as well, perhaps due to the possible gains to be made by some branches at the expense of others. Soviet author I. G. Dragan made explicit reference to this problem in his 1987 biography of Marshal N. I. Krylov:

> In the early 1960s . . . voices were being heard, ever louder and louder—and moreover, on the most diverse levels—that it was time to dismiss the experience of the front [i.e., World War II] all but totally. It was said that [this experience] had become unreliably outdated, and that it was impossible to derive anything practical from it for modern tactics and operational art. Officers and generals who were advocates of this view acted as though these were perfectly obvious facts.[66]

Krylov is presented in this account as having the intellectual foresight to dissent from this view. He argued that nuclear weapons did not replace the need for conventional weapons and operations, but rather forced the necessity of researching means of using those conventional forces under new conditions. The experience of World War II was therefore "priceless," according to Krylov, a judgment in which Dragan notes Krylov was eventually proven correct.[67]

Malinovskii agreed, noting in 1965 that "we consider it premature to 'bury' the infantry, as some people do."[68] Krylov's association with the defense minister as well as his stance on combined-arms operations may have been the motivation behind Malinovskii's insistence that he take over as CINC of the SRF, which he did in March 1963. Malinovskii was probably trying to provide balance to the SRF by naming career Ground Forces man Krylov, who strenuously tried to avoid a job that could only have been considered a major promotion.

The account of Krylov's naming as CINC of the Strategic Rocket Forces is especially interesting, in that Krylov apparently recognized the incongruity of a putting an infantry officer at the head of the

---

[66] Dragan, *Marshal N. I. Krylov*, pp. 215–216.

[67] Ibid., pp. 217–218.

[68] R. Malinovskii, "Historical Exploits of the Soviet People and Their Armed Forces in the Great Patriotic War," *Voennaia Mysl'* 5 (1965), Library of Congress microform, Washington, D.C., p. 25.

strategic deterrent. He was forced to take the job, in a scene reminiscent of Biriuzov's meeting with Gelovani, at the personal behest of Marshal Malinovskii himself, who had been impressed with Krylov when their paths had crossed during assignment to Khabarovsk. Clearly, Krylov did not want the post, and he petitioned Malinovskii to remain commander of the Moscow Military District. Malinovskii, according to a Soviet account, was not pleased: " 'Nikolai Ivanovich, I simply don't recognize you,' Malinovskii said, half-joking, half-serious. 'Remember our long-ago conversation in Khabarovsk. You were vastly more decisive then, although there were more than a few difficulties there.' "[69] Krylov answered that the SRF needed an experienced artillery officer; "I, as you know, am a combined-arms officer [*obshchevoiskovik*]." Malinovskii countered that there were few artillery officers who, like the late Nedelin, had the appropriate breadth for the job. After delaying the decision for a brief time, Krylov assumed the post, but only after being practically ordered to do so. (In 1986, Gorbachev would do the same, replacing the career SRF CINC with a younger Ground Forces man.)

While some officers, like Kurochkin and Krylov, directly attacked the thesis that military history had become inapplicable, others tried to walk a fine line, with commonsense on one side and a very forceful premier on the other.[70] In any event, the Kurochkin piece was recognized for what it was, and a response quickly appeared. The next issue of *Voenno-Istoricheskii Zhurnal*, in September 1961, carried an article by Col. P. Derevianko, an early apologist for the new doctrine, in which Derevianko stressed almost exclusively the importance of nuclear deterrence, and quoted either Khrushchev or recent Party documents no less than six times in eight pages.[71] An article the same month in *Kommunist Vooruzhennykh Sil* took a slightly different tack, praising Khrushchev and pointing out that Soviet strength is in the final analysis dependent upon a healthy economy. "Such is the dialectic of life," wrote Maj. Gen. N. Kiriaev, that "the economically stronger the Soviet nation and the nations of the socialist camp, the stronger its defense capability and the more successful the struggle for

[69] Dragan, *Marshal N. I. Krylov*, p. 220.

[70] See, for example, Grechko's fumbling attempt to reconcile both positions in 1961. A. A. Grechko, "Voennaia istoriia i sovremmenost'," *Voenno-Istoricheskii Zhurnal* 2 (February 1961), p. 4. At the time, Grechko was CINC of Warsaw Pact forces, a post to which he was named in June 1960.

[71] P. Derevianko, "Voennye voprosy v Programme KPSS," *Voenno-Istoricheskii Zhurnal* (September 1961), pp. 8–16. Derevianko also edited the seminal work on the Khrushchevian doctrine, the 1965 anthology *Problemy revoliutsii v voennom dele* (Moscow: Voenizdat, 1965). His writings indicate that he either agreed with the new doctrine, or was simply tasked with its defense.

peace."[72] (Kurochkin's vindication would come in 1965, when he would again make his case—backed up by a supporting piece from Malinovskii—in an issue of *Voennaia Mysl'* devoted to the affirmation of the importance of combined-arms warfare.)[73]

The timing of these criticisms is interesting; from the tone of their articles, it is easy to forget that Derevianko and Kiriaev were composing their responses during the hot summer of the Berlin crisis and the building of the Wall. Although neither Derevianko or Kiriaev referred to the crisis, other officers seized the opportunity to underscore the recklessness of Khrushchev's troop cuts. Three MPA officers, for example, appeared in the pages of *Kommunist Vooruzhennykh Sil* a month before the famous Checkpoint Charlie standoff of October 1961 to repeat Khrushchev's own rhetoric to make their point, including Khrushchev's August 7, 1961, television address in which he said that "the Western powers are pushing the world to a dangerous brink and it is impossible to rule out the arising of the threat of a military attack by the imperialists on the socialist states."[74]

Noted military historian Maj. Gen. P. Zhilin entered the fray with a May 1961 article on the history of the formulation of a "unified military doctrine" in the Soviet Union. It was an obvious attempt to decelerate the escalation of military opposition, and in some ways Zhilin contradicted Frunze himself in order to find middle ground between Khrushchev and the military. In a footnote to the word *doctrine* in the title, for example, Zhilin wrote that "the word doctrine comes from the Latin, and means teaching, or theory."[75] Needless to say, the official definition of doctrine—certainly as Frunze understood it—is phrased somewhat more strongly. It is interesting that Zhilin even found it necessary to mention the Latin root of the word, and his tone suggests that the controversial doctrine was still debatable—indeed, even that doctrine itself is not an iron law. But he also suggests an end to the bickering:

> All of these political and military changes demand a reexamination of many of the principal tenets of our military doctrine. *Now, as never before, it is necessary to have a uniformity of views on all of the most important questions of military art and the use of forces in war. . . .*

[72] N. Kiriaev, "Voprosy ukrepleniia oboronosposobnosti Sovetskogo gosudarstva v proekte Programmy KPSS," *Kommunist Vooruzhennykh Sil* 17 (September 1961), p. 26.

[73] See *Voennaia Mysl'* 5 (1965), Library of Congress microform.

[74] N. Sushko, S. Tiushkevich, and G. Fedorov, "Razvitie marksistsko-leniniskogo ucheniia o voine v sovremennykh usloviiakh," *Kommunist Vooruzhennykh Sil* 18 (September 1961), p. 20.

[75] P. Zhilin, "Diskussii o edinoi voennoi doktrine," *Voenno-Istoricheskii Zhurnal* (May 1961), p. 61.

In the postwar period, Soviet military science has received further creative development. . . . We have worked out fundamental principles of the conduct of modern war. However, it should be noted that in the working out of the military-technical part of doctrine, as M. V. Frunze called it, there are still many arguable and unclear tenets. . . . But in these discussions, regrettably, a unity of views has not been achieved.[76]

Apparently, Zhilin was agreeing that the military can and should discuss issues of doctrine, as long as they are not overtly political issues. However, Khrushchev intended to seize military-technical issues as well as political doctrine (to which the creation of the SRF attests), and this rendered Zhilin's compromise unworkable.

Things did not get better after 1961, despite Khrushchev's eventual public acceptance of the combined-arms concept. By 1963, military writers were talking out of both sides of their collective mouth, supporting the one-war doctrine on one page and then arguing against it on the next. For example, in January 1963 Marshal Rotmistrov made explicit reference to Khrushchev's Supreme Soviet speech, and then went on to argue that the nature of a future war "will demand huge material and human reserves, and the moral and physical strains not only on the army, but on the people and the whole state economy, will be significantly greater in comparison with the last war."[77] This is directly opposed to Khrushchev's intentions in the 1960 speech, in which he emphasized the money saved by nuclear weapons, not the money that would have to be spent maintaining "huge reserves" of men and materiel.

The debate was even more evident in the restricted journal *Voennaia Mysl'*. There, even the combined-arms doctrine was giving way to a spirited defense of the infantry. In August 1963, Maj. Gen. V. Khruchinin wrote:

> Despite the heretofore unheard-of destructive power of the rocket and nuclear weapons, the final victory in a war against a strong, unfriendly coalition is possible only as a result of the combined efforts of the Armed Forces. . . .
> *From the onset of armed conflict the Ground Troops will execute strategic missions in continental theaters* in close coordination with other branches of the armed forces.[78]

---

[76] Zhilin, p. 74, emphasis in original.

[77] P. Rotmistrov, "Prichiny sovremennykh voin i ikh osobennosti," *Kommunist Vooruzhennykh Sil* 2 (January 1963), p. 31.

[78] V. Khruchinin, "Contemporary Strategic Theory on the Goals and Missions of Armed Conflict," in U.S. Air Force, *Selected Readings from Military Thought, 1963–1973* (Washington, D.C.: USGPO, 1982), pp. 3, 9, emphasis added.

Elsewhere in his article Khruchinin generally adhered to the Khrushchev line, but that does not obscure his attempt to defend the importance of traditional forces.

In early 1964, Captain 1st Rank V. Kulakov began an article in *Voennaia Mysl'* by citing Khrushchev's point about the possibilities of raising combat power while decreasing the number of men. Having done his duty, Kulakov quickly turned to the problems of Khrushchev's plan: "The idea of 'replacing men with weapons' very inaccurately reflects reality. New weapons increase the combat capability of men, but do not replace them. In modern war, equipment plays an extremely great, even increasing role. But along with this the role of men, too, in waging armed conflict is constantly increasing." He then warned that "a growth in the role of the individual man in armed conflict is an inevitable consequence, conforming to objective law, of military-technical progress."[79]

In the same issue, Maj. Gen. Kh. Dzhelaukhov of the General Staff Academy went even further, arrogating to himself the task of clarifying doctrine.

> In explaining the idea of "augmentation of strategic efforts in modern conditions," we proceed from the following principles of Soviet military doctrine: *first, recognition that even in modern war massive armies are required;* second, the position that victory over a strong enemy can be achieved by the joint efforts of all the basic types of armed forces with close cooperation among them and with the decisive role of strategic rocket troops.

What this meant, in terms of Khrushchev's plans for force reductions, was this:

> It seems to us that, despite the existence of nuclear weapons in their organization, the augmentation of strategic efforts for [the Ground Forces, the PVO, the Air Force and the Navy] will be achieved mainly by a quantitative increase and a qualitative improvement of their forces and equipment. *A similar position is noted in the military doctrines of all the major powers of the world and in theories of military strategy.* In them is foreseen the creation of massive armed forces and subsequently increasing their numerical strength.[80]

[79] V. Kulakov, "Problems of Military-Technical Superiority," in U.S. Air Force, *Selected Readings*, p. 21.
[80] Kh. Dzhelaukhov, "Augmentation of Strategic Efforts in Modern Armed Conflict," U.S. Air Force, *Selected Readings*, p. 32, emphasis added.

Here, Dzhelaukhov grasps at the straw of citing foreign—imperialist, even—doctrines in his defense of the conventional branches. The timing of his comments is especially ironic: they appeared the very month (August 1964) that Khrushchev eliminated the Ground Forces' command structure.

Dzhelaukhov had gone too far, even for his military comrades. In September 1964, *Voennaia Mysl'* published a series of chastising comments on his article. "Nuclear weapons and other means of mass destruction, not manpower and conventional armament, will now play the main role in strategic groups," admonished Maj. Gen. K. Sevast'ianov.[81] "Nuclear weapons are a primary and necessary means of affecting the augmentation of efforts," continued Maj. Gen. N. Vasendin. "All remaining methods of solving this problem stem from where, when, and how much nuclear means are employed. . . . Thus, the term 'augmentation of strategic efforts' must not be examined in the literal sense."[82] It is not clear whether this criticism was self-policing by the military, or was forced into the pages of *Voennaia Mysl'*. In any event, it was too little and too late, for it was apparent that Dzhelaukhov was not alone.[83]

Dzhelaukhov's reprimand in fact meant little. By 1964, even Marshal Malinovskii was turning a blind eye to the military rejection of Khrushchev's claim to theoretical supremacy. In March, Maj. Gen. S. Kozlov began a discussion of military doctrine by referring to it as, "in the expression of the Minister of Defense, Marshal Malinovskii, tightly interlaced with military science."[84] Military science, in the Soviet usage, is a more elastic term, generally concerned more with military-technical issues rather than politics. It is also the acknowledged preserve of the military professionals, and Kozlov used that fact to make explicit the military claim to influence defense policy: "Like doctrine, military science conditions policy." The remainder of the piece is an attempt to separate the subjects of doctrine and science, but in the end Kozlov is left, in essence, to propose that the military should stop arguing over what he admits to be the politically loaded concept of

[81] K. Sevast'ianov, "Comments on the Article 'Augmentation of Strategic Efforts in Modern Armed Conflict'," U.S. Air Force, *Selected Readings*, p. 58.

[82] Ibid., pp. 60–61.

[83] See, for example the response to Maj. Gen V. Reznichenko's article. Reznichenko apparently discussed the possibilities of non-nuclear combat in early 1964, a position that generated some support as well as criticism in later months. The responses appeared in "Problems of Modern Combined-Arms Combat," *Voennaia Mysl'* 10 (1964), Library of Congress microform.

[84] S. Kozlov, "Voennaia doktrina i voennaia nauka," *Kommunist Vooruzhennykh Sil* 5 (March 1964), p. 9.

"doctrine" proper and instead should shift its discussions to the arena of military science: "Once doctrine is adopted, it is not necessary to continue its discussion . . . in science the struggle of opinions is inherent, it is a law of its development."[85]

These developments in the military press told a simple but significant story: from 1961 to 1964, the military simply wrested the defense issue away from the civilians, and from Khrushchev (who had gone to the trouble in 1964 of having himself named a Hero of the Soviet Union) specifically. Indeed, after 1965, military dissenters such as Khruchinin and Dzhelaukhov would become the core of the General Staff Academy's strategy faculty, training future generations of senior officers.[86] Khrushchev expostulated on what was intended to be the definitive view of future conflict; after a brief period of trepidation, reflection, or both, the military decided to circumvent him, and discuss issues of national, as well as institutional, importance. The Soviet civil-military relationship would never be the same again.

THE NEW MANAGEMENT ARRIVES

In military affairs, the Brezhnev leadership sought to do two things upon arrival. The first was to smooth over the ruffled feathers caused by Khrushchev's reforms. Brezhnev owed a debt to the military, as Georgii Arbatov noted: "I can't judge how actively Biriuzov and then Minister of Defense R. Ia. Malinovskii supported the conspirators (although many knew later through whom Brezhnev tried to establish first contact with Biriuzov)." In any case, Arbatov says, Brezhnev, "from the very beginning of his tenure in the leadership, looked upon the military as a very important base of his own power."[87]

The second priority was to attempt to salvage some of the policies of their predecessor, to avoid throwing out the détentist baby with the radical bathwater. The military was allowed to vent its spleen a bit, and criticize Khrushchev publicly (although not by name), all in an effort to calm jangled military nerves.[88] A 1965 explication of the Party program on defense, edited by military officers, presented the new leadership's military policy as a collective, sober work, thus reflecting military satisfaction with the less extreme course taken by the new

---

[85] Ibid., p. 13.

[86] See *Akademiia general'nogo shtaba*, p. 137.

[87] Arbatov, *Zatianuvsheesiia vyzdorovlenie*, pp. 107, 232.

[88] See Avidar, *The Party and the Army*, pp. 314–318; Wolfe, "Impact of Khrushchev's Downfall," pp. 17–22.

management. Defense policy, the officers wrote, was now "the creation of the collective wisdom of our Party," presumably in contrast to the singular foolishness of the former Premier.[89] They also defended the concept of peaceful coexistence while separating it from Khrushchev personally, writing that "our Party considers peaceful coexistence not as a subjective wish of this or that political figure, but rather as an objective [phenomenon]."[90]

The definition of doctrine itself was returning during this period to the concept of coldly objective law. In 1966, a Soviet military text entitled *Methodological Problems of Military Theory and Practice* defined doctrine as "a system of scientifically based views" on the nature and conduct of war, a far cry from Zhilin's earlier "Latin roots" business. The 1966 definition also reflected the emerging modus vivendi about doctrine that was being reached. No longer was it the premier's private preserve: "Military doctrine is worked out by the political and military leadership of the state. . . . it is not dogma, nor is it an eternal, unchanging category."[91] Agreements apparently had been made, and between 1965 and 1967 the Soviet military took over the business of redefining doctrine, on paper and in the field.

The Revolution Rewritten: Thermidor, 1965–1967

Soviet civil-military friction between 1960 and 1964 was inadvertently to shape the contours of Soviet doctrine for the next twenty years. In the wake of Khrushchev's activism, the Brezhnev leadership retreated from the doctrinal arena, and the military set about the task of rectifying the mistakes of the early 1960s.

The major mistake to be corrected was Khrushchev's overly optimistic assumption that the Americans would be satisfied with a nuclear standoff, in which the missile-centric doctrines of both sides would ensure peace. Sokolovskii correctly noted in 1966 that the West abandoned Massive Retaliation in 1961, because reliance on the threat of global nuclear war was "inflexible" and did nothing to guarantee

---

[89] *Programma KPSS o zashchite sotsialisticheskogo Otechestva*, 2d ed. (Moscow: Voenizdat, 1965), p. 29. The volume, edited by K. Bochkarev, I. Prusanov, and A. Babakov, was sent to press in the summer of 1965.

[90] Ibid., pp. 53–56. At one point, the authors deal with the question of what role the masses could possibly play in war likely to be begun behind closed doors. The answer was that the masses affect the correlation of forces, which even the imperialist must take into account in their plans.

[91] Maj. Gen. S. N. Kozlov is credited with the chapter on military doctrine. *Metodologicheskie problemy voennoi teorii i praktiki* (Moscow: Voenizdat, 1966), p. 85. The volume was sent to press in June 1966.

[85]

the attainment of the imperialists' political objectives.[92] The Soviet military had recognized the same flaw in their own strategy, even if Khrushchev had not, but even within the military approaches to the solution differed, with two tendencies emerging in the early post-Khrushchev period. On one side were the officers arguing for more flexible and realistic scenarios; on the other were defenders of the ICBM-dominant orthodoxy, who apparently saw useful brinkmanship in the Khrushchev approach. In April 1966 Sokolovskii and Maj. Gen. M. Cherednichenko stressed the essential continuity of NATO strategy (flexible response notwithstanding), and argued that the "danger of the aggressor's sudden nuclear attack" was as real and present as ever.[93] At a December 1966 press conference, Sokolovskii repeated his belief that any future war would "immediately become thermonuclear."[94] Sokolovskii was not alone in this belief, although he was one of its most prominent proponents.[95]

If Sokolovskii was not alone, he was also not a majority. (Even Sokolovskii himself would finally retreat from the Khrushchev scenario after 1967, for reasons that probably had as much to do with the Chinese as the Americans.)[96] More detailed criticisms of the "one-war" doctrine emerged quickly after Khrushchev's departure, including Gen. N. Shtemenko's 1965 statement that local wars may not be nuclear wars, an observation that later provided Gen. N. Lomov (Malinovskii's former chief of staff in the Far East) the opportunity to comment that local wars, "fought, as a rule, with conventional arms," could even occur in Europe.[97]

The question of conflict duration was directly related to the issue of nuclear use. Soviet scenarists of the early 1960s were forced to consider only a short, brutal, and decisive ICBM duel. After 1965, this view was tempered somewhat. As Col. I. Grudinin put it in early 1966,

[92] V. D. Sokolovskii, *Voennaia strategiia*, 3d ed. (Moscow: Voenizdat, 1966), p. 72.
[93] V. Sokolovskii and M. Cherednichenko, "O sovremmenoi voennoi strategii," *Kommunist Vooruzhennykh Sil* 7 (April 1966), pp. 63–65.
[94] Quoted in Wolfe, *Soviet Power and Europe*, p. 454n.
[95] See, for example Col. M. Skovorodkin, "Some Questions on Coordination of Branches of Armed Forces in Major Operations," in U.S. Air Force, *Selected Readings*, pp. 141–151. Skovorodkin's piece originally appeared in *Voennaia Mysl'* in February 1967; in it, he defends the primacy of nuclear weapons as well as the apocalyptic Khrushchev scenario.
[96] See V. Sokolovskii and M. Cherednichenko, "Military Strategy and Its Problems," *Voennaia Mysl'* 9 (1968), Library of Congress microform, for Sokolovskii's explicit acceptance of non-nuclear major conflicts.
[97] Quoted in ibid., p. 82.

Along with the possibility of a [short], swift-moving war, there exists the possibility a long, drawn-out war. From this comes the necessity to prepare our Armed Forces simultaneously for winning victory both in a short time and in a lengthy battle.

In the event of a drawn-out war, the early preparation of human and material resources are needed, as well as the ability of the state to expand the means of waging armed conflict quickly in time of war, including conventional sorts of responses.[98]

The message is clear: spend more money now, because later will be too late. Turning Khrushchev's argument on its head, Grudinin cleverly pointed to the immediacy of missile warfare in order to warn that "More *time* is needed now for the production of the latest armaments, as well as more reserves and qualified working hands"[99] One of the authors of the 1965 book on the Party defense program, Col. I. Prusanov, made a similar point in the same issue of *Kommunist Vooruzhennykh Sil*. After a brief nod to the "paramount" role of nuclear missiles in modern warfare, Prusanov wrote that the Soviet armed forces "should be prepared to guarantee the crushing defeat of the enemy not only in conditions of the use of nuclear weapons, but also with only the conventional means of battle."[100]

As these reevaluations progressed, attempts were being made in the field to examine the issues that were being raised. Between 1962 and 1965, inclusive, there were ten Warsaw Pact exercises of varying size and duration. Of these, two each were held in Poland, Czechoslovakia, German Democratic Republic, and Bulgaria; Hungary and Romania each hosted one.[101] After Khrushchev's fall, and the reassessment of his doctrine, there was a significant increase in the number of maneuvers as the Soviets sought to reestablish their conventional combat skills. In 1966, three joint maneuvers (two of which took place in East Germany) were held, the highest number in four years. In 1967, the Pact went on a record seven joint maneuvers in six months, all but three of which were held, again, in the GDR.

The increased frequency of Pact exercises after Khrushchev's departure was matched by a change in emphasis. As early as 1965, Soviet

---

[98] I. Grudinin, "Faktor vremeni v sovremennoi voine," *Kommunist Vooruzhennykh Sil* no. 4 (February 1966), p. 41.

[99] Ibid., p. 41, emphasis in original.

[100] I. Prusanov, *Kommunist Vooruzhennykh Sil*, no. 4 (February 1966), p. 10.

[101] These and other figures in this discussion were taken from the following sources: Jeffrey Simon, *Warsaw Pact Forces* (Boulder, Colo.: Westview, 1985), pp. 27–41; and Wolte, *Soviet Power and Europe*, pp. 477–482.

commanders were exploring more protracted conventional scenarios, an option denied them while Khrushchev was in power. Although Warsaw Pact exercises before 1967 always began with a simulated nuclear exchange, even as early as 1965 pact planners were increasing the scope and broadening the character of their war games. The famous "October Storm" exercise of 1965, for example, involved 50,000 men and stressed the transport of airborne units from outside the combat area; the basic scenario posited a non-nuclear NATO surprise attack and Pact counterattack, during which the West resorts to nuclear weapons.[102] This stands in notable contrast to the 1962 *Vitr* maneuvers, which envisioned a massive Western surprise attack, repulsed in desperation by virtually everything in the Pact armory, including nuclear weapons.[103] By the time the landmark *Dniepr* exercises were conducted in 1967, it was obvious that the Soviets had discarded fundamental aspects of Khrushchev's one-war thinking.[104]

The ultimate synthesis can be seen in this 1970 statement by Marshal Grechko, by then the minister of defense:

> In modern conditions the most important principles of combat, operational and political preparation of the personnel of the Armed Forces are predetermined by the tenets of Soviet military doctrine, according to which a new world war, if it is unleashed by the imperialists, will be a decisive confrontation of two systems. The aggressive imperialist bloc will oppose a coalition of the socialist nations united in their general political and military goals. The chief and decisive means of the conduct of combat will be rocket nuclear weapons. The "classical" types of weapons will be used as well. Certain conditions will allow the conduct of combat operations with units using conventional weapons.
>
> We have given much attention to the reasonable combination of rocket-nuclear weapons and "classical" arms. From strategic nuclear rockets to the newest combat means of the motorized rifle forces—such is the range of our weaponry. Army and navy personnel learn the conduct of combat actions under conditions where nuclear weapons are used, as well as without their use.[105]

Khrushchev's doctrine was dead. More important, its replacement had come not from the Party, but from the General Staff; the civilians

[102] Simon, *Warsaw Pact*, p. 33.

[103] Ibid., p. 19.

[104] *Dniepr*, in Simon's words, "set the tone for future Warsaw Pact exercises," in that it reflected "the notion that war in Europe could now be fought with conventional arms after a long march." Ibid., p. 35.

[105] A. Grechko, "Vernost' leninskim zavetam o zashchite Rodiny," *Kommunist Vooruzhennykh Sil*, no. 7 (April 1970), p. 21.

would never recapture either the absolute powers of Stalin or the brief authority of Khrushchev. Defense policy had changed hands, possibly for good.

THE POLITICAL SYNTHESIS: WHAT DID KHRUSHCHEV WANT?

The details of the military-theoretical effects of Khrushchev's innovation in doctrine are fairly clear, but what do they suggest about the evolution of Soviet civil-military relations? Khrushchev's seizure of defense policy reflected the Stalinist pattern in transition, a weakening of the power of the political center and yet another manifestation of the withering of the totalitarian system of control. Certainly, many aspects of the Stalinist pattern were discernible in the post-1959 reorganization of doctrine and forces. But the fact remained that Stalin was gone, and the open (and partly successful) military opposition to Khrushchev's innovations indicated that Khrushchev could not replicate the original pattern itself.

This is not to say that Khrushchev was a "Stalinist"; rather, he acted in what he saw to be both the national interest and his own political interest. (It is useful to bear in mind Robert Tucker's wise observation that to treat opportunistic behavior in a politician as incompatible with deeply held beliefs is to take a simplistic view of political man.)[106] The Stalinist version of subjective control, the control of military policy by one civilian leader, was the norm, not the exception, when Khrushchev emerged as Stalin's successor. He himself was aware of his political heritage, as he admitted in his memoirs: "I have to admit that . . . Stalin was still belching inside me. Keep in mind, I'd worked under Stalin for years and years, and you don't free yourself from [Stalinist] habits so easily. It takes time to become aware of your shortcomings and free yourself from them."[107] In the final analysis, perhaps Khrushchev simply stepped into a vacuum and attempted to grab the reins of military control left unattended in the wake of Stalin's death. The military, for its part, sought finally to gain greater autonomy, the result of which would be a defense policy that would be both militarily coherent, ideologically consistent, and institutionally gratifying. The contest was inconclusive: Khrushchev was ousted, the military was reorganized, and the most offensive aspects of the new doctrine were deleted while its core concept remained.

[106] Robert Tucker, *Stalinism* (New York: Norton, 1977), p. 97.
[107] Khrushchev, *The Last Testament*, p. 67.

[89]

The Brezhnev regime was in no mood for a rematch with the military, nor did it see any apparent need for one. As the Party's commitment to ideology waned in the 1970s, the military returned even more strongly to its Marxist roots. For a time, this did not lead to immediate conflict, and the Soviet civil-military relationship proceeded more smoothly in the next decade, with neither side unduly affronting the other. This would last only so long as civilian indifference and the supply of rubles lasted, but for a time it seemed that the Party and Army had had enough of a struggle that had been bruising to both.

Back to the Future

The next chapter describes the "golden age" of Soviet civil-military relations and shows how the unraveling of that consensus created the predicament in which Gorbachev found himself. Although the expansion of Soviet capabilities in the 1970s generated huge amounts of work for Soviet strategists, "doctrine" did not reemerge as an issue of contention until 1985, and then primarily because Gorbachev had chosen to make it one. This was preceded by a growing unease in the military, as in 1954, about changes in American policy and developments in military technology. While Brezhnev spoke of "military détente" and stable deterrence, the military began to paint dark pictures of potential disaster.

[4]

The "Golden Age" and After: Brezhnev's Retreat and Military Ascendance

Brezhnev, from the very beginning of his tenure in the leadership, looked upon the military as a very important base of his power. And so he therefore tried to give them practically everything they asked for.
—Georgii Arbatov, September 1990

We thank the Central Committee of the Party, the Politburo and Leonid Il'ich Brezhnev personally for their continuing and tireless concern about the Armed Forces of our state.
—Marshal A. A. Grechko, January 1975

THE CIVILIAN RETREAT

The struggle over defense policy in the early 1960s had not been kind to either the Party or the military, and by 1965 both sides were ready for a more cooperative relationship. This cooperation took the form of a civilian retreat, in the wake of which defense issues were largely left to the soldiers. This period of relative tranquility, however, did not reflect a general resolution of the civil-military problem in the Soviet Union; rather, it reflected only a truce, in which the military was given a share of political power and the Party was given an oath of political peace. Just as the turbulent 1960s produced Kolkowicz' descriptions of Party-Army conflict, so the torpid 1970s led to the images of accommodation and symbiosis described by Odom. What the civilians failed to realize was that influence, once given, is difficult to rescind.

And influence was indeed given. The Brezhnev era has come to be widely regarded in Western writings as, in Jeremy Azrael's terms, a "golden age," in which "the Soviet high command got almost everything it wanted in terms of resources, programs, status, and freedom of action in developing Soviet strategic concepts."[1] Brezhnev's passivity came to create problems of its own, however, and the expansion of military influence in foreign and defense affairs proved difficult to scale back. According to Brezhnev adviser Arbatov, the compromise was simple: defense issues fell largely to the generals (and ex officio to Brezhnev and Defense Minister Dmitrii Ustinov) while "the remaining members of the Politburo simply decided not to interfere in military matters," with the possible and occasional exceptions of Andropov and Gromyko.[2]

For various political and practical reasons both the Party and the military welcomed the civil-military truce that followed in the wake of Khrushchev's forced retirement. From the perspective of national security, it became ever more obvious through the 1960s that the Khrushchev doctrine was no more viable in the Soviet Union than Massive Retaliation had been in the United States in the 1950s; theoretical and practical flaws left both East and West pondering the question of what should be done in cases less than all-out war. Even as Massive Retaliation was evolving into Flexible Response (an evolution codified by NATO in 1967), many Soviet officers also saw a need for options other than annihilating civilization in wartime, and Brezhnev's doctrinal cease-fire meant that these issues could be more openly evaluated by the military without constant interference from the Party.

From a political standpoint, the civilian leadership had little reason to want a continuation of the civil-military tensions that plagued the Khrushchev regime. At the least, Brezhnev and his partners had more respect for the uniformed military than did Khrushchev, whose disdain for professional soldiers was barely concealed. But the Brezhnev leadership's more flexible stance served a more political purpose as well, for the civil-military rift had made policymaking more difficult, leaving the USSR lacking clear direction in the accelerating (and increasingly global) Soviet-American military competition. Moreover, the ire of the generals and officers threatened to raise uncomfortable questions of the Party's legitimacy—questions that would reemerge in 1989—in a state that predicated much of its own

[1] Jeremy Azrael, "The Soviet Civilian Leadership and the Military High Command, 1976–1986," RAND R-3251-AF, p. 2.

[2] Georgii Arbatov, *Zatiamuvsheesiia vyzdovrovlenie (1953–1986 gg.)* (Moscow: "Mezhdunarodnye otnosheniia," 1990), p. 233.

rectitude on the accumulation of massive military power. In the end, the new arrangement met the military's demand for autonomy, satisfied the leadership's desires for obedience, and mitigated almost everyone's concerns about the nonviability of Khrushchev's military doctrine.

Despite the emergence of an apparently more modern civil-military relationship, this arrangement did not represent a move toward objective control. Indeed, the primary obstacles to the development of objective control were the attitudes of both groups. For its part, the leadership did not seek a rational division of labor between soldiers and civilians, choosing abdication of responsibility rather than a solution to the problem. Objective control implies trust, and none was given or asked on an institutional level. Instead, personal arrangements of loyalty were made, with military appointments becoming more, rather than less, politicized—hardly a surprise, given the increase in general cronyism under Brezhnev. Likewise, on the part of the military, there was a growing insularity among the military professionals that represented deepening arrogance rather than increasing professionalization. These two tendencies, the fading strength of civil authority and the increasing encroachment of military specialists, would collide in the early 1980s, when the Brezhnev leadership would seek to regain control of military issues.

PRESTIGE, GUNS, AND MONEY

The first step in reconciling Party and Army in the 1960s was the restoration of both prestige and budgetary latitude to the high command. It was evident at the outset that the new collective leadership intended to provide the military with new weapons, an open state purse, and a renewed respect. One of the most important symbolic as well as practical steps in the restoration of the Soviet military took place in 1964, when Marshal Zakharov was returned to his post as chief of the General Staff and allowed to make scathing remarks about "hare-brained schemers." In 1967, Marshal of the Soviet Union Andrei Grechko was appointed minister of defense after Malinovskii's death. This was another victory for the military, since Grechko was every inch a career combat officer and, like Malinovskii, therefore one of their own. Grechko represented more than just the continuity of keeping a military professional in the Defense Ministry; he soon came to personify the ascending influence of the military in civil councils of power.

[93]

Concrete plans for rebuilding the military were also proceeding apace, in part because the rapid growth of the Soviet economy in the late 1960s would defer any painful decisions about guns and butter. The Party leaders made this plain during the XXIII Party Congress of 1966, the first of the Brezhnev-Kosygin collective leadership. Soviet military commentary in the wake of the Congress was generally positive, although there was, of course, brief concern about Kosygin. One group of military authors seized on Kosygin's comment about the increasing cost of military hardware, warning that "military affairs are continuing to develop quickly. The imperialist states are making every effort to gain an advantage over us in the military area. Therefore now the significance of military science, the correct scientific-technical policy of the CPSU, and the all-around development of our economy has especially increased."[3] They need not have worried, since even Kosygin's watered-down economic reforms would be defeated soon enough, and the explosive growth of the Soviet military would commence.[4]

"All-Azimuth" Buildup

The military had good material reason to be initially content with the Brezhnev leadership. Soviet strategic and conventional capabilities (including naval power) increased dramatically, and previously oppressed branches were restored to positions of respect, a process that culminated in the restoration of the high command of the Ground Forces in 1967.

The expansion of the Soviet military during the late 1960s and into the 1980s has been documented at length elsewhere, and will not be recounted in detail here.[5] A few figures give some idea of the scale of the buildup: between 1967 and 1977, the number of fixed-wing aircraft in Europe alone increased by 20 percent (tactical air power rose 25 percent overall); the number of tanks grew by 31 percent (40 percent overall); artillery, by 38 percent (60 percent overall), and armored personnel carriers by an impressive 79 percent. In the same period, growth in strategic forces culminated with the 1975 SS-18 ICBM deployments, the ten-warhead weapon that generated the mathematics

[3] *KPSS i stroitel'stvo sovetskikh vooruzhennykh sil* (Moscow: Voenizdat, 1967), p. 372.
[4] See George Breslauer, *Khrushchev and Brezhnev as Leaders* (London: Allen and Unwin, 1982), for a more complete history of the Kosygin reforms.
[5] One straightforward chronology of this process is available in James Hansen's *Correlation of Forces* (New York: Praeger, 1987).

of the "window of vulnerability."[6] Naval expansion was also undertaken: while the submarine fleet (a favorite Khrushchev project anyway) grew by only 6 percent, the naval air inventory increased 29 percent; cruisers and destroyers increased by 33 percent (with the number of missile-armed ships more than tripling) and frigates and escorts by 44 percent.[7]

Clearly, the civil-military truce had carried a price. Through the early 1970s, the military commanded huge resources because, as David Holloway has noted, "in the late 1960s the doctrinal debates of that decade were settled in an open-ended way, which provided a framework within which all elements of the armed forces could press their claims. The Party leaders accepted this settlement and thus left themselves open to military pressure."[8] Thus, the high command was allowed to prepare for almost every contingency it identified. The Soviet military took advantage of this "open-ended" resolution (that is to say, no resolution) to engage in the "all-azimuth" planning that characterized Soviet military policy in the 1960s and 1970s.[9]

The result, according to Arbatov, was that the "military and the military-industrial complex were a government within the government," whose sphere was "perfectly untouchable." Brezhnev, Arbatov claims, "was more than a little indebted to the support of the military . . . over the years he became the chief party curator of the military industry, and the generals and the military designers got used to being refused practically nothing."[10] Military satisfaction with this blank financial and theoretical check was evident, as Soviet officers made regular reference in the 1970s to their "first-class" weapons. In return, they tempered their gloomy assessments of the world to make mention of the positive changes in the international environment and the correlation of forces, crediting the Party for these im-

---

[6] The United States at the time had 1,000 Minuteman silos and 54 Titan missiles, making a total of 1,054 land-based targets. The Soviets deployed 308 SS-18s making a total of 3,080 warheads. The reasoning went that the Soviets could reliably destroy the entire American land-based deterrent (targeting 2 warheads per silo) and still use only a fraction of their missile force. The issue was a potent one in the 1980 U.S. presidential election.

[7] See W. Y. Smith, "Soviet Military Capabilities: Status and Trends," in *The USSR and the Sources of Soviet Policy*, Kennan Institute Occasional Papers, no. 34, 1977.

[8] David Holloway, "Decision-Making in Soviet Defence Politics," *Adelphi Paper*, no. 152 (1981), p. 28.

[9] For one of many such examples, see "Ispytannym leninskim kursom," *Kommunist Vooruzhennykh Sil*, no. 1 (January 1967), pp. 3–5.

[10] Arbatov, *Zatiamuvsheesiia vyzdorovlenie*, p. 194.

provements rather than relating them to the relentless growth of Soviet military capabilities and the relative (and, as time would tell, temporary) military decline of the United States.[11]

It is evidence of military complacency that the common theme reflected professional concerns about the assimilation of weaponry, rather than its acquisition. Marshal Kulikov, for example, wrote during his tenure as chief of the General Staff in 1973 that the armed forces had everything necessary for "struggle with a strong opponent," but that technology alone could not provide victory if the weapons were handled by incompetent soldiers.[12] As John Erickson pointed out at the time, Kulikov spoke of this process of receiving the most modern weapons "as if it were now the established and natural order of things, wholly irreversible."[13]

The Takeover of Doctrine

The arms buildup was not undertaken for its own sake; much-needed changes in strategy were under way as well. The military, freed from Khrushchev's narrow dictates, began to make provisions for serious and protracted conflict in Eurasia as well as elsewhere. The General Staff Academy held several conferences on out-of-area conflicts in 1969, attended by Generals N. A. Lomov, N. A. Sbitov and M. Cherednichenko, some of the earliest "local war" theorists. (There could be no doubt, of course, that one such area was China.)[14] And although the Soviet military expected a nuclear war in Europe, the advent of parity and the arrival of Mutual Assured Destruction (as a fact if not as a desirable policy) meant that it preferred a conventional war, if possible, and Soviet strategists planned—and spent—for the event should it arise.[15] Indeed, the bulk of the research work on this subject was carried out at the Voroshilov Academy, where some of Khrushchev's most blunt military critics had become instructors after

[11] See, for example, M. Cherednichenko, "Nauchno-tekhnicheskii progress i nekotorye problemy voennoi nauki," *Kommunist Vooruzhennykh Sil* 3 (July 1976), p. 9; S. G. Gorshkov, "Opyt istorii i sovremennost'," *Voprosy Filosofii* 5 (1976), p. 37. For an earlier such comment, see M. V. Zakharov, "Uroki istorii," *Kommunist* 9 (September 1971), p. 75; E. Mal'tsev, "Leninskie idei zashchity sotsializma," *Krasnaia Zvezda*, February 14, 1974, pp. 2–3.

[12] V. Kulikov, "Vysokaia boegotovnost'—vazhneishee uslovie nadezhnoi zashchity rodiny," *Kommunist Vooruzhennykh Sil* 6 (March 1973), p. 18.

[13] John Erickson, "Trends in the Soviet Combined-Arms Concept," *Strategic Review* (Winter 1977), p. 39.

[14] *Akademiia general'nogo shtaba* (Moscow: Voenizdat, 1987), p. 146.

[15] See Phillip Petersen and John Hines, "The Conventional Offensive in Soviet Theater Strategy," *Orbis* (Fall 1983), esp. pp. 695–705.

1965. The innovative wrinkle bought by all this hardware was the ability to indulge a heavy emphasis on the rapid conventional neutralization of NATO nuclear and conventional forces, essentially a conventional pre-emptive strike.[16]

Thus, the Brezhnevian civil-military rapprochement meant more than a hardware buildup; it also meant a civilian retreat on the right to define defense policy more broadly. Repeatedly, Soviet officers made claims for military science and military strategy that were in theory strictly the preserve of the Party. Although Khrushchev had only inadvertently opened the door to military influence on defense policy, Brezhnev now accepted it as part of what was hoped to be a more harmonious relationship with the Soviet high command.

The military leadership quickly adopted this enlargement of their role as a right rather than a privilege. A subtle but clear sign of this attitude appeared in 1968 in the restricted pages of *Voennaia Mysl'*, when Marshal V. Sokolovskii and Maj. Gen. Cherednichenko defined "military strategy" thusly:

> It seems to us that the general subject of military strategy as a science may be stated as: determination of the nature, character and condition of the outbreak of various types of wars; the theory of organization of the armed forces, of their structure, and development of a system of military equipment and armament; the theory of strategic planning; the theory of strategic deployment, establishment of strategic groupings, and the maintenance of the combat readiness of the armed forces; the theory of the preparation of the economy and the country as a whole for war in all respects, including preparation of the population in a moral sense, the creation of reserve supplies of arms, combat equipment and other material resources; the development of methods of conducting armed struggle, of types and forms of strategic operations; determination of forms and methods of strategic leadership of the armed forces; the development of command systems; the study and evaluation of a probable enemy; the theory of strategic intelligence; and the theory on the possible results of a war.[17]

In other words, the subjects of military strategy, and therefore properly the legitimate prerogatives of the military, are everything con-

---

[16] See John Sloan, Ali Jalali, and Guhlam Wardak, "Soviet Front Level Planning Methods" (McLean, Va.: Science Applications), November 15, 1985.

[17] V. Sokolovskii and M. Cherednichenko, "Military Strategy and Its Problems," *Voennaia Mysl'* 9, 1968, Library of Congress microform, Washington, D.C., p. 35. The earlier comment about strategy and policy may be found in V. Sokolovskii and M. Cherednichenko, "O sovremennoi voennoi strategii," *Kommunist Vooruzhennykh Sil* 7 (April 1966), p. 61.

nected with defense policy. In theory, military strategy is subordinate to military doctrine, but it is clear that by 1968 both were dominated by the General Staff. Because this definition accurately reflected the state of affairs at the time (evident from the statements of Marshal Grechko as well), the Soviet military therefore had good reason to consider their political situation under Brezhnev to be the best they had ever enjoyed.[18]

The growing encroachment of the military on defense policy reappeared time and again in the military press of the late 1960s and early 1970s. Marshal Zakharov himself, back in his old office as General Staff chief, turned the structure of military doctrine upside down in 1968 when he claimed that Soviet military science, the product of the military professionals, had provided the basis for successful Party policies in military matters, and that military doctrine must be based on military science, rather than vice versa.[19] (This claim, as will be seen, persisted into the 1980s.) These and other such comments represented a trend among military writers to eschew the use of the term "doctrine" altogether and instead refer to Soviet military strategy, military science, or military theory, even when it was clear that the reference was to issues that were instantly recognizable as military doctrine.[20]

Nor was this some sort of detached, theoretical debate; the military took seriously its new powers in doctrine. Arbatov tells, for example, of how Marshal Grechko made a last-ditch effort to torpedo SALT I,

---

[18] See, for example, A. Grechko, "Torzhestvo leninskikh idei o zashchite sotsialisticheskogo Otechestva," *Kommunist Vooruzhennykh Sil* 20 (October 1967), esp. pp. 34–35; A. Grechko, "Vernost' leninskim zavetam o zashchite Rodiny," *Kommunist Vooruzhennykh Sil*, no. 7 (April 1970).

[19] M. Zakharov, "Soviet Military Science over Fifty Years, *Voennaia Mysl'* 2 (1968), Library of Congress microform, p. 36.

[20] One such example was the 1970 declaration by the then-deputy political chief of the SRF that the combined-arms doctrine was a product of military "theory," perhaps an inadvertent admission of the true source of combined arms. N. Leont'ev, "Raketno-iadernyi shchit rodiny," *Kommunist Vooruzhennykh Sil* 20 (October 1970), p. 37. Col. Gen. Baskakov followed suit in an article about war and society in which he made constant reference to military "theory," even when discussing the structure and preparation of the armed forces for war. V. Baskakov, "O sootnoshenii voini kak obshchestvennogo iavleniia i vooruzhennoi bor'by," *Kommunist Vooruzhennykh Sil* 1 (January 1971), p. 41. Likewise, military academic A. Milovidov in 1973 chastised Soviet civilians who wrote on military issues from a strictly quantitative perspective, reaffirming that military theory and the problem of war needed to be based on military science, defined as "the unified system of knowledge about the laws of armed combat, the character and peculiarities of modern wars, and the means and methods of their conduct in the interests of the defense of the socialist Fatherland." A. Milovidov, "Filosofskii analiz voennoi mysli," *Krasnaia Zvezda*, May 17, 1973, p. 2.

inadvertently revealing the degree to which the Soviet military had come to see itself as the stewards of Soviet defense policy. Until Brezhnev became ill, he

> not only objected to, but actually entered into conflict with, the military. This happened, for example, during the discussions of SALT I. In the Politburo, Marshal Grechko expressed his objections to the already agreed upon text, declaring that he, *as the one responsible for the security of the nation*, could not give his assent. Brezhnev, the chairman of the Defense Council and the Commander in Chief, reasonably thought that he above all was responsible for the security of the nation. The Minister of Defense's declaration stung him deeply, and he then insisted on [the treaty's] approval from the Politburo, after sharply setting Grechko straight.[21]

Arbatov says that Grechko later apologized, but makes it clear that this sort of usurpation continued and accelerated as Brezhnev's health declined.

It should be understood that this struggle for military doctrine and defense planning took place among a select group of the military leadership. As a rule, the typical junior and mid-level Soviet officer was told that military issues were subordinate to political priorities. This does not change the fact, however, that the senior military had managed to appropriate issues that had been formerly out of their reach.

Nor is it to deny that the political leadership did still make doctrinal pronouncements. But more and more these pronouncements, whatever their intention, were primarily rhetorical, devoid of genuine impact on the Soviet military establishment.[22] On occasion these statements were similar in style to military rhetoric; such statements, however, almost never led to the same conclusions or recommendations reached by military authors, and they tended to be directed at audiences of foreign Communists with whom Soviet spokesmen might be expected in any case to be more ideologically orthodox.

All in all, the outlines of the civil-military deal were clear: the military would have a substantial say in defense policy, including deep participation in arms control and other security-related matters, while the political leadership would conduct more routine diplomacy and consult with their military colleagues on important issues of defense.

[21] Arbatov, *Zatianuvsheesiia vyzdorovlenie*, p. 233, emphasis added.

[22] The case of Brezhnev's famous Tula speech, discussed later, is one example. The speech, given in January 18, 1977, appears in L. Brezhnev, *Na strazhe mira i sotsializma* (Moscow: Politizdat, 1979), pp. 487–493.

This bargain was made explicit in the 1967 book, *The CPSU and the Construction of the Armed Forces*, in which the military described the leading role of the Party in the creation of doctrine.[23] The doctrine described therein, of course, was the one designed and polished by the military. The Party finally had an acknowledgment of its own primacy in military doctrine, but at the expense of allowing that doctrine to be created by the military itself.

Although this arrangement kept the civil-military peace—that is, preserved the social contract of mutual support between the high command and the political leadership—in the 1960s, it became increasingly apparent to the Brezhnev leadership that the abdication of defense policy would threaten the domestic gains of détente in the 1970s.

THE DETERIORATION OF DÉTENTE AND THE NEW COLD WAR

Into the early 1970s, Brezhnev could claim with some credibility that his attempts to maintain détente, and to pursue arms negotiations in the face of his emerging military critics, had paid off. The record from 1967 onward was generally good, and reflected undeniably impressive foreign policy gains for the USSR. Even the opprobrium over the invasion of Czechoslovakia—Brezhnev's handling of which, ironically, seemed to solidify his ascendance over the other members of the Politburo—eventually faded as Brezhnev's *Westpolitik* picked up momentum in the early 1970s.[24] As Adam Ulam has described it, Soviet policy at this time was "patient and subtle," designed to "emphasize Soviet Russia's new respectability as contrasted with America's recently displayed [i.e., in Vietnam] irresponsibility."[25] The result, it was hoped, would be the dilution of American influence in Europe as the citizens of the continent began to question which superpower was really the more dangerous and unpredictable.

Of course, the political leadership had good reason to press for better relations with the West. A more immediate but narrow issue was the need to contain China, whose radicalism was a source of

---

[23] There was even an echo of the strange 1961 business about the "Latin root" of the word "doctrine"—this time, the word was translated more strictly in accord with the Soviet understanding of the term. *KPSS i stroitel'stvo*, p. 407.

[24] See Anthony D'Agostino, *Soviet Succession Struggles* (Winchester, Mass.: Unwin Hyman, 1988), p. 206.

[25] Adam Ulam, *Expansion and Coexistence*, 2d ed. (New York: Holt, Rhinehart, 1974), p. 722.

apprehension to military and civilians alike. Moreover, the Soviets were beginning to fear a hostile encirclement, caught between China and NATO. As far as the eastern borders were concerned, this was hardly a fantasy; there were some 400 border skirmishes between Soviet and Chinese troops in 1969 alone, several of them quite serious.[26] The Chinese situation was creating problems for the political leadership both at home and abroad: in the Politburo, Marshal Grechko called for debate on the issue of using nuclear weapons against China in 1969, while still only a candidate member of that body.[27] Meanwhile, Sino-Soviet tensions provided the Americans with leverage against both sides, and the Soviets knew it.[28]

More broadly, between 1968 and 1972 the Soviets were finally on the verge of attaining a rough nuclear parity with the United States, and this drove much of the push for détente in both the East and West.[29] Moscow hoped that this achievement would lead to the treatment of the USSR as an equal on a global scale, which would in turn allow the Soviets to compete with the Americans for influence in Europe and elsewhere while claiming the rights of a fellow status-quo power. This acknowledgment of equality came in the Basic Principles agreement of May 1972, signed three days after SALT I. Brezhnev spelled out what the agreement meant at the XXV Congress in 1976, citing it as part of Soviet achievements to create "a solid political and legal basis for the development of mutually advantageous relations between the USSR and the USA on the principles of peaceful coexistence," despite the fact that "it is no secret that there are certain difficulties" which had arisen from Washington's policies.[30]

Despite the "difficulties," Brezhnev had managed to overcome military objections to the détentist line. In the mid-1970s, the USSR would reach both the height of its international powers, and the turning point on the path to eventual disintegration. As the Soviet position (and Brezhnev's health) worsened throughout the 1970s, Brezhnev remained determined to preserve détente, while the military stood even more firmly in defense of its ideological and material prerogatives.

In 1975, the Soviets reached what they might well have considered

---

[26] Hansen, *Correlation of Forces*, p. 99.

[27] Brezhnev, said Shevchenko, would have vetoed any such use anyway. John Newhouse, *War and Peace in the Nuclear Age* (New York: Knopf, 1989), p. 218.

[28] See ibid., pp. 223–226, and Arbatov, *Zatianuvsheesiia vyzdorovleniie*, pp. 195–199.

[29] The Soviets built more than 1,000 land-based and submarine missile launchers between 1968 and 1972. Hansen, *Correlation of Forces*, p. 95.

[30] *Materialy XXV s"ezda KPSS* (Moscow: Politizdat, 1977), pp. 20–21.

a high-water mark in their foreign policy. The appearance of the SS-18 heavy ICBM had, rightly or wrongly, intensified U.S. insecurity about the "window of vulnerability" ostensibly opened by dramatic Soviet strategic gains. Overseas, Saigon fell, and the Americans soon made it clear—in their reticence with regard to the Angolan situation—that the United States had had enough of overseas adventures for the time being. Marshal Grechko had no such reservations, however, and he warned that the Soviets would henceforth be more active in support of national liberation struggles "in whatever distant region of our planet" they may appear.[31] A year later, Cuban soldiers headed for Luanda, and the overall number of Soviet advisers in the Third World topped 7,000, despite a setback in the loss of their Egyptian client.[32] The U.S. Congress remained unimpressed, as did the American people, who in 1976 elected a president whose foreign policy decried an "inordinate fear of Communism."

Within the Kremlin as well Brezhnev had reason for optimism; his position after the XXV Congress, at least vis-à-vis the other members of the civilian leadership, was unarguably strengthened. By 1977, Brezhnev had vanquished potential rivals Piotr Shelest and Aleksandr Shelepin (dismissed in 1973 and 1976, respectively) and Nikolai Podgorny (promoted into irrelevance in 1977). More important, Grechko had passed away in early 1976, opening an opportunity for Brezhnev to try to gain more control over the Defense Ministry. Grechko had been a thorn in the leadership's side, an uncompromising, aggressive, anti-Western officer who was viewed by Brezhnev as "unreliable" and difficult.[33] Brezhnev was apparently determined not to make the same mistake twice; in early 1976, he appointed a civilian defense industrialist, his old friend (and later "Marshal"), Dmitrii Ustinov, as defense minister.

Certainly, more control over the military was going to be crucial to Soviet economic health in the late 1970s, whatever Brezhnev may have thought of Grechko.[34] Whereas common estimates indicate that Soviet growth slowed to about 2 percent in the late 1970s, some Soviet economists now believe that in fact the USSR was at zero-growth by

---

[31] Cited in Hansen, *Correlation of Forces*, p. 134.

[32] Ibid., p. 136.

[33] Arbatov, *Zatianuvsheesiia vyzdorovlenie*, p. 286.

[34] See Abraham Becker, "Ogarkov's Complaint and Gorbachev's Dilemma: The Soviet Defense Budget and Party Military Conflict," RAND R-3541-AF, December 1987, for the actual statistics on the military impact of the Soviet economic slowdown in the late 1970s. See also Azrael, "Soviet Civilian Leadership," pp. 6–7.

1976, which would mean that military expenditures were still rising even as the nonmilitary economy shrank.[35] (This did not apparently faze Marshal Grechko, who had continued to insist until his death that "developed socialism" could and would continue to provide the material resources the military wanted.[36]) Naming Ustinov to the post of defense minister at the time was no doubt part of the plan to prepare the military for the scaling back of financial and political influence to be attempted by the Brezhnev leadership in the late 1970s and early 1980s.[37] But Ustinov was the wrong man for the job; quite possibly he took to his new rank and post and became part of the military in his own way. As Arbatov has described him, "it was as if Ustinov was trying to prove that a civilian minister could do even more for military departments than a professional soldier."[38]

It would be unfair to lay too much of the blame for the decline of Soviet foreign policy (and the deterioration of the civil-military relationship) on Ustinov's epaulets. (Indeed, even the Soviet military cleared Ustinov in a sort of mini-rehabilitation in 1988, claiming that Ustinov did the best he could within the confines of the ossified Brezhnev leadership).[39] Nothing could change the fact that by 1976, military control of defense policy had metastasized too far, and the leadership had become too weak (politically and physically), to mount an effective challenge to military priorities.

The Brezhnev leadership reacted too slowly and incompetently to stop the military takeover of defense policy in the late 1960s and early 1970s, but in the last years of the Brezhnev-Andropov period it appears that civilian leaders made an effort at some sort of damage control. Specifically, Brezhnev and others tried to depict the international situation in ways that would undermine military alarmism, a tactic attempted by Khrushchev in 1959, and one that Gorbachev would try again in 1985 and 1986. As early as the XXIII Party Congress in 1966, Brezhnev could be seen pushing for a more relaxed relationship with the West even at the height of the Vietnam War, decrying

[35] See "Survey: Perestroika," *Economist*, April 28–May 4, 1990, p. Survey 5. The two economists cited are Grigorii Khanin and Vasilii Seliunin.

[36] A. A. Grechko, "Rukovodiashchaia rol' KPSS v stroitel'stve armii razvitogo sotsialisticheskogo obshchestva," *Voprosy Istorii KPSS*, no. 5 (May 1974), p. 41.

[37] For more on Ustinov's appointment, see Azrael, "Soviet Civilian Leadership," pp. 5–6.

[38] Arbatov, *Zatianuvsheesiia vyzdorovlenie*, p. 233

[39] In part, this was because military officers found his reign as defense minister in the end not as odious as they might have expected it to be when he first took office. See "'Kakovo delo rukh tvoikh, takova i chest'," *Krasnaia Zvezda*, October 29, 1988, p. 2.

American aggressiveness in one statement and then advocating expanded East-West relations in the next.[40]

This pattern became more obvious after 1977, as Brezhnev offered more detailed statements about Soviet foreign policy. This is important, because it suggests that the "Gorbachev line" of the mid-1980s was not new, but rather an extension of Brezhnev's efforts in years before. Indeed, the similarity between Brezhnev's rhetoric in his last years and the first strains of Gorbachev's "New Political Thinking" is striking, and it suggests that the juxtaposition of military aggressiveness with Party pragmatism is not new.

Whatever other disagreements may have arisen between the leadership and the high command, it was undeniable that détente itself had begun to deteriorate almost as soon as it was achieved. Many factors contributed to this deterioration on both sides, including differing Soviet and American perceptions of the relationship, the erosion of the Nixon administration, the ossification of the Brezhnev leadership, Soviet successes and American failures in the Third World, and the inexorable pressure of technological advance. By 1976, the word "détente" would be banned from the White House, thousands of Soviet military advisers would be scattered throughout the Southern Hemisphere, the Americans would be in the midst of a wrenching election, and the prospects of greater Soviet-American cooperation began to fade quickly. The Soviets themselves, as Georgii Arbatov admits, were responsible for fumbling away much of the progress made in superpower relations in the 1970s; in adventures from Africa to Asia to Latin America, the Soviets squandered their image as a status-quo power.[41]

The Turning Point: 1979–1980

By 1979, détente, the arms control process, and superpower relations in general lay in ashes. In the West, the turning point in the military's assessment of the political changes—and two major defeats for Brezhnev—occurred in 1979, generated by the one-two punch of theater nuclear missile modernization and the Carter administration's official acceptance of a "counterforce" nuclear strategy. The knockout blow, delivered within days of NATO's "two-track" decision approving INF deployments, would be the invasion of Afghanistan and the

---

[40] *23rd Congress of the Communist Party of the Soviet Union* (Moscow: Novosti, 1966), pp. 50–52.
[41] Arbatov, *Zatianuvsheesiia vyzdorovlenie*, p. 235.

simultaneous collapse of détente and the SALT process. The Soviet military shared culpability for all three events, but that did not stop them from exploiting the deterioration in relations to press their case.

The Intermediate-Range Nuclear Forces Decision

In 1977, the Soviet Union began to deploy the SS-20 missile, a three-warhead weapon fielded supposedly as the replacement for aging SS-4s and SS-5s. But the Europeans—even the French, who called the SS-20 *"le grand menace"*—and particularly the West Germans, saw things differently.[42] Although the extra military capacity bought by the more accurate and more destructive SS-20 was questionable, the political impact of the weapon was undeniable. The SS-20 deployments (coupled with President Jimmy Carter's fumbled neutron-bomb decision the same year) galvanized NATO into accepting modernized American theater nuclear forces consisting of Pershing II and ground-launched cruise missiles. Although there was considerable domestic opposition to these weapons in most of the NATO nations, all members agreed at a December 1979 meeting to accept them on their soil, including even the Dutch and the Belgians. Worse yet, the two-track decision turned out to be only one aspect of an all-around effort aimed at raising NATO's nuclear *and* conventional capabilities.[43]

The SS-20 debacle was a defeat of the first order for Soviet policy, and it had been brought on by the Soviet military. Arbatov, who has argued bluntly that the SS-20s led directly to the NATO INF decision, claims that most of the diplomatic and foreign policy establishment was against the SS-20 deployments, including Gromyko. Gromyko, in this account, refused to oppose the Defense Ministry, and Ustinov personally, "because he was somewhat afraid of Ustinov, above all because he was already thinking about what might happen after Brezhnev."[44] Arbatov then went to Andropov, who also stonewalled him, probably for the same reason. In the end, Arbatov believes that Brezhnev might have opposed the SS-20s had his health been better.[45]

But the SS-20s were deployed as planned. Negotiations on theater

---

[42] Hansen, *Correlation of Forces*, p. 109.

[43] For the report of the European Security Study, see ESECS, *Strengthening Conventional Deterrence in Europe* (New York: St Martin's, 1983). The study was initiated in mid-1981.

[44] Arbatov, *Zatianuvsheesiia vyzdorovlenie*, pp. 236–237.

[45] Ibid.

arms were about to flicker out; SALT II remained. Within days of the INF decisions, a second Soviet blunder would take care of that as well.

Into Afghanistan

If the SS-20 deployments had reawakened the Americans and their European partners to a Soviet threat, the rest of the world quickly joined that assessment in the last days of 1979 when the Soviet Union invaded and occupied Afghanistan. The international reaction was one of outrage, and even if there had been no previous qualms about SALT II (and there were), there was now no way for the U.S. Senate to ratify the treaty. The damage done to the superpower relationship was deep and swift; "détente," in any form, was buried, Jimmy Carter, locked in electoral combat with Ronald Reagan and disillusioned by Soviet actions, emerged as a "born again" Cold Warrior, and the Soviets watched as some twelve years of hard diplomatic work went up in flames. In the end, Afghanistan was only the last and heaviest straw on the camel's back, a burden that included a trail of Soviet meddling from Ethiopia to Angola to Nicaragua. The SALT talks, as Zbigniew Brzezinski had said, might have lain buried in the Ogaden, but détente itself disappeared into the snows of the Afghan mountains.

It should be noted, as Bruce Porter has convincingly demonstrated, that Afghanistan never became a serious issue of civil-military contention.[46] There were several reasons for this: first and foremost was that the high command and the Party leadership shared the blame for the Afghan decision. Although the military now claims that the decision was opposed by many senior officers, Arbatov and others have countered that the Ministry of Defense itself was the "chief advocate" of intervention.[47] In any event, all of the major decision makers— including Brezhnev, Ustinov, Gromyko, and Andropov—were dead by the time Afghanistan became the quagmire it did, and there was no point in either soldiers or civilians assigning blame to each other.

Another fact to be kept in mind about Afghanistan is that the Soviet commitment, while large, was still not large enough or far enough away to produce the kinds of dislocations so familiar to Americans during Vietnam. As a measure of comparison, Porter points out that

---

[46] See Bruce Porter, "The Military Abroad," in Timothy Colton and Thane Gustafson, eds., *Soldiers and the Soviet State* (Princeton: Princeton University Press, 1990).
[47] Arbatov, *Zatianuvsheesiia vyzdorovlenie,* p. 230.

over 21 percent of total U.S. forces were deployed in Vietnam in at the peak of that conflict, while the corresponding figure for the Soviet Union in Afghanistan was only 2.1 percent in 1985, or ten times smaller; as a percentage of total national population, the Soviet toll in Afghanistan was less than one-fifth that of the United States in Vietnam.[48]

This is not to say that Afghanistan did not create severe social and political liabilities over the ten years of the conflict; in particular the social impact of returning veterans has been a visible and troubling aspect of the Soviet scene in the 1980s. Rather, it is to point out that the war in Afghanistan did not displace other, more central concerns in the civil-military agenda, at the top of which always remained the strategic relationship with the United States.

Presidential Directive 59

Afghanistan may have been the proximate cause of the final collapse of détente, but there were strategic trends that would have complicated Soviet-American relations in any case. Specifically, the Americans were seeking a way out of the corner into which parity, and later, the new threat of the SS-18s, had placed them. The result was embodied in PD (Presidential Directive) no. 59.[49]

Officially adopted in the summer of 1980, PD-59 was a nuclear war plan with a twist. Rather than seeking merely to destroy cities or even military targets, PD-59 sought to create a strategy designed to destroy what the Soviets valued most: Communist control of the Eurasian land mass. To this end, PD-59 envisioned striking everything from Soviet command and control facilities to the Soviet leadership bunkers themselves.[50] Although PD-59 was more a targeting "wishlist" of questionable executability than an actual war plan, the Soviet military reaction was, as might be expected, singularly hostile. Military analysts argued that PD-59 was nothing less than a conscious attempt to gain first-strike superiority through decapitating attacks. Even a more moderate critic like Gen. M. A. Mil'shtein (retired and working as an "Americanist" for Arbatov's USA/Canada institute)

---

[48] Porter, "The Military Abroad," p. 294.

[49] See Newhouse, *War and Peace in the Nuclear Age*, pp. 286–287, for an explanation of the policy genesis of PD-59.

[50] See Lawrence Freedman, *The Evolution of Nuclear Strategy* (New York: St. Martin's, 1983), pp. 393–394, and Newhouse, *War and Peace*, p. 286; for a detailed critique of the counterforce strategy, see Robert Jervis, *The Illogic of American Nuclear Strategy* (Ithaca: Cornell Press, 1981).

accused the United States in May 1980 of turning away from the stable deterrence of the 1970s, claiming that America's commitment to mutual deterrence had become purely rhetorical.[51]

Worse, from the point of view of Soviet-American relations more broadly, was that PD-59 eradicated any difference between Carter and then-candidate Reagan in the Soviet military view.[52] In the wake of Afghanistan, Carter had moved dramatically to the right both in terms of his attitude toward the Soviets and his concrete decision to begin a serious strategic buildup that would include the MX missile. To the Soviet military (and to many other critics of PD-59), this was no longer a struggle between American hawks and doves, but rather a watershed in U.S. policy that transcended personalities—a point echoed by Ogarkov in 1981 when he wrote that PD-59 had been "gladly" picked up by the new Reagan administration.[53] Later Soviet analyses would mark 1979 as turning point in American foreign policy and describe PD-59 as the root of the Reagan administration's family tree of subsequent military concepts.[54] Although there was a recognition in some Soviet circles that Soviet behavior had to some extent brought Reagan to the White House, the military, according to Arbatov, actually profited from the 1980 election; Reagan's rhetoric bolstered the arguments of the high command, he claims, despite the fact that Reagan, "it must be acknowledged, came to power not without our help."[55]

THE "APOGEE OF STAGNATION" AND THE END OF THE GOLDEN AGE

Brezhnev's increasing efforts to gain some control over the defense agenda were evident especially in his evolution from the XXV to the XXVI Party Congresses (1976 to 1981), a period Arbatov rightly calls

[51] M. A. Mil'shtein, "Nekotorye kharakternye cherty sovremennoi voennoi doktriny Ssha," *SShA* 5 (May 1980), p. 11. Mil'shtein was one of the "institutchiki" supporting Gorbachev's New Thinking, and a more optimistic proponent of better relations with the United States than his many of his former military colleagues.

[52] L. Semeiko, "Stavka na potentsial pervogo udara," *Krasnaia Zvezda*, August 8, 1980, p. 3; see also L. Semeiko, "Direktiva no. 59: Evolutsiia ili skachok?" *Novoe Vremia* 38 (1980), pp. 5–7.

[53] N. Ogarkov, "Na strazhe mirnogo truda," *Kommunist* 10 (Oct. 1981), p. 81.

[54] See, for example, *Gonka Vooruzhennii: Prichini, Tendentsii, Puti Prekrashcheniia* (Moscow: Mezhdunarodnaia Otnosheniia, 1986), p. 61; V. Beletskii, *Potsdam 1945: Istoriia i sovremennost'* (Moscow: Mezhdunarodnaia Otnosheniia, 1987), pp. 298–299.

[55] Arbatov, *Zatianuvsheesiia vyzdorovlenie*, pp. 241–242.

the "apogee of *zastoi*," the stagnation that has come to be associated with the Brezhnev era.[56]

As Bruce Parrott has noted, Brezhnev's commitment to keeping the civil-military truce by continual emphasis on military power began to fade as early as 1974.[57] This turnaround was probably due to three factors. First, Brezhnev no doubt wanted to consolidate his personal power, and the military was a natural target after the removal of his rivals in the Politburo. Second, Brezhnev and the rest of the Politburo leadership (including, to some extent Grechko shortly before his death) were looking ahead to the increasingly poor performance of the already sclerotic Soviet economy; measures had to be taken to undermine the military's apparently insatiable claim on Soviet resources. Finally, there is some possibility that Brezhnev was beginning to have some understanding of the meaning of nuclear parity and the implications of a major war. Although Brezhnev, according to Arbatov, was "weak" as a theoretician, "he always had his feet on the ground," and he understood even by the late 1960s that keeping the peace while improving the Soviet Union's international situation had to be the highest priority.[58]

But Brezhnev's change of heart, sincere or otherwise, was not supported either by the high command or by events in the real world. Claims like those made by Chief of the General Staff Ogarkov and Warsaw Pact CINC Kulikov for greater ideological and diplomatic militancy were supported by the steady worsening of superpower relations from the mid-1970s to the early 1980s; yet in this period Brezhnev's tone seems to become more conciliatory even as tensions became more pronounced. Brezhnev's attempts to recapture the military agenda became, due as much to his growing infirmity as to his acceptance of his own cult of personality, increasingly (and with heavy-handed ineptitude) the tactics of subjective control.

"Marshal" Brezhnev

The successes of détente and the growth of the Brezhnevian cult on Brezhnev's attitude toward the military were evident. His 1965 Victory Day speech contained references to the heroism of the armed forces, along with a description of the perfidy of the Western ap-

---

[56] Ibid., p. 219.
[57] Bruce Parrott, "Political Change and Civil-Military Relations," in Colton and Gustafson, *Soldiers and the Soviet State*, p. 56.
[58] Arbatov, *Zatianuvsheesiia vyzdorovlenie*, p. 191.

peasers who had hoped Hitler would smash the Soviet Union. By 1975 the glorification of the military had been toned down, and Brezhnev stood in the Kremlin to "welcome esteemed guests from the nations of the anti-Hitlerite coalition" of Britain, the United States and France, all of whom were greeted with applause.[59]

After 1975, Brezhnev accelerated his efforts to enshrine himself at the head of the armed forces, including the accumulation of ranks and awards. At the 1976 Victory Day celebration, incredulous military officers would be treated to the spectacle of Brezhnev immodestly awarding himself the rank of Marshal of the Soviet Union, mentioning his own contributions to the war effort before those of the armed forces as a whole.[60] In addition to the Hero of the Soviet Union medal given him in 1966, Brezhnev awarded himself that title three more times in 1976, 1978, and 1981, in addition to the eight Orders of Lenin, two Orders of the October Revolution, and countless other medals he had acquired in the 1970s.[61] By contrast, Khrushchev named himself a Hero of the Soviet Union only once, choosing instead to acquire several Hero of Socialist Labor awards; Gorbachev was never named a Hero of the Soviet Union.[62] This avalanche of honors for Brezhnev grated on men who knew what trials had to be endured to attain honors such as the gold and platinum Victory Medal, normally reserved for giants of combat such as Zhukov (who in the end was buried with fewer medals than "Marshal" Brezhnev). Zhores Medvedev writes that "everyone knew he was conferring the awards on himself" and that such "absurdities contributed to the growing disillusionment of the military with Brezhnev's leadership."[63] Military writings in later years pointedly ignored these additions to Brezhnev's titles.[64]

Defense of Détente, 1976–1981

As the domestic economic crisis deepened, Brezhnev clung to détentist rhetoric more tenaciously, despite the deterioration of East-

---

[59] Brezhnev, *Na strazhe mira i sotsializma*, pp. 17–20, 377.

[60] Ibid., p. 440.

[61] A joke making the rounds in Brezhnev's day told of an earthquake in Moscow caused by Brezhnev's jacket falling from a coatrack.

[62] See the entries for both leaders in the biographical reference *Geroi sovetskogo soiuza*, vols. 1–2 (Moscow: Voenizdat, 1987), for the full listing of military awards held by Khrushchev and Gorbachev.

[63] Zhores Medvedev, *Andropov* (New York: Norton, 1983), pp. 102–104.

[64] See, for example, the several references to Brezhnev in the introduction of *V. I. Lenin i sovetskie vooruzhennye sily*, 3d ed. (Moscow: Voenizdat, 1980), where Brezhnev is referred to only by his Party and state titles.

West relations and the growth of anti-Sovietism in the United States and Europe. In 1976, Brezhnev presented his peace program to the XXV Congress, pointing to improvement in Soviet-American relations, while chastising the United States for its refusal of Soviet strategic arms proposals.[65] He also fired a shot across the military's bow, warning that the Soviet Union "will not increase its military budget, nor will it decrease, but rather [it will] steadfastly increase allocations for the well-being of the people."[66] Of course, he then leavened this with the promise that the Party would continue "do everything" to provide the military with "all necessary means" for defense.[67] Later in 1976 Brezhnev repeated his offer to reduce military expenditures in concert with the Americans, pointing out to a conference of European communists that the Soviet Union was alone among the great powers in its refusal to increase its defense budget annually.[68]

Shortly after the XXV Congress (and less than two years after his own arrival as a full member of the Politburo), KGB chief Iurii Andropov echoed Brezhnev's call for a continued constructive relationship with the West. It was common practice in Soviet political rhetoric to criticize the West as a means of criticizing domestic opposition, and this may have been the motivation for Andropov's reference to "enemies of détente," the term later applied to the regime's most prominent military critic, Marshal Ogarkov:

> Arguments about détente have become part of the internal struggle that has arisen in many Western nations. The enemies of détente are trying to become active. . . . The policies of the Cold War and the "position of strength" are unthinkable and dangerous. They are dangerous for everyone, for the cause of peace. They are dangerous and unthinkable for the West itself.[69]

Like Brezhnev at the XXV Congress, Andropov also added the caveat that material sacrifices would continue to be made in the cause of defense, but also that "objective processes of international relations demand the preservation and strengthening of detente."[70]

---

[65] *Materialy XXV s"ezda KPSS*, pp. 22–23.

[66] Ibid., p. 22.

[67] Ibid., p. 83.

[68] L. Brezhnev, "Vo imia mira i sotsial'nogo progressa," *XXV s"ezd KPSS: Edinstvo teorii i praktiki*, vol. 1 (Moscow: Politizdat, 1977), pp. 51–52.

[69] The statement was part of Andropov's 1976 Lenin's birthday speech. Iu. Andropov, "Leninizm—nauka i iskusstvo revoliutsionnogo tvorchestva," *XXV s"ezd KPSS: Edinstvo teorii i praktiki*, p. 150.

[70] Ibid., p. 150.

The civilian leadership seemed determined throughout this period not to allow the inexorable disintegration of détente to be exploited by anti-Western elements in the Soviet Union, including the military high command. Brezhnev argued continually that the Soviet Union must not fall prey to the provocations of the enemies of détente, and that Soviet foreign policy would remain centered on the political process in general and arms negotiations in particular.[71] Even when Brezhnev was at his most hostile and accusatory, as during an early 1980 interview, he still maintained that Europe was a safer and better place than it was in the early 1970s, a rather startling assertion given the decline of Soviet power, the debacle of Afghanistan, and the resurgent aggressiveness of the United States and NATO at the time.[72]

The Politburo, of course, was itself divided about American intentions, with figures such as Suslov among the most militant critics of U.S. policy.[73] The existence of intracivilian tensions, however, did not alter the fact that the leadership wanted to resolve such issues within civilian councils, without the intervention of military pressure. Whatever the members of the Party leadership felt about the future of détente, they seemed resolved to regain control of the issue from the military. Brezhnev even tried to use the deterioration of relations to his advantage in a 1980 speech.

> From the very start it was clear that only a stubborn *political* struggle could reliably guarantee peace and detente. Détente is in the peoples' interests. Its necessity is understood by responsible, realistically thinking politicians. But against it are great forces who directly or tangentially work in the capitalist states on the preparations for war: the military clique, with the monopolists, and their protégés in the state apparatus and in the mass media.
>
> And the more the possibilities decrease for the imperialists to rule over other nations and peoples, the more furiously their most aggressive and short-sighted spokesmen react to this. Only power and the reasonable policy of the peace-loving states, and the decisiveness of the peoples to frustrate the dangerous plans of the pretenders to world domination, can restrain this aggressiveness.[74]

[71] See, for example, Brezhnev's September 1978 speech awarding the Order of Lenin to the city of Baku in *Na strazhe mira*, p. 646.

[72] L. Brezhnev, "Otvety na voprosy korrespondenta gazety 'Pravda,'" *XXV s"ezd KPSS: Edinstvo teorii i praktiki*, vol. 7 (Moscow: Politizdat, 1981), p. 19.

[73] M. A. Suslov, "Istoricheskaia pravota idei i dela Lenina," in *XXV s"ezd KPSS: Edinstvo teorii i praktiki* (Moscow: Politizdat, 1981), pp. 119–120.

[74] L. Brezhnev, "Rech' na vstreche s izbirateliami baumanskogo izbiratel'nogo okruga g. Moskvy," *XXV s"ezd KPSS: Edinstvo teorii i praktiki* 7:29, emphasis added.

Here, Brezhnev argued that the American repudiation of détente actually represented the successes of Soviet policy, in the sense that American hostility was a response to Soviet ascendancy. More important, note how Brezhnev blames the defense community (the *voenshchiny*) in the United States, and not right-thinking politicians, for the destruction of détente. To whom was he speaking? It is hard to believe, in the midst of military attacks on détente at the time, that Brezhnev was not also making a point to a domestic audience.

Later that year, Brezhnev again defended the inviolability of détente. Speaking to an audience in Alma-Ata, he said that international problems could not be resolved through the American insistence on the "position of strength," and that "sooner or later, even the leaders of the USA will again draw that conclusion. Better sooner than later, of course." He immediately added that the "valorous" Soviet Armed Forces had "everything necessary to rebuff any aggressor."[75] This outdated formulation was no longer accepted by the military, anymore than the idea of détente was still acceptable to either Jimmy Carter or then-candidate Ronald Reagan. At a point where Brezhnev's foreign as well as domestic policies had to be considered both as failures, he nonetheless hewed to his optimistic line, taking a position increasingly divorced from international realities.

Although U.S.-Soviet relations had degenerated to open animosity by the time of the XXVI Party Congress in February 1981, the détentist line remained fixed in leadership rhetoric. Brezhnev told the Congress:

> A genuine military threat hangs over the USA, as well as over all the other states in the world. But its source is not the Soviet Union, or its mythical superiority, but the arms race itself which maintains tensions in the world. Against this authentic, not imaginary threat, we are ready to struggle hand in hand with America, with the European states, with all the nations of the planet.

Brezhnev concluded this passage with his now-famous statement that "to count on victory in nuclear war is dangerous madness."[76]

The 1981 Alert: Operation RYAN

This effort to salvage détente, and in the process to control military interference, now seems especially desperate in light of recent revela-

---

[75] L. Brezhnev, "Rech' na torzhestvennom zasedanii v Alma-Ate, posviashchennom 60-letniiu Kazakhskoi SSR i kommunisticheskoi partii Kazakhstana," *XXV s"ezd KPSS: edinstvo teorii i praktiki*, vol. 8 (Moscow: Politizdat, 1978), p. 35.

[76] *Materialy XXVI s"ezda KPSS* (Moscow: Politizdat, 1981), p. 23.

tions about a war-alert issued to the KGB in 1981. "Reagan's evil-empire rhetoric," according to KGB defector Oleg Gordievsky, "combined with Moscow's paranoia about Western conspiracies to produce a potentially lethal mixture":

> In May 1981 Brezhnev denounced Reagan's policies in a secret address to a major KGB conference in Moscow. The most dramatic speech, however, was given by Andropov. The new American administration, he declared, was actively preparing for nuclear war. There was now the possibility of a nuclear first strike by the United States.[77]

Andropov then approved Operation RYAN, an acronym for *Raketno-Yadernoe Napadenie*: nuclear missile attack. All KGB stations were put on alert and told to watch for any signs of imminent nuclear attack against the USSR. But Gordievsky claims there was no doubt within the KGB as to the origins of the alert:

> Andropov's apocalyptic vision of the nuclear threat from the West was regarded by the main American experts at the Center [i.e., KGB headquarters] as seriously alarmist. While they did not doubt his genuine alarm at Reagan's policies, *they believed that pressure for Operation RYAN originated with the high command*. Its leading advocate in the Politburo was probably the veteran defense minister, Marshal Ustinov . . . [who] would also prove to be one of Andropov's key supporters in the struggle to succeed Brezhnev.[78]

This account is supported by Arbatov's revelations about Andropov's explicit desire to maintain his relationship with Ustinov. Indeed, Arbatov even claims that Andropov "was, of course, an advocate of détente and the bettering of relations with [the United States]," whose "doubts" about Reagan did not become "certainty" until the outpouring of "stormy antisovietism" that broke out after the Soviets shot down a South Korean airliner in 1983—the last year of Operation RYAN.[79] In the end, Operation RYAN appears to have been an attempt to undermine the Brezhnev line by translating alarmist rhetoric into policy; it is unlikely that Ustinov, Andropov or anyone else actually expected an American nuclear attack.

In any case, by 1981 Brezhnev and the military were on completely different tracks, RYAN notwithstanding. While Brezhnev looked to

[77] Christopher Andrew and Oleg Gordievsky, *KGB: The Inside Story* (New York: HarperCollins, 1990), p. 583.
[78] Ibid., p. 583, emphasis added.
[79] Arbatov, *Zatianuvsheesiia vyzdorovlenie*, p. 323.

strategic arms control and the possibility of doing business with realistic Westerners, the military looked only to a new and unavoidable round of intense Soviet-American confrontation. In addition, the military was rapidly becoming obsessed with the dangers of the new conventional battlefield and the renewed NATO unity on holding the Central European line. In the end, Brezhnev was selling a correlation of forces that had supposedly turned irreversibly in favor of socialism, but the Soviet military wasn't buying. Instead, the line many chose to repeat from the XXVI Party Congress concerned the increasing aggressiveness of the West, not the positive change in the correlation of forces.[80] Brezhnev's opponents in the military were looking ahead to a coming political and technological storm that, in their view, threatened to undo the Soviet Union's "irreversible" progress.

THE NEW TECHNOLOGICAL BATTLEFIELD

The more specific problem for the military was not so much that a new round of weapons *procurement* was required, but rather that a new round of strategic and conventional weapons *development* was imminent. The advances of science in the late 1970s and early 1980s were seen by Soviet military figures as qualitatively different from the technological challenges that had preceded them in the 1950s, and they foresaw a new kind of challenge, a steepening of the curve of technological progress that was both unprecedented and dangerous.

There were, of course, objective developments that made military anxiety understandable. The American technological challenge in the late 1970s was characterized by advances that were relatively new in degree, if not entirely in kind, including a more immediate dependence on basic science, the incorporation of a wider array of new components and materials (necessitating broader innovation and more complex management) in new weapons systems, and the unprecedented importance in military-industrial innovation of software and human skills (e.g., CAD/CAM, programming, etc.) By the early 1980s, as Thane Gustafson has pointed out, the nature of the military-technological challenge struck the Soviets at their weakest link—industrial innovation—and they were therefore apprehensive with good reason.[81]

[80] One of many such examples is General Ivan Tret'iak's chapter in *Sovetskie sukhoputnye* (Moscow: Voenizdat, 1981), p. 211.

[81] See Thane Gustafson, "Responses to Technological Challenge, 1965–1985," in Colton and Gustafson, *Soldiers and the Soviet State.*

Moreover, the military saw the technological threat within the context of a reemergent political danger. In the military view, the technological threat and the political threat were two interrelated aspects of the same general deterioration of the world situation. Advances in technology were linked to what many officers believed (correctly) to be a genuinely new escalation of American anti-Sovietism; concepts such as PD-59 and weapons systems such as the B-1 bomber, the Trident submarine, and the MX missile were a perfect and deadly match in the eyes of the high command.

Many Soviet officers, however, saw developments in conventional military affairs in the early 1980s as even more dangerous than strategic improvements, largely because they were buttressed by renewed NATO commitment and redesigned NATO doctrine in an arena where conflict was more likely, as opposed to central nuclear war. (Of course, the announcement of the Strategic Defense Initiative in March 1983 would reunite the strategic and conventional threats.) Although predictable concerns about American strategic modernization programs appeared as early as 1976, military writers then began an all-out campaign of alarmism on the issue of conventional technologies in the early 1980s.[82] (As early as 1980, *Krasnaia Zvezda* accurately noted that conventional weapons were becoming more like weapons of mass destruction, an observation that became common in the Soviet press.[83]) Both of the major Soviet military academies intensified their general research activities during this period, widely held in the military to have been among the most dangerous in recent memory.[84]

The special object of Soviet military vitriol was a group of proposals within NATO that came to be known as the "Rogers Plan," named for former NATO Supreme Allied Commander General Bernard Rogers. Briefly, the Rogers Plan was centered on FOFA, or the Follow-On Forces Attack, which envisioned using NATO air superiority and high-technology weapons to offset Soviet numerical superiority without resort to nuclear weapons. The point was to disrupt or even destroy rear-area Warsaw Pact units before they reached the front, negating Soviet plans to overwhelm Western forces in successive

[82] See, for example, Maj. Gen. R. Simonian's three part series in *Krasnaia Zvezda*: "Voiny glazami pentagona," May 27, 1976, p. 3; "Kontsepsiia 'strategicheskoi dostatochnosti,'" August 24, 1976, p. 3; and "Kontsepsiia 'vybora tselei,'" September 28, 1976. The last of the three is the most relevant here in that it discusses James Schlesinger's statements on counterforce, the predecessor of the hated PD-59.

[83] Hansen, *Correlation of Forces*, p. 166.

[84] *Akademiia general'nogo shtaba* (Moscow: Voenizdat, 1987), pp. 159–160; *Voennaia akademiia M. V. Frunze* (Moscow: Voenizdat, 1988), pp. 242–244.

waves. This would have turned a European war into a drawn-out affair—precisely the type of war that the USSR wished to avoid.[85] The assumption is that the Soviets would be deterred by the idea of a contest in which NATO's superior technology and GNP would come into play, forcing the kind of long war that raised Soviet fears about politico-military cohesion and domestic stability.

This reinvigoration of NATO defenses struck a rather raw nerve in the Soviet military—as the Strategic Defense Initiative would again in 1983—and touched off the second stage of the growing debate in the USSR about Western aggressiveness and national priorities. The attempt to revitalize NATO conventional defenses, even in theory, was greeted with a blast of Soviet hostility characteristic of the strained superpower relationship between 1981 and 1985. Even some civilian writers were as heated in their accusations as their military counterparts. One analyst wrote in the August 1984 edition of *SShA* (the journal of Soviet "Americanologists") that the Soviet attainment of parity had led the Americans to seek to "localize" European conflicts in both scale and location, even if it meant sacrificing the Europeans.[86]

Soviet military authors had picked up on this theme as early as 1980, and by 1984 several articles had appeared on FOFA and the Rogers Plan.[87] Marshal Vasilii Petrov, then CINC of the Ground Forces, said in 1983 that the Western adoption of AirLand Battle (the U.S. Army version of FOFA) "leaves nobody in doubt about the Pentagon's endeavor to ensure, together with the other NATO countries, superiority over the Warsaw Pact and to create and make use of the potential for a 'disarming' first [conventional] strike and concluding the war under conditions favorable" to the United States and NATO.[88] By late 1984, Petrov stopped referring to the Soviet Armed Forces as having "everything necessary," and instead claimed only

---

[85] For more detailed discussions of the Rogers Plan, see the following articles by Gen. Bernard Rogers: "Greater Flexibility for NATO's Flexible Response," *Atlantic Community Quarterly* (Fall 1983); "Enhancing Deterrence—Raising the Threshold," *NATO Review* (February 1983); "FOFA: Myths and Realities," *NATO Review* (December 1984). For official U.S. Army doctrine at the time, see U.S. Army, *FM 100–5* (Washington, D.C.: U.S. Army, 1982), section 7.

[86] V. S. Shein, "Debaty vokrug voennoi doktriny NATO," *SShA* 8 (August 1984), pp. 28–29.

[87] For examples, see I. Vorob'iev, "Sovremennoe oruzhie i taktika," *Krasnaia Zvezda*, September 15, 1984, p. 2. Other articles are cited in Michael J. Sterling, "Soviet Reactions to NATO's Emerging Technologies for Deep Attack," RAND N-2294-AF, August 1985.

[88] Quoted in ibid., pp. 8–9. The remark was made in an interview in *Sovetskaia Rossiia*, December 1, 1983.

that the Party saw the need to support combat might at a "high level" in the face of "the growth of a real danger of war."[89] Marshal Kulikov likewise argued in early 1984 that NATO was seeking conventional superiority in order to defeat Warsaw Pact forces in the initial period of war without nuclear weapons. While Kulikov warned that this should not be taken to mean that NATO had given up on nuclear weapons (which remained "key" in NATO doctrine), he also claimed that "air-land operations" represented a "qualitative change" in American views of war.[90]

This public rhetoric represented more than just inflammatory phrasings of military interests; it also represented a serious reappraisal of Soviet strategy. One insight into this process appeared in a book written during 1984, Col. Gen. M. A. Gareev's *Frunze—Military Theoretician*. Although *Frunze* is a biography, Gareev (deputy chief of the General Staff in the military science department) used this military-historical forum to make a military-theoretical endorsement of the need to rethink strategy.

Gareev took narrow-minded thinking about the future battlefield to task and dismissed large sections of Marshal Sokolovskii's classic *Military Strategy* in the process. While praising Sokolovskii as good in his day, Gareev openly stated the need to revise Soviet military thinking, a point supported by Gareev's nominal superior at the time, Marshal Sergei Akhromeev.[91] In particular, Gareev was concerned about the shorter mobilization required by modern war, and he took Sokolovskii to task for underestimating both the problems of surprise and the provocative political nature of long mobilizations, "from which a turn back to a peaceful situation is very difficult to do." "Therefore", he wrote, *"one of the most important tasks of military science is the investigation of ways to further raise the combat readiness of the Armed Forces, and their capability to conduct decisive actions toward the utter crushing of any aggressor in any conditions of the start of a war."*[92] Gareev's book, however circumspect and academic his discussion of the unsolved problems of Soviet military research, is evidence of the genuine military concern about the West that accompanied the political

[89] V. Petrov, "S uchetom trebovanii sovremennogo boia," in *Voprosy voinskogo vospitaniia* (Moscow: Voenizdat, 1985), p. 3.

[90] V. Kulikov, "Obuzdat' gonku vooruzhenii," *Pravda*, February 21, 1984, p. 3.

[91] See Akhromeev's comments as quoted in Dale Herspring, "Marshal Akhromeev and the Future of the Soviet Armed Forces," *Survival* 27, no. 6 (November–December 1986), p. 526.

[92] M. A. Gareev, *Frunze—Voennyi Teoretik* (Moscow: Voenizdat, 1985), pp. 242–243, original emphasis.

challenge emerging from the military in the 1980s. More telling, it was a continuation of the line of reasoning defended by Gareev's boss, the man fired as chief of the General Staff in 1984, Marshal Nikolai Ogarkov.

Ogarkov's Alarms

The Brezhnev leadership had no more dedicated opponent than the chief of the General Staff himself. Marshal Nikolai Ogarkov was a brilliant officer who had been deeply involved in arms control and military planning for most of his distinguished career, including a stint as a senior SALT negotiator in the early 1970s. He remains a popular figure, as his 1989 election to the chairmanship of the national Soviet veterans' organization attests. Articulate, stubborn, and arrogant, he was exactly the kind of respected military leader who—especially with the power derived from Ustinov's tacit backing—could be a major obstruction to the leadership's plans if he wanted to be.[93] And he obviously wanted to be: little wonder that a Soviet diplomat confided to American officials that "unpartylike tendencies" had been part of the reason for Ogarkov's dismissal.[94]

In 1977 in Tula, Brezhnev gave a now-famous speech in which he rhetorically accepted the basic tenets of Mutual Assured Destruction, or MAD. Benjamin Lambeth was probably correct when he suggested the "Tula line" was intended largely for a foreign audience, and there is little evidence that it produced any substantive change in the Soviet strategic posture.[95] Ogarkov, however, made no attempt to pretend that he agreed with it, or even to play along for the sake of foreign consumption. The Tula declaration and other such ex cathedra statements by Brezhnev on doctrine were, in Azrael's words, "adding insult to injury" where the military was concerned.[96]

Insofar as the Tula line was directed at a domestic audience, it represented the first movements of the Soviet leadership toward a kind of Soviet version of James Schlesinger's "essential equivalence,"

[93] As one example of this power, Arbatov claims that Ogarkov vetoed, practically single-handedly, a nuclear-free zone proposal in 1982. Arbatov, *Zatianuvsheesiia vyzdorovlenie*, p. 240

[94] Bernard Gwertzman, "Soviet Dismissal Now Being Laid to Policy Split," *New York Times*, September 13, 1984, p. 1.

[95] "My own inclination," Lambeth wrote, "is to regard the emergence of the Tula position . . . as a result of mounting Soviet embarrassment at their own doctrinal hyperbole." See Benjamin Lambeth, "The State of Western Research on Soviet Military Strategy and Policy," RAND N-2230-AF, October 1984, pp. 29, 52–54.

[96] Azrael, "Soviet Civilian Leadership," p. 7.

a rough match of capability rather than a strict numerical balance. In late 1977 Brezhnev told a joint session of the Central Committee and the Supreme Soviet, "The Soviet Union is effectively concerned about its defense, but does not and will not seek military superiority over any side. We do not want to upset the approximate equilibrium of military forces that now exists between East and West in Central Europe or between the USSR and the USA. But at the same time we demand that nobody else try to upset it in their favor.[97] This had to be irritating to the military leadership. It was bad enough to have to deal with economic restraints; how much worse it must have seemed to them to have to listen to Brezhnev expound first on strategic doctrine and now on the conventional balance, especially as the Americans were about to bring their frightful technological advantage to bear in Europe.

Military dissatisfaction was expressed through Ogarkov, and his response was neither subtle nor flexible. In 1978, barely a year after the Tula declaration, Ogarkov warned:

> Despite the détente in international tensions, achieved thanks to the titanic efforts of our party, the imperialist states continue to strengthen their aggressive military blocs, to modernize their armed forces, and to spend huge sums on weapons. In the development of means of the conduct of war, a further perfecting of existing weapons systems is evident, as well as the working out of new forms of weapons based not only on known, but also on fundamentally new physical principles, with even greater destructive and striking properties.[98]

This left little doubt about where Ogarkov stood on any ill-defined or "approximate" equilibriums. And to eliminate any doubt about his position, Ogarkov a year later directly reaffirmed the idea of victory in nuclear conflict, a concept banned from public discussion at the time, whether or not the leadership still agreed with it.[99]

In 1981, his patience with indirect rhetoric running out, Ogarkov implied that the Soviets were in danger of losing the ongoing technological struggle. He resorted to barely veiled criticism of the leadership's priorities: "Military art," he wrote in October of that year, "has

[97] L. Brezhnev, "Velikii oktiabr' i progress chelovechestva," *XXV s"ezd KPSS: Edinstvo teorii i praktiki*, vol. 3 (Moscow: Politizdat, 1978), p. 68.

[98] N. Ogarkov, "Voennaia nauka i zashchita sotsialisticheskogo otechestva," *Kommunist* 7 (May 1978), p. 116.

[99] See "Strategiia voennaia," in N. V. Ogarkov, ed., *Voenno-Entsiklopedicheskii Slovar'* (Moscow: Voenizdat, 1979).

no right to lag behind the combat possibilities of the means of armed struggle, especially in the modern stage, when on the basis of scientific-technical progress basic systems of weapons change practically after every 10–12 years."[100] The implication here was that Soviet industrial capacity was more than capable of meeting the Western challenge, and that the real problem lay in leadership priorities. By this time, even the obligatory references to détente were gone, and Ogarkov openly argued that Soviet defenses should be reoriented toward an ability to make a quick transition to a war footing.[101]

In mid-1981, Marshal Kulikov supported Ogarkov's attack on détente, citing public statements by Alexander Haig and Richard Pipes to the effect that the United States was actively seeking war with the Soviet Union, and warning that these were "not accidental, passing phrases."[102] In particular, Kulikov zeroed in on two admittedly hard-line statements: Haig's assertions that "there are things more important than peace" and that Americans have always liked to fight, and Pipes's comment that the USSR would face, in the final analysis, the two choices of change or war. Given the rapidly deteriorating situation in Poland—marital law was just months away—it is easy to see how Kulikov, the Warsaw Pact CINC, could have taken such challenging remarks to heart.

This sea change in military opposition did not escape the leadership, and initial measures were taken, particularly with regard to the Main Political Administration, to ensure that the officers were vaccinated against the malady overtaking their superiors. Turnover among senior MPA officers, for example, rose sharply to 30 percent annually from 1980 to 1982.[103] Another sign of Party concern with military obedience was the early 1982 revision of the military textbook on *Party-Political Work in the Soviet Armed Forces*. The contrast with the 1978 version is striking; the 1978 text opens with a description of the role and purpose of the Soviet military, whereas the 1982 edition begins with a much stronger emphasis on the primacy of the Party in military matters.[104] Shortly thereafter, the Frunze Academy instituted

---

[100] Ogarkov, "Na strazhe mirnogo truda," p. 86.

[101] N. Ogarkov, *Na Strazhe mira i sotsializma* (Moscow: Voenizdat, 1981), pp. 86–89.

[102] V. Kulikov, "Obuzdat' sily agressii," *Krasnaia Zvezda*, June 21, 1981, p. 2.

[103] See Parrott, "Political Change," p. 67.

[104] Not one author or editor of the 1978 edition is found in the 1982 version, now designated as a part of the "officer's library" series. See *Partiino-politicheskaia rabota v Sovetskikh Vooruzhennykh Silakh* (Moscow: Voenizdat, 1978), pp. 3–28; and *Partiino-politicheskaia rabota v Sovetskoi Armii i Voenno-Morskom Flote* (Moscow: Voenizdat, 1982), pp. 3–30.

a "complex state examination" on Party history and Marxism-Leninism. This examination was not meant so much to improve the level of Marxist indoctrination among the military—there was clearly enough of that—but rather to bolster propaganda relating to the policies of the Party itself.[105]

Despite the presence of other military critics of Party policy, Ogarkov was still the chief of the General Staff and in the end it would be Ogarkov's comments that would serve as a lightning rod. Among the efforts to restrain Ogarkov was a 1982 editorial in *Kommunist*. This was an extraordinary step, in which the leadership actually felt the need to use the main Party journal to warn off their own top military officer. The centerpiece of the editorial was a stern warning to unnamed "declared enemies of peaceful coexistence," a clear reference to the chief.[106] Ogarkov was nonetheless undeterred. Soon after the *Kommunist* piece, Ogarkov published *Always in Readiness to Defend the Fatherland*; actually, Ogarkov was probably sending *Always in Readiness* off to press even as the *Kommunist* editorial was being written. If he was given the chance to reedit his book in light of this pending criticism, he chose not to take advantage of it.

Always in Readiness was undiluted in its stridency. Among the more serious accusations, Ogarkov claimed, among other things, that the United States had returned to a newer version of Massive Retaliation (a generally accurate charge also leveled at the time by many Western critics of the Reagan administration).[107] He repeatedly stressed the effects of renewed American aggressiveness, and new Western weapons, on Soviet mobilizational procedures and economic policy.[108] It was clearly a polemic, aimed at a Party leadership that Ogarkov felt was blind to a real threat of war. Worse, Ogarkov believed that however slim the chances of nuclear war, the Soviets were even more unprepared for a conventional contest. This shift in emphasis from the strategic level to the theater (with its implicit acceptance of strategic stability) was evident in statements Ogarkov made in 1983 and 1984, when he deemphasized the strategic nuclear threat: "What was possible 20 or 30 years ago to achieve with nuclear weapons is now becoming impossible for an aggressor," he said in 1983. "A crushing nuclear counterstrike awaits him!"[109] Until his removal in 1984, he

---

[105] *Voennaia akademiia imeni M. V. Frunze*, p. 261.

[106] See Azrael, "Soviet Civilian Leadership," pp. 22–24.

[107] N. Ogarkov, *Vsegda v Gotovnosti k Zashchite Otechestva* (Moscow: Voenizdat, 1982) p. 17. My thanks to Larry George for his contributions on this point.

[108] Ibid., pp. 10, 13, 36, 58, 60.

[109] N. Ogarkov, "Pobeda i Sovremmenost'," *Izvestiia*, May 9, 1983, p. 2.

continued to press his case that the development of new conventional weapons had to be undertaken "right now."[110]

Perhaps the most important aspect of Ogarkov's 1984 reassignment was that it did not mean the end of Ogarkov-like writings by senior officers, even into 1988. In part, this was because Ogarkov's removal was not a complete fall from grace, since he went from the General Staff to commander in chief of the Western Theater.[111] Azrael and others have suggested that the proximate cause of Ogarkov's removal was the imminent death of Defense Minister Ustinov, after which Ogarkov would be a natural contender for Ustinov's post.[112] Ustinov was mortally ill by 1984, and the civilian leaders would have had understandable reasons for wanting Ogarkov out of the halls of the Kremlin before his death, in order to avert his claim to the Ministry. Ogarkov was in many respects the logical choice to become the next defense minister (after all, Ustinov the civilian was the anomaly, not the rule) but that would have given the military a more militant voice in the Politburo than it had ever had, even under Zhukov.

Some confirmation of this hypothesis can be found in Arbatov's memoirs. Arbatov claims that tensions between Andropov and Ogarkov ran high and reflected not only personal enmity but classic civil-military tensions:

> [Andropov] felt a political mistrust (or maybe, uncertainty?) about certain military figures, including N. V. Ogarkov. At one point in my presence he was talking to a certain someone on the telephone, and he called him a "napoleonchik" (I would remind you of how soon after Andropov's death he was removed from his post as Chief of the General Staff.)[113]

Parrott has speculated (rightly, in my view) that Ogarkov was saved from obscurity after his dismissal by one of the few natural allies the military had in the Politburo: Grigorii Romanov, soon to emerge as a contender for the leadership against Gorbachev.[114]

[110] Quoted in Azrael, "Soviet Civilian Leadership," p. 34. See Ogarkov's V-E Day piece in *Krasnaia Zvezda*, May 9, 1984.

[111] Ogarkov's biography in the 1986 *Voennyi Entsiklopedicheskii Slovar'* serves to confirm what the Soviet rumor mill and the intelligence community already knew. His duties since 1984 were labeled with the standard phrase, "assigned to other responsible duties," which appears in all officers' biographies where the CIA has confirmed a Theater Command appointment. See Thomas Nichols, "New Soviet Military Dictionary," *Radio Liberty Reports*, RL 186/87, May 15, 1987, p. 3.

[112] Azrael, "Soviet Civilian Leadership," p. 35.

[113] Arbatov, *Zatianuvsheesiia vyzdorovlenie*, p. 323.

[114] Parrott, "Political Change," p. 74.

Only under Gorbachev was Ogarkov removed from substantive military command, probably in connection with a still-undisclosed elimination of the four TVD, or theater-level, commands.[115] He continued to be spotted in Moscow (for example, at Gorbachev's 1990 Lenin Day speech and again atop Lenin's tomb a month later on Victory Day) and now heads a national veterans' association.

Ogarkov's writings signaled more than just his own fears. They also heralded the end of the "golden age," as the Party leadership was treated to open castigation from their senior professional officers. Ogarkov was arguing that the gains of the 1970s were in danger, that measures had to be taken to avert the coming danger, and they had to be taken immediately. By 1981, it was evident that the military was in broad agreement with Ogarkov.

ANDROPOV AND THE GENESIS OF THE GORBACHEV LINE

Andropov did not abandon Brezhnev's foreign policy, even if the KGB chief-cum-general secretary had other plans for Brezhnev's corrupt cronies in the apparatus. On Lenin's birthday in 1982, Brezhnev was already in precarious health, and so Andropov defended the Brezhnev line in the traditional Kremlin address, noting that "the Soviet Union has never proceeded from the position that a firm peace may be achieved only through military force and that therefore our policy should be based on it. Such a policy could only lead, not to peace, but to an arms race, confrontations, and in the final analysis—war."[116] Like Brezhnev, Andropov argued that the major capitalist nations had essentially chosen the path of peaceful coexistence, despite the recalcitrance and hostility of some Western hawks.[117] And at the Central Committee meeting held after Brezhnev's death in November 1982, Andropov rejected the idea that the useful Soviet-American relationship of the 1970s was an accident or passing phase, emphasizing that "the future belongs to détente."[118]

At first glance, Andropov seems tougher, less flexible, and more anti-American than the desperate Brezhnev, clutching at détente in

[115] This is conjecture on my part, based on the fact that all four TVD, or *teatr voennykh deistv*, commanders were relieved within months of each other, with no clear replacements emerging. The TVD concept is associated with Ogarkov, and may have been scrapped when he was no longer in a position to be its advocate.

[116] Iu. Andropov, "Leninizm—neizcherpaemyi istochnik revoliutsionnoi energii i tvorchestva mass," *XXVI s"ezd KPSS: Edinstvo teorii i praktiki*, 3:87.

[117] Ibid., 3:90.

[118] Iu. Andropov, "Rech' na plenume TsK KPSS," in ibid., 3:108.

his final days. But it must be remembered that superpower relations were at their lowest point since the Cuban Missile Crisis, with each side trading increasingly hostile rhetoric, and conducting the Soviet-American relationship through the media rather than through diplomacy. President Reagan did not even meet with a senior Soviet official until 1984, when he greeted Andrei Gromyko in an inconclusive meeting at the White House. For their part, the Soviets were taking the Americans to task for rejecting Soviet proposals that were unworkable to begin with, all the while expecting Washington to carry on business as usual without reference to the invasion of Afghanistan.

Each side had a vested interest in continuing the war of nerves. For the Reagan administration, it was imperative to deliver on the candidate's promise to rebuild the American military establishment. Anti-Soviet rhetoric not only reflected the president's personal feelings, it represented the mood of the electorate as well. But Andropov, by contrast, had good reason to continue Brezhnev's détentist line as well. John Newhouse has correctly pointed out that "Brezhnev was winning the propaganda war on points when he died."[119] More pressing for Andropov was the growing military resistance to virtually every major arms initiative proposed by the Soviets in 1981 and 1982, including the no-first-use pledge, the halting of SS-20 missile deployments in the western USSR, and the yet-unannounced testing moratorium. By late 1982, Ustinov himself had to deny in *Pravda* that such moves were not a sign of weakness—a sure sign that such a charge was exactly the criticism being leveled at the time.[120] (Gorbachev, by 1982 a full member of the Politburo, should have taken closer notes: he would face the same charges barely three years later.)

Andropov was a tougher and smarter man than Brezhnev, even for a leader forced to divide his time between policymaking and dialysis, and he did not suffer military recalcitrance lightly despite his failing health. Instead, he went on the offensive, slamming domestic critics and the Reagan administration at the same time.

Specifically, Andropov attacked the aspect of U.S. policy that Soviet military figures found most disturbing, the idea of victory in a limited or even protracted nuclear war. (Even the normally more restrained Vice President George Bush had supported the idea of nuclear victory as a candidate in 1980.)[121] Of course, the Soviet military was obsessed

---

[119] Newhouse, *War and Peace in the Nuclear Age*, p. 352.
[120] See Azrael, "Soviet Civilian Leadership," p. 24.
[121] Newhouse, *War and Peace in the Nuclear Age*, p. 337.

with this turn in American thinking because they themselves were strong believers in nuclear victory as well.[122] Andropov railed at both sides: "Our position on this question is clear: a nuclear war must never be allowed to happen—not a small one, not a large one, not limited, not total."[123] Andropov then went on to remind his listeners—on whichever side of the Atlantic they might be—of the achievements of Soviet-American arms diplomacy.

Like his predecessor, Andropov tried to insulate arms control from the overall deterioration of the Soviet-American relationship, a perfect compliment to the U.S. effort to create "linkage" between arms control and Soviet international behavior. "I think," Andropov said in a New Year's Eve 1982 interview with an American journalist, "that our two countries could jointly undertake much that would be useful for ourselves as well as for other nations and peoples," particularly arms measures.[124]

The military, of course, did not share this optimistic view. The authors of *Marxist-Leninist Teachings on War and the Army* (led by MPA agitprop chief Volkogonov) chose to focus on Andropov's more confrontational side, as when he described a "sharpening of the struggle" between the two world systems in a June 1983 speech to the Central Committee.[125] But the military authors *had quoted Andropov out of context*. The full text of that speech reveals that Andropov was actually speaking about problems within the socialist movement (in other words, about the terrible situation in Poland), and he returned to his more doggedly détentist line shortly thereafter in the same speech when he downplayed the aggressiveness of some in the West: "In the modern capitalist world there is also another tendency, which more realistically takes account of the situation in the international arena. They understand that irreversible changes have already taken place in the world, and they understand the necessity and mutual advantageousness of the continued peaceful coexistence of states

---

[122] Ogarkov affirmed this in the 1979 *Voenno-entsiklopedicheskii slovar'* in the entry under "military strategy," and Volkogonov again raised the issue in 1986 as will be seen in the next chapter. The idea refused to die: in May 1989, I was told by members of the Foreign Ministry that certain elements of the General Staff had accepted the INF Treaty because it seemed to open new possibilities for the use of tactical nuclear weapons.

[123] Iu. Andropov, "Shest'deciat let SSSR," *XXVI s"ezd KPSS: Edinstvo teorii i praktiki*, 3:125.

[124] Iu. Andropov, "Otvety na voprosy amerikanskogo politicheskogo obozrevatelia Dzh. Kingsberi-Smita," in ibid., 3:131.

[125] D. A. Volkogonov, ed., *Marksistko-leninskoe uchenie o voine i armii* (Moscow: Voenizdat, 1984), p. 3.

with different social structures."[126] The authors were well aware of this latter part of Andropov's speech, but it did not stop them from presenting their own analysis and tasking the Party accordingly, in a passage that seems to answer Andropov directly:

> However, the détente in international tensions observed in recent years has not eliminated the military threat from imperialism, and this threat continues to exist. Militarism is growing stronger in the USA and other nations, the arms race is mounting, and new types of weapons of mass destruction are being created. Hot spots of military danger which have arisen in various regions of the world are fraught with serious threats. This demands of the CPSU an ever more deep and thoroughgoing analysis of the changes taking place in the correlation of class forces in the world arena, a timely evaluation of the tendencies and perspectives of military construction in the largest imperialist states, the preservation of the established parity (equality) of military forces between East and West in Central Europe, as well as between the USA and the USSR.[127]

Andropov rejected both the appraisal and the advice, but he would not live long enough to put his own program into place.

The Gorbachev Inheritance

Military alarm in 1983 and 1984, continuing themes that arose in 1979, now seem only a prologue to the intense military criticism of the West that erupted in 1986 and 1987. By contrast, civilian rhetoric—with the exception of a few comments such as Romanov's 1983 description of the international situation as "white-hot"—was soon to cool considerably, while military rhetoric continued to heat up.[128] A good example is Volkogonov's 1984 book *Psychological Warfare*. On the very first page, Volkogonov (a brilliant and prolific writer who would later emerge prominently in the debates under Gorbachev) made clear his pessimism: "The planetary struggle of two worlds," as he called it, "has reached an especially high [level] of tension and acuteness."[129] In his discussion of the "myth of the Soviet threat," Vol-

---

[126] Iu. Andropov, "Rech' na [June 15, 1983] plenume TsK KPSS," *XXVI s"ezd KPSS: Edinstvo teorii i praktiki*, vol. 4 (Moscow: Politizdat, 1984), p. 58.

[127] *V. I. Lenin i sovetskie vooruzhennye sily*, 3d. ed. (Moscow: Voenizdat, 1980), p. 168.

[128] G. V. Romanov, "Velikaia zhiznennaia sila idei i dela oktiabriia," in *XXVI s"ezd KPSS: Edinstvo teorii i praktiki* (Moscow: Politizdat, 1984), 4:425.

[129] D. A. Volkogonov, *Psikhologicheskaia Voina*, 2d ed., exp. (Moscow: Voenizdat, 1984), p. 3. The book was sent to press in July 1984.

kogonov agreed with Kulikov and others; the Western bourgeoisie "are *not ready* to acknowledge the just thesis of *equal security* of states of two systems."[130] By 1986, even as Mikhail Gorbachev was taking steps to reform defense policy, these warnings had become widespread in the Soviet military press, as well as the civilian press. (Even Ogarkov got in a parting shot: in mid-1985, just a few months after Gorbachev's accession, he published *History Teaches Vigilance*, a look back on the fortieth anniversary of the victory over Nazism in which Ogarkov again warned of the West's preparations for war.)[131]

Gorbachev's portfolio in this period was agriculture and, later, general supervision of the economy. He would, after Chernenko's brief reign and undignified funeral, continue the Brezhnev-Andropov line with renewed energy. But in many respects, Gorbachev entered office in 1985 with the civil-military deck stacked against him. Brezhnev and Andropov had failed to reassert Party dominance, the former because of neglect and the latter perhaps only due to poor health. Brezhnev's passivity had both averted a showdown and subverted an opportunity to define the civil-military relationship. The high command controlled access to crucial information; they had established themselves on the high ground of military-patriotic rhetoric; they exploited legitimate fears of a technological arms race the USSR could not win; and conveniently, they faced an American president whose own fiery anti-Soviet rhetoric would make almost any political accommodation look like appeasement.[132] More pressing, they held the key to economic reorganization and therefore to Gorbachev's political survival: by 1985, defense plus fixed defense investment was absorbing some 45 percent of Soviet output, twice the average Western rates.[133]

Gorbachev was left to face a military with very detailed concerns and very broad authority, a military that had fended off several threats from Party leaders better entrenched than the new general secretary. And although Gorbachev was at first only following through on Andropov's initial vision of an improved Soviet economy and revitalized

[130] Ibid., p. 219, emphasis in original. Volkogonov complimented his book with a prominent and strident appearance in *Pravda* in June 1984. D. Volkogonov, "Zashchita sotsializma i sovremennyi mir," *Pravda*, June 29, 1984, pp. 2–3.

[131] N. Ogarkov, *Istoriia uchit bditel'nosti* (Moscow: Voenizdat, 1985), esp. pp. 88–91. For a summary of the book, see George Weickhardt, "Ogarkov's Latest Fulminations on Vigilance," *Radio Liberty Reports*, RL 325/85, September 27, 1985.

[132] By 1984 even Ustinov was blaming Reagan by name for the resurgence of American aggressiveness. D. Ustinov, "Borot'siia za mir, ukrepliat' oboronosposobnost'," *XXVI s"ezd KPSS: edinstvo teorii i praktiki*, 4:474.

[133] Arthur Alexander, "Perestroika and Change in Soviet Weapons Acquisition," RAND R-3821-USDP, June 1990, p. 5.

Communist Party, the changes in social priorities even this limited reform would require meant that continued civil-military tension would now turn from a probability to a certainty. In the end, Gorbachev's fight would be uphill all the way, in large part due to decisions made by Leonid Brezhnev twenty years earlier in a very different world.

[5]

Reform and Resistance: Gorbachev and the Military, 1985–1986

> The proposed reduction will in no way reduce the firepower of our armed forces, and this is the main thing after all. . . . We shall continue to have all the means necessary for the country's defense, and an opponent will be well aware of this.
> —Nikita Khrushchev, January 14, 1960

> With all responsibility, we may say today: the defensive might of the USSR is supported at that level which allows the peaceful labor and the peaceful life of the Soviet peoples to be reliably defended.
> —Mikhail Gorbachev, February 25, 1986

GORBACHEV AND THE DILEMMA OF MILITARY REFORM

The Gorbachev era in civil-military politics is naturally the most fascinating; it is also the most important, both the West and to the peoples of the former Soviet Union itself. The processes of post-Soviet disintegration and reformation have only just begun, and the position of the military—Soviet, Russian, Ukrainian, or otherwise—is one of the crucial security issues the 1990s. During the first three years of Gorbachev's rule, questions about the scope of military influence on the Soviet political process became intimately bound to issues of reform, as Gorbachev reneged on the longstanding Party tradition of insulating the military from the difficulties and burdens faced by the rest of Soviet society. Reforms, whether economic decentralization or the lifting of restrictions on free speech, were now of paramount concern to the officer corps, as it fought not only for material resources but for its own, previously privileged, place in society. The dramatic—and traumatic—changes after 1989 led to increased concern in the West and in the USSR about the military's power over the fragmented political agenda, concerns that persist even in the wake of the dissolution of the Soviet state.

Despite Gorbachev's dramatic reforms in other areas of society, his problems with the military were notably similar to those faced by his predecessors. Like Khrushchev, Gorbachev sought to gain control of the military by gaining control of military matters, especially military doctrine. And like Brezhnev, he chose to forge personal relationships with individual military leaders rather than to confront head-on the exasperating problem of institutional control. This is why, in 1989 and after, efforts to impose a legal-constitutional framework on the civil-military relationship met with little success: like those before him, Gorbachev succumbed to the temptations of subjective control, due as much to the economic necessity of reining in military spending as to the utter frustration of earlier, more reasonable efforts at a dialogue with the military.

In the first two years of Gorbachev's reign, some sort of compromise may have been within reach. This window was short-lived, however, as Gorbachev made a forceful play for civilian supremacy in defense and security matters. Although Gorbachev's attack on the military was more eloquent than Khrushchev's, the theme was the same. It was music the military recognized.

The First Days

When Mikhail Gorbachev took his seat in March 1985 at the head of the Soviet Communist Party, he inherited a state and a society that was, by his own admission, in precarious condition. His immediate predecessors, Chernenko and Andropov, had failed to make headway either at home or abroad, in no small measure because of the failures of their own predecessor, Brezhnev. The Soviet economy was at a painful standstill, poised only for further decline; meanwhile the United States embarked on an active and dedicated recapturing of its role as a global superpower, flanked by a revitalized, modernized, and heavily rearmed NATO. Indeed, the foreign and domestic policy failures of previous Soviet leaders were united in a powerful synergy by 1985; the collapse of détente in 1979 had led to a sharpened arms race in which the United States took an early and commanding lead, and one that the Soviet Union could ill afford. The Soviet system was headed, economically and politically, for a free fall into chaos. Regaining control of the economy meant gaining control of the budget, which meant gaining control of military spending. The new general secretary had his work cut out for him.

[131]

Gorbachev came to power without any successful precedent to follow in civil-military affairs in general, or security policy in particular. Gorbachev arrived in Moscow only in 1980, by which time the Brezhnev leadership was struggling with the Ogarkov-led military opposition, a contest Gorbachev could only watch from the sidelines in his post as agriculture secretary in the Central Committee.

It is hard to imagine that Gorbachev would have been the military's choice for general secretary. That honor probably would have gone to Grigorii Romanov—according to Arbatov, a "perfectly odious" man— the former Leningrad party leader who supported the military attack on détente in the early 1980s.[1] But Romanov was bellicose to the point of frightening (he was the one who had thundered about the "white-hot" international situation in 1983), and rumors in Moscow depicted him as an unstable character. Gorbachev prevailed in the councils of the Party, and within the year, Romanov would be expelled from the Politburo and into obscurity.

The high command knew that it had lost the kind of powerful representation within the Politburo it had enjoyed in the 1970s. Not only was Romanov gone, but Ustinov had died barely three months before Gorbachev's arrival. His replacement was Marshal Sergei Sokolov, a decorated war hero but a nonentity in political terms. And even if Sokolov had been a more forceful individual, he was still only a nonvoting candidate member of the Politburo, and would remain so until his dismissal in 1987. Finally, the most prominent military representative in Moscow, Marshal Ogarkov, had been fired as chief of the General Staff, depriving him of his seat at the policy table, despite his transfer to the important Western Theater command.

The military leadership had other resources at its disposal, however. Gorbachev knew nothing of military affairs, and the General Staff still had a monopoly on the kinds of indispensable knowledge and expertise needed even to begin the reform of national security policy. The mechanisms designed to facilitate control by the general secretary, particularly the Defense Council, had fallen into disuse due to the personalized style that evolved under Brezhnev; according to Gorbachev himself, the Defense Council, a highly secret group of government, Party, and military decision makers, was virtually defunct, and its functions had migrated to the Defense Ministry and General Staff.[2]

---

[1] Arbatov claims that Andropov was a poor judge of character at times, and Romanov was proof. Arbatov, *Zatianvsheesiia vyzdorovlenie (1953–1986 gg.)* (Moscow: "Mezhdunarodnye otnoshenie," 1990), p. 304.

[2] Paul Quinn-Judge, "Gorbachev Hints at Troubles in the Military," *Christian Science Monitor*, July 12, 1989, p. 1.

Thus, Gorbachev took office with great formal powers as general secretary but virtually none of the informal powers that would allow him to contest the stranglehold over defense issues successfully maintained by the military throughout the 1970s and 1980s. Moreover, the military sought to undermine the new leadership by exploiting the worsening of superpower relations, the strategy they had used to such effect against Brezhnev and Andropov. Recognizing the limitations of a new leader with an as yet unarticulated foreign policy, the military press began this period by conducting a stridently alarmist, anti-Western campaign.

Gorbachev, showing that he had learned Khrushchev's lessons well, bided his time and carefully prepared his eventual attack, rather than blundering ahead in neo-Stalinist fashion as Nikita Sergeevich had done thirty years ago. For Gorbachev it was not so much a matter of gaining control as of *re*gaining it, a far more difficult task. Khrushchev at least had the good fortune to have inherited Stalin's military; Gorbachev had the bad fortune to inherit Brezhnev's, and reasserting civilian supremacy turned out to be even more daunting a task than Khrushchev had undertaken.

1985: An Abortive Truce?

Before Gorbachev's official arrival, and during the first months of his tenure, there was still at least the possibility of a general reconciliation between the leadership and the military. Gorbachev began by promising in his March 11 valedictory that the military would be supported during this tense time in Soviet-American relations:

> In the complex international situation, as never before, it is important to support the defense capability of our nation at such a level that potential aggressors will know well: encroachments on the security of the Soviet nation and its allies, on the peaceful life of the Soviet peoples, will be met with a crushing retaliatory strike. Our glorious Armed Forces will continue to be provided with everything necessary for this.[3]

It was a line hinted at in earlier Gorbachev statements, and it seemed to lead some senior officers to make tentative attempts to moderate their rhetoric.

One officer who was willing to support a more constructive relationship with the political leadership was Marshal of the Soviet Union Sergei F. Akhromeev, Ogarkov's replacement as chief of the General

[3] M. S. Gorbachev, *Izbrannye rechi i stat'i* , vol. 2, (Moscow: Politicheskoi literatury, 1987), p. 132.

Staff and therefore a potentially valuable ally. Because the position of defense minister was technically a state position that could be occupied by a civilian, the chief was in fact the top professional military officer in the USSR, so he could set the tone for a large part of the military establishment overall. Akhromeev's early attitude was apparently one of cautious optimism; he began 1985 with a mixed message that warned of American aggressiveness while acknowledging the possibilities for peace. Discussing World War II in the party journal *Kommunist* three months before Gorbachev was elected general secretary, Akhromeev saw in the war a lesson for the present, even "in conditions of the strengthening of the aggressiveness of imperialism." He argued that "it is possible to prevent war only through the collective efforts of all nations and peoples. If in its time the alienation of peace-loving forces in the West allowed the Hitlerites to unleash the Second World War, then today the situation has fundamentally changed. Although the cause of wars, in the person of imperialism, has persisted, the CPSU considers it possible and necessary to prevent war."[4] This was complimented in the same month by a typically harsh excoriation of American policy before the more specialized readership of *Krasnaia Zvezda*, although the *Kommunist* piece nonetheless represented a moderation of the even tougher stance Akhromeev had taken in a discussion of the war the year before.[5]

This conciliatory line appeared somewhat more widely after Gorbachev's arrival. Minister of Defense Sergei Sokolov wrote in *Kommunist* in April 1985 that "the economic potential and defense might" of the Soviet Union was growing, as was the well-being of the socialist commonwealth.[6] He also repeated an important theme common at the time, that "there is no force in the world that can destroy socialism."[7] Like Akhromeev, Sokolov was also quite complimentary to the Soviet Union's allies in World War II, noting the "great contribution" made by the "peoples and the armies of the USA, Great Britain,

[4] S. Akhromeev, "Prevoskhodstvo sovetskoi voennoi nauki i sovetskogo voennogo iskusstva—odin iz vazhneishikh faktorov pobedy v velikoi otechestvennoi voine," *Kommunist* 3 (February 1985), pp. 59–60.

[5] S. Akhromeev, "Na strazhe mira i sotsializma," *Krasnaia Zvezda*, February 22, 1985, p. 2; for the more harsh 1984 assessment, see S. Akhromeev, "Rol' Sovetskogo Soiuza i ego Vooruzhennykh Sil v dostizhenii korennogo pereloma vo vtoroi mirovoi voine i ego mezhdunarodnoe znachenie," *Voenno-Istoricheskii Zhurnal* (February 1984), p. 22.

[6] S. Sokolov, "Velikaia Pobeda," *Kommunist* 6 (April 1985), p. 55.

[7] Ibid., p. 63. Lizichev repeated this formula in his book as well, as it was apparently a dominant political theme in the wake of the plenums that followed the XXVI Party Congress.

France, China, and other nations of the anti-Hitler coalition."[8] The new top political officer, Col. Gen. Aleksei Lizichev (appointed chief of the MPA after the death of his predecessor in 1985), agreed, noting that "we, the Soviet people, have many reasons for optimism" both at home and abroad despite the efforts of some in the West to raise "anti-Soviet hysteria."[9] (His deputy, Adm. A. Sorokin, was less convinced, however, and said so in an anti-Western article in April.[10])

If these high-level pronouncements were meant to be taken as the authoritative line among the military, they failed miserably.[11] Despite the warming of some of the top officers to the new general secretary, few in the senior officer corps were willing to adopt this early "wait and see" attitude toward Gorbachev's foreign policy; overall the military attitude deteriorated soon after Gorbachev's arrival. A month before the Sokolov piece, the chief political officer of the Strategic Rocket Forces, Col. Gen. P. Gorchakov, warned that "aggressive imperialist circles, above all the United States of America, ignoring the lessons of history, have declared a new 'crusade' against socialism."[12] Ground forces CINC Vasilii Petrov (promoted to marshal of the Soviet Union in 1985, before Gorbachev's attempted moratorium on peacetime marshals), like Akhromeev earlier, used a discussion of World War II to make his point. Petrov, however, came to different conclusions, in which he lashed out at the Western powers and warned that even now "the imperialists are doing everything possible to ensure a first disarming strike against the USSR."[13] Another military academic drew a parallel between Nazi aspirations and current Western policy aimed at the "destruction of socialism," adding that there was now an increased "immediate risk of war" due to U.S. "material and moral preparations for war."[14]

Deputy MPA chief D. A. Volkogonov, one of Gorbachev's most

---

[8] Ibid., p. 57.

[9] A. D. Lizichev, *My-patrioty, internatsionalisty* (Sovetskii Obraz Zhizni), (Moscow: DOSAAF, 1985), pp. 10, 14.

[10] A. Sorokin, "Surovyi urok agressoram," *Krasnaia Zvezda*, April 19, 1985, p. 2.

[11] Ground Forces CINC E. Ivanovskii at least did not harp on the "tense" international situation in his April 1985 article—but he also chose not to mention Allied help in his discussion of World War II. Ivanovskii, "V edinom boevoi stroiiu," *Krasnaia Zvezda*, April 17, 1985, p. 2.

[12] P. Gorchakov, "Torzhestvo marksistko-leninskoi ideologii," *Kommunist Vooruzhennykh Sil* 6 (1985), p. 37.

[13] V. Petrov, "Reshaiushchaia rol' Vooruzhennykh Sil SSSR v razgrome fashistskoi Germanii," *Voenno-Istoricheskii Zhurnal* (July 1985), p. 21.

[14] S. Tiushkevich, "Uroki, kotorye zabyvat' nel'zia," *Kommunist Vooruzhennykh Sil* 8 (1985), p. 33.

eloquent and consistent critics in the 1980s, also offered a much more pessimistic view of the world. In early 1985, with Chernenko's death imminent, Volkogonov noted the preparations for the upcoming XXVII Party Congress and said that the Party would be approaching its work in the midst of a "complex and dangerous" international situation: "The actions of international imperialism today are becoming ever more aggressive. The USA and its allies are forcing preparations for war, [and] trying to change the fully developed equilibrium of military forces in their favor. The tense opposing struggle of two systems," Volkogonov concluded, "goes on."[15]

In August 1985, Volkogonov appropriated Brezhnev's line from the XXVI Congress—that counting on victory in nuclear war is "dangerous madness"—in order to point out that it is a madness nonetheless engaged in by "the aggressive wing of modern imperialism."[16] At the time responsible for agitprop in the MPA, Volkogonov was soon promoted to colonel general, and he appeared with increasing frequency and increasing conservatism in both the civilian and the military press in the next few years.

Warsaw Pact CINC Marshal Kulikov also turned up the rhetorical heat in 1985. Praising Soviet arms control efforts, he warned (as he would so many times to come) that the West was not amenable to civilized solutions: "However, the peaceful initiatives of the Warsaw Treaty nations have not yet met a positive response in the USA and NATO . . . the imperialist circles stubbornly continue on the risky path of militarist preparations, and are giving birth to criminal plans for the unleashing of a new war."[17] Worse, Kulikov resurrected Ogarkov's line on weapons: "To this end, the USA has expanded the arms race on an unprecedented scale, above all [in] nuclear [arms], accumulating reserves of weapons of mass destruction and creating qualitatively new types of them."[18] Likewise, military academic R. G. Simonian spoke for many of his colleagues in a 1985 book which argued that NATO and America had entered a new phase of aggressiveness under Reagan (a common observation) and that the United States was prepared for every contingency from strategic nuclear war down to conflicts in selected regions of a theater. He also made brief mention of a concept hinted at by Kulikov, which was to be a hot topic in the coming year, *vseobshchaia obychnaia voina*, or

[15] D. A. Volkogonov, "Vyshe deistvennost' ideologicheskoi raboty," *Kommunist Vooruzhennykh Sil* 2 (February 1985), p. 8.

[16] D. A. Volkogonov, "Voina i mir v 'iadernyi vek'," *Pravda*, August 30, 1985, p. 3.

[17] V. Kulikov, "Nadezhnyi shchit mira," *Kommunist* 8 (May 1985), p. 73.

[18] Ibid., p. 73.

"general conventional war." The "White House bosses" change the names of their doctrines, Simonian wrote, but the essence remains the same: "aggression."[19]

A December 1985 piece in *Krasnaia Zvezda* followed Simonian's line of reasoning and set the tone for the year to come in the military press. Lt. Gen. M. Proskurin asked, "What Lurks Behind the Rogers Plan?" He then answered his own question: The essence of the Rogers Plan "lies in the creation of military superiority over the Warsaw Treaty states in conventional weapons, and therefore the favorable conditions for the conduct of combat actions aimed at the utter destruction of opposing armed forces in the beginning period of war without the use of nuclear weapons." Proskurin was very specific about both the technology involved as well as his convictions about its intended uses. At the end of his argument, Proskurin sent an unsubtle message to the new leadership by juxtaposing Gorbachev's statement that the Warsaw Pact would not allow the West to achieve superiority with a citation of Secretary of Defense Caspar Weinberger's remark that the United States is seeking "full and unarguable military superiority."[20]

Thus, while some senior members of the high command such as Sokolov and Akhromeev seemed willing to let Gorbachev take the lead, other segments of the professional military seized upon Chernenko's illness and later, the change in leadership, to press their case even more strongly. Gorbachev's top military leadership proved ineffective at controlling the military debate: Sokolov and Akhromeev were practically ignored, while one of Lizichev's own deputies in the MPA (Volkogonov) proved to be more vocally conservative than the chief himself. Indeed, even as the military war-scare got under way in earnest in 1986 and 1987, Lizichev's writings seemed to indicate a certain obliviousness on his part to the controversy swirling about him (in part due, as it was later revealed, to the fact that he suffered a heart attack in 1986.)[21]

---

[19] R. G. Simonian, *Real'naia Opasnost': Voennye bloki imperializma* (Moscow: Voenizdat, 1985), p. 71. The book was sent to press in June 1985. This was a return to form for Simonian, who had critiqued Western strategies in a similar three-part series in *Krasnaia Zvezda* in 1976. R. Simonian, "Kontseptsiia 'strategicheskoi dostatochnosti,'" *Krasnaia Zvezda*, August 24, 1976, p. 3; His other two pieces appeared in *Krasnaia Zvezda*, May 27 and September 28, 1976.

[20] M. Proskurin, "Chto kroetsia za 'Planom Rodzhersa,'" *Krasnaia Zvezda*, December 3, 1985, p. 3.

[21] See, for example, "Boevoi gotovnosti voisk—partiinuiu zabotu," *Kommunist* 3 (February 1986), pp. 88–97. Lizichev discussed his heart attack in *Kommunist Vooruzhennykh Sil* 10 (May 1991), p. 51.

To be fair, there can be little question that the Soviet military leadership, from its own perspective, had good reason to be concerned about Washington. The U.S. military buildup was proceeding apace, and events from Central America to the Middle East suggested that the United States was no longer reticent about exercising newfound muscle and resolve, particularly where Soviet clients were concerned—indeed, *especially* where Soviet clients were concerned. If the Soviets believed that President Reagan's foreign policy activism was going to be rebuffed at the polls in 1984, they were disappointed; Reagan won a smashing electoral victory that promised more of the same, which in later months complicated Gorbachev's attempts to argue that Washington's aggressive circles did not represent the will of the American people. In Europe, meanwhile, conservative, anti-Soviet leaders were securely positioned, and NATO modernization plans continued unaffected by Soviet protest or vocal domestic opposition. All indications were that the Soviet position in Europe and the world was eroding rapidly.

In 1986, elements in the military continued to press for a vigilant expansion of Soviet capabilities and issued dire warnings of potential defeat in Europe. Gorbachev, meanwhile, had declared a moratorium on SS-20 missile deployments in April 1985, lending credence to Arbatov's claim that a healthier Brezhnev wanted to do the same all along. And in January 1986, in the wake of an inconclusive but cordial meeting with Reagan in Geneva two months earlier, Gorbachev called for a nuclear-free world by the year 2000, a proposal probably more sincere than thought by the Reagan administration at the time.[22]

The nuclear-free world proposal wasn't taken very seriously in the United States, and in this the Americans and the Soviet high command had something in common. Rather than concern themselves with Gorbachev's gauzy images of world peace, military spokesmen offered more down-to-earth and frightening scenarios. In particular, the military stressed two related themes: the danger of surprise attack (unlikely in reality though it was), and the possibility of quick conventional defeat. These alarms were a resurrected and intensified extension of the Rogers Plan flap (described in the previous chapter), and for understandable reasons: U.S. military research and development, spurred by the twin engines of the Strategic Defense Initiative and the Rogers Plan, had shifted into high gear by 1985. In this if nothing else the Soviet marshals had it right: the 1980s and 1990s promised a

[22] See Newhouse, *War and Peace in the Nuclear Age*, pp. 387–388; for the January 1986 proposal, see Gorbachev, *Izbrannye rechi*, 3:133–144.

technological acceleration of arms research that would quickly overwhelm the Soviet capacity to compete, financially or intellectually.

A typical example of this sort of accusation came from Col. V. Alekseev, a vocal critic of NATO policies. In January 1986, Alekseev warned that "general conventional war" had become an established part of American military doctrine, now that advanced technologies had "created the prerequisites for the conduct of prolonged conventional war in Europe." The aims of this war, perhaps launched under the pretext of maneuvers and carried out under both the "Eurostrategic" and U.S. strategic nuclear umbrellas, would be nothing less than "to liquidate the socialist system in the Eastern European countries of the Warsaw Pact, and to weaken the Soviet Union significantly to force it to give up the armed struggle under conditions favorable to the West."[23]

From the political leadership's standpoint, the year was no doubt off to a bad start.

CIVILIAN REACTION: THE NEW POLITICAL THINKING

Gorbachev assumed his office facing the seemingly impossible task of reimposing order and authority on this rather woolly defense debate. Gorbachev's plans for domestic economic and political reforms—as yet untested, and in part undefined, concepts such as "democratization," "acceleration," *glasnost'*, "new thinking," and "the human factor"—were all aimed at rejuvenating Soviet society and the Soviet economy. The implications of his program included greater worker discipline, more rational use of resources, a cultural and political thaw, and international retrenchment; overall, these plans necessitated either unwilling subordination or cooperative political acquiesence on the part of the military. Whatever the substantive faults or merits of Gorbachev's plans, however, they were tactically flawed, in that the early civilian reaction to the military challenge was generally slow, confused, and ineffective, and did little to curb military opposition to Gorbachev's more optimistic views.

Perhaps seeking to avoid Khrushchev's reputation for thoughtless blundering, Gorbachev tried to make his reform of defense policy intelligible to both Soviet military elites and the West with a set of concepts that came to be known as the "novoe politicheskoe mysh-

---

[23] V. Alekseev, "'Obychnye' voiny v planakh pentagona i NATO," *Krasnaia Zvezda*, January 17, 1986, p. 3.

lenie," or "new political thinking." The New Thinking, which made its appearance in the wake of the April 1985 Plenum of the Central Committee, served two purposes. First, it signaled Gorbachev's desire (and provided him a rationalization other than "détente") for better relations and renewed efforts at arms control with the West. Second, it served as the philosophical groundwork for a civilian counteroffensive, aimed at wresting control of the security agenda from the military.

It is interesting to consider what might have happened had this philosophical campaign taken root in the military. The New Thinking, as will be seen, included the importance of military subordination to political power *for its own sake*—in essence, a Soviet affirmation of the idea of objective control. The failure of this campaign perhaps indicates the degree to which both Party and Army had come to accept subjective control as the natural order of the civil-military relationship. In any case, Gorbachev's commitment to this aspect of the New Thinking was short-lived, but it suggests that the leadership, even if only briefly, had an initial notion of the sort of modern military it was hoping to create.

Early Aspects of the New Thinking

Gorbachev officially initiated his reform program at one of the key Soviet political events of the decade, the April 1985 Plenum of the Central Committee. Expanding on his foreign policy concepts, Gorbachev told the members of the Central Committee,

> Our readiness to improve relations with the United States of America is well-known. . . . There isn't some sort of fatal unavoidability of confrontation of the two nations. If the positive as well as negative experiences of the accumulated history of Soviet-American relations, recent as well as distant history, are interpreted, then it follows that the most reasonable [path] is to find the way leading to the smoothing of relations, [and] to build bridges of cooperation, but to build them from both sides.[24]

Here, Gorbachev went beyond denying the inevitability of war, to denying even the inevitability of confrontation. At both the plenum and afterward, Gorbachev stated that he was aware of the West's

[24] M. S. Gorbachev, *Izbrannye rechi*, 2:171.

recalcitrance, but held out the hope that the American position could be "corrected."[25]

Indeed, Gorbachev's speeches throughout 1985 contain, side by side, condemnations of American stubbornness and hopes of American reasonability. In his 1985 Victory Day speech, Gorbachev invoked the memory of the Grand Alliance and set the tone that was to be emulated by Marshal Sokolov and others. "Noting Victory Day," he told his Kremlin audience, "we give due credit to the fighting prowess of the soldiers of the allied armies—the USA, Great Britain, France."[26] Moreover, Gorbachev struck a conciliatory tone when recounting the lessons of the war.

> The whole experience of the anti-Hitlerite coalition unarguably proves: states, opposite in their social nature, can join forces in a struggle with a common enemy. . . .
>
> The Soviet people have not forgotten the material help that the allies rendered our nation. True, it wasn't nearly as great as they like to say it was in the West, but we remain grateful for that help, considering it as a symbol of joint actions.[27]

Gorbachev then took his point even further with his acknowledgment of the military importance of the Allied opening of the second front (traditionally a sore point with the Soviets), however late it may have been.

A fundamental aspect of Gorbachev's redefinition of Soviet security needs was his estimation that an improved relationship with the West would be not only possible but beneficial. On his first day in power, Gorbachev told the Central Committee,

> We will firmly follow the Leninist course of peace and peaceful coexistence. The Soviet Union will always answer good will with good will, trust—with trust. But all should know that we will never forgo the interests of our *Rodina* [motherland] and her allies.
>
> We value the successes of the détente in international tensions achieved in the 1970s, and are ready to participate in the continuation of the process of getting under way the peaceful, mutually beneficial cooperation between states on the bases of equal rights, mutual respect, and noninterference in internal affairs.[28]

[25] Ibid., p. 171. See also Gorbachev's remarks in Warsaw, April 26, 1985, ibid., 2:176–179.
[26] Ibid., 2:193.
[27] Ibid., 2:201.
[28] Ibid., 2:131.

In light of military rhetoric of the period (early 1985) and after, it is easy to see how Gorbachev's words could be interpreted as overly trusting of the West and only tepidly defensive of Soviet interests. Almost as soon as the military had managed to bury détente (one is reminded, of course, of Ogarkov's scathing 1981 remarks), Gorbachev resurrected it, ten years after Gerald Ford had banned the term from the White House and six years after even Jimmy Carter had abandoned it in the wake of the invasion of Afghanistan.

Gorbachev's rhetoric did not generate serious public objections among his colleagues, since an acceptance of the basic rationality of the West, despite its aggressiveness, was a line traceable back to the XXVI Party Congress and to the Brezhnev era in general.[29] This left the military in 1985 and 1986 facing a fairly monolithic leadership; whatever disagreements there were in the leadership on this topic, they were not at this point aired with any detailed publicity, and the military was not able to utilize divisions in the leadership in any apparent way.[30]

An Early Gorbachev Victory: The Attack on the Strategic Rocket Forces

If anyone in the high command was in doubt about the practical implications of Gorbachev's rhetoric, they needed to look no farther than the Strategic Rocket Forces for confirmation of the general secretary's seriousness. In 1985 and 1986, the top political and command posts were overturned in the SRF. The Strategic Rocket Forces have always been the jewel in the Soviet military crown; indeed, even Khrushchev may have questioned his own decision to create a military organization with so great a sense of identity, attached to so

---

[29] To take but one of many examples, KGB chief Viktor Chebrikov echoed Gorbachev's upbeat assessments in 1985. Speaking on the eve of Revolution Day in the Kremlin, Chebrikov defended the position of the XXVI Congress (and Gorbachev's) that the nature of modern war left "no reasonable alternative" to arms control. Furthermore, despite the admitted aggressiveness of the West, Chebrikov summarized the international situation by asserting that "time works against those who are trying to block détente, the transition to disarmament, and peaceful cooperation." See V. Chebrikov, *Pod znamenem oktiabria—k novym rubezham sovershenstvovaniia sotsializma* (Moscow: Politizdat, 1985), pp. 22, 28.

[30] One possible source of objections was Egor Ligachev, formerly cadres chief and later the ideology boss on the Politburo. See E. K. Ligachev, *Kursom oktiabria, v dukhe revoliutsionnogo tvorchestva* (Moscow: Politizdat, 1986), p. 30, in which he promises continued high military expenditures. In October 1988, Ligachev was put in charge of agricultural affairs, an evident demotion that served to distance him from foreign policy. See "Gorbachev's Main Rival Has Slipped from No. 2 Post, Kremlin Suggests," *Boston Globe*, October 18, 1988, p. 3.

specific a technology, and praised as second only to the Party itself as the guarantor of Soviet security. (This may be the reason behind the emergence of terminology in 1985 and 1986 emphasizing the "strategic nuclear forces." This phrase served to decentralize the role—and therefore the glory—of strategic weapons, and helped to deemphasize the SRF.)[31] It is evident that Gorbachev was seeking to reduce the immense prestige of the service branch least likely to see combat, thereby to prepare them for the cuts they were about to take under Gorbachev's renewed arms control initiatives. The SRF CINC until 1985, Marshal V. Tolubko, was probably replaced because of his strong service identification. Tolubko was a forceful writer, uncompromising in his pride in the SRF.[32] Certainly, it was clear that the SRF would not (and did not, for a time) accept Gorbachev's plans for nuclear disarmament and renewed détente, especially with Reagan.

In the end, the demands of subjective control force politicians to escalate or accommodate, and so Gorbachev chose to escalate. In a move with a clear parallel in the Khrushchev era, a reliable Ground Forces officer (an *obshchevoiskovik*) was chosen to fill the post, an obvious and stinging slap in the face of the SRF.[33] (Imagine the indignation and destruction of the esprit de corps of, say, the U.S. Marines if the president were to assign them a career air force or army officer as commandant.) Tolubko's successor, Col. Gen. Iurii Maksimov, played the role of the good soldier, rather than the service protector, defending Gorbachev's policies both foreign and domestic.[34] The SRF also lost a vocally conservative political chief in Col. Gen. Gorchakov, who

[31] A 1985 *Krasnaia Zvezda* editorial may have been alluding to this new emphasis when it said, "Now all types of the Armed Forces have rocket weapons, and [these weapons] are one of the most important components of combat power [*boevoi moshchi*]." "Raketchiki," *Krasnaia Zvezda*, February 10, 1985, p. 1. See also the lecture notes for Rocket/Artillery Day, "Nadezhnyi shchit otchizny," *Kommunist Vooruzhennykh Sil* 19 (October 1986).

[32] For typical example, see "Vysokoi meroi boegotovnosti," *Kommunist Vooruzhennykh Sil* 10 (May 1985). Also see "Vsegda v boevoi gotovnosti," *Krasnaia Zvezda*, April 25, 1985, p. 2. This sort of service pride does not seem to be as pronounced in one of Tolubko's subordinates passed over for the job of CINC, Col. Gen. Iu. Iashin; Iashin may have been disqualified primarily because he was a career SRF man. See Iu. Iashin, "Rezerv na vydvizhenie," *Krasnaia Zvezda*, February 15, 1986, p. 2.

[33] The story of the appointment of Marshal N. Krylov is worth reading. Krylov, supposedly like Maksimov later, didn't want the job, and Krylov's biographer relates the clear arm-twisting Malinovskii used before practically ordering Krylov to take the post. See I. G. Dragan, *Marshal N. I. Krylov* (Moscow: Voenizdat, 1987), pp. 221–222, and chap. 3 of this book.

[34] See, in particular, "Pod boevymi znamenami," *Krasnaia Zvezda*, May 9, 1988. In 1988, Maksimov published an unremarkable piece on training and education, "Voennomu delu uchitsia nastoiashchim obrazom," *Kommunist Vooruzhennykh Sil* 4 (February 1988).

declined to join in the generally optimistic rhetoric of 1985. Within a year, Gorchakov was retired from his position (one he had held since 1970) and replaced by V. S. Rodin, formerly the political officer in the Southwestern Theater, a not inconsequential post in itself. Rodin was far less controversial than his predecessor; in one of his first Rocket Forces Day pieces, he established his later style by avoiding any mention of international politics, sticking instead strictly to party-political work.[35]

The SRF did not take these affronts lightly, and they tried to defend themselves by taking their case to the public. "What stress [these missileers] suffer on duty!" one military journalist wrote. "By the age of 40, they have high blood pressure and suffer from insomnia." Significantly, this piece was aimed not at the specialized readership of *Krasnaia Zvezda*, but at the general readership of *Izvestiia*.[36] Another example is a book in which the military decided to provide a more detailed look at the lives and personalities of Soviet missile officers, dramatically titled *U Pultov Strategicheskikh* ("At the Strategic Launchers"; a more visceral translation would read, "With Their Fingers on the Buttons," or something similar).[37]

With the SRF firmly in hand, Gorbachev seemed poised to gain control of the military situation at the XXVII Party Congress. He failed, however, to put forward a detailed program the way Khrushchev had, and by mid-1986, the discussion would again be out of control. Still, Gorbachev's statements at the Congress constituted his most complete exposition of his defense philosophy, despite the lack of details.

The military needed no details. The contours of the Gorbachev program were clear to them early on, and they deduced the details from the general line. Even in March, only five days after Gorbachev's valedictory, the editors of *Krasnaia Zvezda* weighed in with a reminder to the new general secretary of his promise made to the March Plenum of the Central Committee; the quid pro quo was that the military

[35] V. Rodin, "Sovetskaia Armiia—shkola vospitaniia," *Voenno-Istoricheskii Zhurnal* (November 1986). In a similar vein: Col. A. Fedorov (inspector of political work in the SRF), "Kommunist—pritsipal'nyi boets partii," *Kommunist Vooruzhennykh Sil* 9 (May 1985). Rodin was a bit more boastful in his *Krasnaia Zvezda* piece for Rocket Day in 1986, as might be expected for that readership, one that includes the rank and file; this was toned down the following year in a Rocket Forces Day interview, "Vo imia boevoi gotovnosti," *Krasnaia Zvezda*, November 19, 1987, pp. 1–2.

[36] "Missile Officers' Training Described," FBIS-SOV-87-228, November 27, 1987, p. 74.

[37] A. V. Belousov, *U Pultov Strategicheskikh* (Moscow: Voenizdat, 1987). Belousov, a military journalist, is himself a former SRF missileer.

explicitly accepted the primacy of rebuilding the consumer economy, at least rhetorically.[38] The next month, however, the editors may have been speaking to the leadership when they said that the "aggressive appetites of imperialism have been reliably restrained by the military-strategic equilibrium attained between the fraternal countries and NATO. No one will be allowed to violate that equilibrium."[39]

Gorbachev went to the Party Congress thus forewarned, and he set out early to undermine exactly the kind of obsessive thinking about the military balance that could only serve to harm his plans for reform. Unfortunately, to accomplish this would require the same sort of major intrusions into military policy so characteristic of Khrushchev. The parallels did not, as it turned out, go unnoticed.

THE XXVII PARTY CONGRESS

In 1986, as the military conservatives became more vocal, the "new political thinking" emerged more fully. At the XXVII Party Congress in February 1986, Gorbachev set out four basic tenets of Soviet foreign policy. In military eyes, each was contentious at best, and foolish at worst.

The first theme taken up by Gorbachev at the congress was a direct rebuttal of military warnings about advanced weaponry, as Gorbachev presented his own interpretation of the technological developments (including the Rogers Plan and SDI) that had the soldiers so worried: "The character of present weapons does not leave a single state with the hope of defending itself only by military-technical means, in other words, through the creation of new weapons—even the most powerful. The guaranteeing of security ever more appears as a political problem, and it can be resolved only by political means. Above all, the will is needed to embark on the path of disarmament." Here, Gorbachev intended to kill several birds (hawks?) with a single stone. This passage served three purposes: to allay possible fears among the delegates about American technology, to undercut the

---

[38] "Krepit' moguchestvo rodiny," *Krasnaia Zvezda*, March 16, 1985, p. 1. A week later an editorial appeared reassuring the readership that none of this consumerism meant that the USSR was abandoning its international obligations. "Politika posledovatel'-naia, printsipal'naia," *Krasnaia Zvezda*, March 21, 1985, p. 1.

[39] "Navstrechu XXVII s"ezdu KPSS," *Krasnaia Zvezda*, April 25, 1985, p. 1. A few days earlier, the editors had voiced the military complaint common in the days of the first Reagan term, that the United States was seeking military superiority over the USSR. See "Revoliutsionnoe znamiia epokhi," *Krasnaia Zvezda*, April 21, 1985, p. 1.

military argument about weaponry, and—most important—to establish explicitly the problem of security as being within the exclusive purview of politicians rather than soldiers. Gorbachev reinforced this last point by saying that new weapons systems shorten the time to make *"political* decisions on the questions of war and peace" during a crisis.[40]

Gorbachev's second and third points on foreign policy at the XXVII Congress also seemed to anticipate military objections. In a return to language similar to the days of the Soviet Union's reliance on collective security in the 1930s, Gorbachev emphasized that security must be mutual in the case of Soviet-American relations, and general in the case of international relations at large. And while he acknowledged the aggressiveness of the U.S. military-industrial complex, he also noted that "the interests and goals of the military-industrial complex are not entirely one and the same with the interests and goals of the American people, [nor with] the underlying national interests of that great nation."[41] Needless to say, military commentators then and since chose to eschew the depiction of America as a "great nation," with many instead arguing that the interests of the military-industrial complex were indivisible from American interests.

Finally, Gorbachev sought to move the debate on security away from strictly military considerations. In the tradition of Western socialists and social democrats, Gorbachev embraced a broadened definition of security that relied more on social justice to strike at the causes of conflict, rather than on armaments to defend against conflicts. In essence, he argued that the cause of peace cannot be furthered without "a thoroughgoing system of international economic security."[42] The same phrase had also appeared, predictably enough, in Gorbachev's welcoming remarks before his 1985 meeting with Willy Brandt.[43]

Initial support for the Gorbachev program was quick to appear, and again the military faced what appeared to be closed civilian ranks. Nikolai Ryzhkov, for example, said after the Congress, that "the Leninist principles of our foreign policy" now "actively serve the struggle which the Soviet government has carried on for the basic restructuring of international relations. In this struggle we are directed by the new political thinking, which reflects the realities of today's world—the full contradictions and conflicts, as well as its

[40] Gorbachev, *Izbrannye Rechi*, 3:245, emphasis added.
[41] Ibid.
[42] Ibid., 3:246.
[43] For the Brandt speech, see ibid., 2:238.

unity and interrelatedness." After referring to the historical symbol of the New Thinking, the Bolshevik "Decree on Peace," Ryzhkov added: "Our new philosophical view of peace proceeds from this: that in the present era security cannot be built on nuclear terror or other kinds of politics of force."[44] Gorbachev could not have said it better. And abroad, of course, Gorbachev protégé and Minister of Foreign Affairs Eduard Shevardnadze brought Gorbachev's message before the world in his address to the forty-first session of the UN General Assembly.[45]

At the XXVII Party Congress, the two military delegates who were allowed to speak were predictably supportive of the Gorbachev program, although without evident conviction. Indeed, what is striking about the Congress is not the tone of military comment, but rather the lack of it. Minister of Defense Sokolov had unkind words about Western aggressiveness, but labeled the American response to Soviet arms initiatives only as "unconstructive." The Soviet Armed Forces, he maintained, were being "supported at the requisite level."[46] Elsewhere during the congress, the head of the Gagarin Air Force Academy, N. M. Skomorokhov, repeated the Gorbachev sentiment that the arms race "is not only leading the world to global nuclear war, but also is exerting a ruinous influence on the economy and on social development in the capitalist as well as socialist and developing countries."[47] Even though this was obviously the Party's preferred line, it is interesting that the only officer available to make Gorbachev's case was so minor a figure as Skomorokhov.

After the Congress: Military Rejection of the New Thinking

If Gorbachev had hoped that the forceful renewal and expansion of the Brezhnev-Andropov line at the Party Congress would serve to stifle the military opposition, he was disappointed. If anything, Gorbachev's more detailed statements at the congress led to intensified military warnings about the West that, through 1986 and 1987, verged at times on hysteria. The examples are numerous, as the chorus of military Cassandras pressed their case. Col. Gen. V. S. Nechaev of the

[44] N. Ryzhkov, "Leninizm—osnova teorii i praktiki perestroiki," *Izvestiia*, April 23, 1986, pp. 2–3.

[45] E. A. Shevardnadze, *Za novoe myshlenie v mirovoi politike: Vystuplenie na 41-i sessii General'noi Assamblei OON* (Moscow: Politicheskoi literatury, 1986).

[46] *XXVII S"ezd Kommunisticheskoi Partii Sovetskogo Soiuza: Stenograficheskii otchet*, vol. 1 (Moscow: Politizdat, 1986), pp. 452, 454.

[47] Ibid., 3:10.

MPA wrote in early 1987 that "the ruling circles of the United States have not rejected the course of stirring up war-hysteria."[48] (Notice that this is an accusation against the actual American leadership rather than the more limited accusation against "certain" circles used by other Soviet writers.)[49] Likewise, Nechaev referred to the failure of arms initiatives and the dangerous American attitude it revealed, promising that "the Soviet Union, of course, cannot fail to take into account the militaristic actions of the United States."[50] Ground Forces CINC E. F. Ivanovskii agreed, concurring with many of his colleagues that the West was simply unprepared to live peaceably with the USSR. "Now," he wrote in mid-1986, "when the imperialist states spurn the peace-loving, clear and honorable proposals of the Soviet government, strengthen military preparations, and seek to carry the arms race into space, it is especially necessary that our tireless struggle for peace be organically combined with the readiness to rebuff any aggressor."[51] Ironically, both Ivanovskii's and Nechaev's comments appeared in a series of pamphlets whose ostensible purpose was to explain and support the work of the XXVII Congress.

The deputy minister of defense for armaments, Gen. V. Shabanov, also put it bluntly that summer: "Through the fault of imperialistic circles in the USA the international situation remains complicated. The aggressiveness of imperialism not only is not decreasing, but on the contrary, it is getting greater."[52] Although Shabanov (a former civilian in the Ustinov mold) remained faithful to the Gorbachevian line that weapons alone do not win wars, his depiction of the external danger is far more bleak than Gorbachev's, and his listing of every major improvement in American weapons systems left little doubt as to the focal point of his concerns. (In 1989 Shabanov broke his silence and simply admitted that he objected to the cuts in defense spending,

[48] V. S. Nechaev, *Reshaiushchii istochnik boevoi moshchi* [series: Resheniia XXVII S"ezda KPSS—v Zhizni] (Moscow: Izdatel'stvo DOSAAF, 1987) p. 23.

[49] For Nechaev's statements on more prosaic matters, see "Bliznost' k liudiam kak faktor splocheniia voinskogo kollektiva," *Kommunist Vooruzhennykh Sil* 4 (February 1987); "Voinskii byt: Novye kriterii i podkhody," *Kommunist Vooruzhennykh Sil* 7 (April 1988).

[50] Nechaev, *Reshaiushchii istochnik boevoi moshchi*, p. 33. Nechaev also reveals his traditionalist view of the Soviet Armed Forces in this work; on page 92 he reaffirms the SRF as the basis of Soviet military power, noting that the "tactical-technical characteristics of ballistic missiles allow for strikes on any of the aggressor's objectives, and with sufficiently high accuracy," a formulation that sounds more like 1965 than 1985.

[51] E. F. Ivanovskii, *Na Strazhe Rodiny* [series: Resheniia XXVII S"ezda KPSS—v Zhizn'] (Moscow: Izdatel'stvo DOSAAF, 1986), p. 88.

[52] V. Shabanov, "Material'naia osnova oboronnoi moshchi," *Krasnaia Zvezda*, August 15, 1986, p. 2.

noting that "although this is something I do not agree with, we cannot help it.")[53]

Through the spring and summer of 1986, military alarmism continued unabated. The specter of all-out nuclear war was not forgotten in the rush to point out the danger of conventional conflict. Col. V. A. Zubkov, for one, added a nuclear twist to the surprise attack argument in the March 1986 *Voenno-Istoricheskii Zhurnal* lead editorial. Zubkov wrote that the West was planning the nuclear destruction of both military and civilian targets, and he used this threat to argue (as Ogarkov had in previous years) for greater militarization of the economy: "The militarist circles of the USA and NATO are planning on the massive use of rocket-nuclear weapons not only against groupings of forces and military objectives, but also against the rear and throughout the entire depth with the goal of the destruction or the essential undermining of military-economic potential, disruption of the system of economic communications and control and the demoralization of the population."[54] Zubkov argued point-blank that this mobilizational requirement was a policy problem, not a structural problem. "A level of development of science and technology has been achieved in our country," he writes near his conclusion, "that allows the successful solving of the most complex technical problems and the creation in a short period of any kind of weapon on which the aggressors are counting."[55] Zubkov suffered little in the way of a rebuke; the following month an unsigned article appeared where Zubkov's had, with a similar title, on the same subject, tepidly disagreeing with his recommendations by ignoring them.[56] If the follow-up article was meant as a reprimand or a rejoinder, it was a weak one.

Other officers integrated the threats of nuclear attack and general conventional war into similarly nightmarish scenarios. Col. G. Lukava warned in June 1986 that the United States had returned "to the adventuristic anti-Soviet conceptions" of the 1940s and 1950s, and had staked its hopes on "the factor of surprise and the offensive character of the use of all types" of "the most destructive" nuclear and conventional weapons. (Lukava's rank belies his importance, as he is

[53] "Reaction to 8.2 Percent Cut in Defense Budget: Deputy Minister Shabanov," FBIS-SOV-90–003, January 4, 1990, p. 103.

[54] V. A. Zubkov, "Zabota KPSS ob ukreplenii ekonomicheskikh osnov voennoi moshchi sotsialisticheskogo gosudarstva," *Voenno-Istoricheskii Zhurnal* (March 1986), p. 6.

[55] Ibid., p. 7.

[56] "XXVII s"ezd KPSS o dal'neishem ukreplenii oboronosposobnosti strany i povyshenii boevoi gotovnosti Vooruzhennikh Sil," *Voenno-Istoricheskii Zhurnal* (April 1986), pp. 3–12.

one of the more senior and influential instructors at the Lenin Military-Political Academy.)[57] That same month, Lt. Gen. V. A. Aleksandrov, in a historical review of the development of U.S. military strategy, identified Secretary of Defense Weinberger personally as the author of the new American approach to global war and claimed that the United States was preparing both for prolonged nuclear war as well as for conventional victory over the Warsaw Pact.[58]

Maj. Gen. L. Korzun expanded on this a month later, when he claimed that the Rogers Plan concepts envisioned a preventive, rather than preemptive, Western strike against both echeloned Warsaw Pact forces and strategically important targets in Eastern Europe using every means of combat—chemical, conventional, and nuclear.[59] Korzun's only disagreement with his fellow officers was that they did not depict the threat starkly enough; to him, there was nothing "conventional" about NATO strategy, and he pointed to the plethora of NATO nuclear forces to make his point. The concept of preventive war, of course, implies premeditated aggression, even more perfidious than the Nazi attack of 1941 (launched, at least, in the midst of a major, preexistent conflict between signatories of a nonaggression pact). The accusation that NATO was planning a preventive war carried especially serious connotations for both civilian foreign policy and military preparation, and it is doubtful that the impact of the term could have escaped the general.

The "New Thinkers" Counterattack

Gorbachev's supporters did not remain silent, although their first act was to try to silence the military. One indication of this was the virtual closure of the Party's main theoretical journal, *Kommunist*, to the high command. In 1985, there were substantive appearances in *Kommunist* by Akhromeev, Y. Epishev, Kulikov, and Sokolov; in 1986 only Lizichev and Volkogonov (and the ubiquitous and predictable propagandist Col. Gen. Nikolai Chervov) made it past the editors, the last appearances by senior officers for the next two years.

[57] G. Lukava, "Faktor vnezapnosti v agressivnoi politike imperializma," *Kommunist Vooruzhennykh Sil* 11 (June 1986), p. 24. In 1986, he published a brief book that underscored his conservative themes, *V. I. Lenin o zashchite zavoevanii sotsializma* (Moscow: Voenizdat, 1986). I am indebted to Sergei Zamascikov of the RAND Corporation for these insights into Lukava's career.

[58] V. Aleksandrov, "Evoliutsiia amerikanskikh vzgliadov na vozmozhnyi kharakter voin," *Voenno-Istoricheskii Zhurnal* (June 1986), p. 62.

[59] L. Korzun, "NATO—Udarnyi kulak imperializma," *Krasnaia Zvezda*, July 15, 1986, p. 3.

In any case, *Kommunist*—once the forum for criticizing Ogarkov—had no time to publish military articles; it was too busy publishing defenses of the New Thinking. One key architect of Gorbachev's foreign policy, former ambassador to the United States Anatolii Dobrynin, put forward an explication of Gorbachev's ideas in a seminal June 1986 article that served as one of the first detailed descriptions of the New Thinking. Dobrynin restated Gorbachev's themes of political primacy and technological subordination, arguing that "weapons themselves have never played a 'pacifying role.' Not one new weapon has meant the end of wars; rather, they have only given war an even more destructive scale. Scientists know this no less than politicians."[60] Bruce Parrott has noted the pointed nature of this last comment, in which "military men, including Soviet military men, were conspicuously absent from Dobrynin's formula."[61]

Dobrynin was probably right to exclude military men from his discussion, since the summer of 1986 had shaped up to be a hot one in the military press. Dobrynin single-mindedly hammered home Gorbachev's admonition that "weapons never bring peace, however complicated and expensive they may be."[62] The new political thinking, Dobrynin wrote, recognizes the mutuality of security interests, and this necessitates "a qualitatively new approach to the problem of national security. . . . The new political thinking presupposes a qualitatively higher level of flexibility in foreign policy, a readiness to proceed to reasonable compromises with its partners in negotiations."[63] Dobrynin moved from this to a defense of one of New Thinking's more concrete manifestations, the Soviet nuclear test moratorium. There is some evidence that the moratorium, not surprisingly, was unpopular with the senior military, as was much of the New Thinking.[64]

Other academics contributed intellectual support to the New Thinking, particularly in the pages of *SShA*, the journal of the USA/Canada Institute of the Academy of Sciences in Moscow. (The institute's original chief, Georgii Arbatov, would enter into direct political combat with Marshal Akhromeev in 1990.) Vitaly Zhurkin, an official of the institute, opened 1986 in the pages of *SShA* with a reasoned and

[60] A. Dobrynin, "Za bez"iadernyi mir, navstrechu xxi veka," *Kommunist* 9 (September 1986), p. 20.
[61] Bruce Parrott, "The Soviet Union and Ballistic Missile Defense," *SAIS Papers in International Affairs*, 14 (1987), p. 66.
[62] Dobrynin, "Za bez"iadernyi mir," p. 21.
[63] Ibid., p. 24.
[64] See Parrott, *The Soviet Union and Ballistic Missile Defense*, passim.

carefully worded discussion of strategic stability that sounded almost as if it had been written from an advance draft of Gorbachev's XXVII Party Congress remarks. Zhurkin made six general points about strategic stability, one of which indirectly attempted to divorce military policy from ideology, probably reflecting the realization that ideological arguments were more useful to the military than to Gorbachev. Zhurkin's points sustained, once again, the Gorbachevian argument that peace and stability are manipulable exclusively through political means: "Strategic stability (or instability)," he claimed, "is the result of state policy. . . . The creation of this or that weapons system is the result of a political decision."[65] Furthermore, Zhurkin attacked technological determinism and bean-counting: "The structure of strategic forces is the result of free choice by each side. In comparing their potentials, the point is not in the structure, but in overall qualitative and quantitative parity."[66]

So much for the strategic situation, but what of the nefarious Rogers Plan in Europe? Soon after Zhurkin's discussion, one of his colleagues undermined military warnings about the NATO conventional threat. Parity, according to S. A. Ulin, meant (and in this he was correct) that the Europeans had begun to have doubts about the reliability of American leadership. In particular, Ulin claimed that the introduction of new American missiles in Europe hurt the solidarity of the alliance, while offering no relief from the nuclear stalemate.[67] Furthermore, Ulin described the Rogers Plan primarily as a reflection of the American desire to force the Europeans to assume a greater share of the hefty spending on NATO conventional forces, and he showed that it was unsuccessful even in that.[68] All in all, Ulin's was a far less alarmist view of Atlantic developments, and one that stood in direct opposition to the overwhelmingly dominant military line at the time.

The Campaign against Clausewitz

The theme that the nature of the modern era is itself the rationale for Gorbachev's approach was complimented by the rather unusual civilian tactic of attacking the Soviet military's admiration of Clausewitz. One irony here, of course, is that Clausewitz was a strong champion of the cause of civilian control of the military. The civilians,

---

[65] V. V. Zhurkin, "O strategicheskoi stabil'nosti," *SShA* 1 (January 1986), p. 13.
[66] Ibid., p. 16.
[67] S. A. Ulin, "Krizisnye iavleniia v NATO," *SShA* 4 (April 1986), pp. 15–16.
[68] Ibid., p. 21.

however, used Clausewitz as shorthand language for outdated military thinking, no doubt well aware of the honored place Clausewitz holds in the Soviet military pantheon.[69]

In an early 1986 account of the 1985 Geneva summit, Soviet political analyst Fedor Burlatskii aggressively attacked traditional military thinking through Clausewitz. Referring to Clausewitz as "that classic of militarism," Burlatskii opined that Lenin only intended to use Clausewitz's formula as an indictment of the corrupt society that produced it.[70] (No doubt the Soviet officer corps would find that to be an interesting assertion; even Lenin's Western biographers would be hard-pressed to defend it.) This traditional thinking, for Burlatskii, was part and parcel of the traditional system of international relations that had failed to provide alternatives to the postwar security dilemma.

Apparently, Burlatskii and others were speaking to those who were less visionary than they—but where? Aleksandr Bovin, in the summer of 1986 (as the military war-scare was reaching a peak) excoriated those, ostensibly in the West, who were blind to new realities in the atomic age. Some scholars, he admitted, in the early postwar days realized the importance of what had happened in the skies over Hiroshima and Nagasaki. Others were less perceptive. "Politicians and generals, as always, prepared for 'the previous war.' From their point of view, nuclear weapons had changed tactics and strategy, but had left the philosophy of war, the traditional view of it as a fully rational means of achieving political goals, inviolable: everything was approximately the same, only the scale was different."[71] One wonders which generals and politicians Bovin really intended to criticize, because he then turned his attention to the inapplicability of Clausewitzian thought to modern war, arguing that the German general had indiscriminately assigned equal weight to peaceful and forceful means of politics, and "it is precisely here that Clausewitz has become outdated."[72]

---

[69] In the 1957 version of *Marxism-Leninism on War and the Army*, the authors wrote that it was "natural" that Lenin had referred to Clausewitz in discussing war, "insofar as it was Clausewitz himself who first put forward the formula of war as a continuation of politics by violent means." This formulation was without doubt a contribution to the development of military thought, and therefore the classics of Marxism-Leninism have greatly valued Clausewitz as an outstanding military thinker. See I. N. Levadov, B. A. Belyi, and A. P. Novoselov, eds., *Marksizm-leninizm o voine i armii* (Moscow: Voenizdat, 1957), p. 5.

[70] F. Burlatskii, *Zheneva: vchera, segodnia, zavtra* (Moscow: Mysl', 1986), p. 107.

[71] A. Bovin, "Novoe Myshlenie—trebovanie iadernogo veka," *Kommunist* 10 (July 1986), pp. 113–114.

[72] Ibid., p. 116.

Another source of ire for the Soviet military had to be Bovin's kind words for President Reagan. Choosing instead to blame the Pentagon for American aggressiveness, he quoted Reagan's 1986 speech in Japan. There Reagan, after referring to having witnessed four major wars, said that he spoke not only as the president, but also as a husband, father, and grandfather. Thus, according to Bovin, "In the words of American leaders it is acknowledged that a nuclear war cannot be won," a direct refutation of the accusations made against the Reagan administration by Soviet military commentators. In analyzing U.S. military policy, however, it was clear to Bovin that "the Pentagon has not lost the hope of rehabilitating Clausewitz, of breaking out of the stalemated situation, to create a 'strategy of victory.' "[73] Bovin concluded with guarded optimism that the West, despite its failings, may change and accept the realities of the nuclear era: "I suggest that Reagan, and even Weinberger, do not want to go to war with the Soviet Union."[74]

The next issue of *Kommunist* took up Bovin's argument, with commentator Iu. Zhilin agreeing that Clausewitz had become outdated. In the modern age, according to Zhilin, war "would not be war in the traditional sense of the word, in that there would be neither victors nor vanquished, because in the final analysis there would be nobody."[75]

This shelling of Clausewitz, and the moral behind it, did not go unnoticed by the military. Clausewitz, with his bourgeois background, had never been an easy subject for military ideologists who, like Lenin before them, nonetheless admired his lucidity and detachment. Indeed, this was hardly the first time that Soviet thinkers encountered this dilemma; this time, however, it was especially problematic because the issue was openly forced by the leadership. There was a sense in the military that the criticism of Clausewitz went too far, no doubt in part because it was in reality a criticism aimed at them.[76]

One attempt to deal with the indictment of Clausewitz was made by a prominent commentator on the New Thinking in the military press, Lt. Gen. V. Serebriannikov, a deputy chief of the Lenin

[73] Ibid., p. 117.
[74] Ibid., pp. 122, 124.
[75] Iu. Zhilin, "Faktor vremeni v iadernyi vek," *Kommunist* 11 (July 1986), p. 115.
[76] For an analysis of earlier examples of Soviet writing on the problem of war and Clausewitz, see Christian Hacke and Wolfgang Pfeiler, "Soviet Approaches to Limited War," *Soviet Union/Union Sovietique* 10 (1983), p. 273.

Military-Political Academy.[77] On the question of the New Thinking's analysis of the relationship between war and politics, Serebriannikov found himself in a difficult spot, and he reverted to the formulation that emerged from the late 1960s: namely, all wars are necessarily a continuation of politics, in the sense that they represent the political interests of those waging them, even if war itself should be rejected as a policy option. Here, war has a political nature because it has a moral nature. Serebriannikov also sent along a warning to civilian commentators about limits on the discussion of Clausewitz:

> The definition of war as a continuation of politics by violent means is well known to Marxist-Leninists. This formulation allows understanding of the new quality of modern war, linked to deep changes in politics as well as in the means of armed struggle. Modern war—large or small, nuclear or conventional—cannot be anything other than a continuation of politics, and consequently it is subject to a socio-class evaluation: it is either just or unjust.[78]

In other words: let us not be infected by our own propaganda. While Serebriannikov gladly defended the regime's efforts at peaceful coexistence in the international arena, he was far less comfortable with the undercutting of a basic rationale behind the armed forces' existence and rectitude, an issue that would reemerge with a vengeance in 1987. In the end, the question of the status of Clausewitz was never settled, and it reappeared regularly in the Soviet press over the last few years of Gorbachev's time in office.

VOLKOGONOV'S ATTACK

Beyond the Congress, there were a few mild attempts to defend New Thinking in the military press, with no extensive results. (Articles on the subject briefly appeared in *Krasnaia Zvezda* under the rubric "New Thinking: A Look at the Problem," not exactly enthusiastic as Soviet slogans go.) Overall, the term did not work its way into

---

[77] Serebriannikov (like Volkogonov) has a Ph.D. in philosophy and the rank of professor. He was in charge of scholarly and scientific work at the Lenin Military-Political Academy, according to an introduction to one of his articles in *Na putiiakh perestroiki* (Moscow: Voenizdat, 1987), p. 153.

[78] V. Serebriannikov, "Zashchita sotsializma v iadernyi vek," *Krasnaia Zvezda*, December 19, 1986, pp. 2–3.

common usage among the military in any but the most jargonistic way.[79]

Even these feeble attempts at getting the New Thinking into the military mainstream after the XXVII Party Congress were accompanied by signs of trouble. That trouble emerged in the persona of Colonel General, Deputy Chief of the Main Political Administration, Doctor of Philosophy, and Professor Dmitrii A. Volkogonov. In the next chapter, we will see how Volkogonov led the fight to protect military prestige and Soviet patriotism (and later, his change of heart and how he finally broke with the Soviet system); here, we will examine his differences with the general secretary on defense policy and the nature of the Western threat in 1986.

In a May 1986 article in *Partiinaia Zhizn'*, Volkogonov dutifully repeated the foreign policy formulations of the XXVII Congress. Thus, it was all the more striking when Volkogonov then reaffirmed his belief that the West was simply blind to reason.

> As long as imperialism is not fully ready to adopt in practice the logic of peaceful coexistence, we have found it necessary to assign the highest importance to the matter of strengthening the defense capability of the nation and the defense of the socialist Fatherland. . . . today, it is impossible not to take into account that, although imperialism could not win a nuclear war, it is in a position to unleash one.[80]

Volkogonov even took a parting shot at Gorbachev's insistence that war is not fatalistically unavoidable, noting that "this doesn't mean the automatic exclusion of [war] from social life. Moreover, imperialis-

---

[79] There appeared to be, however, at least one change of heart among the military (albeit not in one of the more prominent journals): in early 1986, Maj. Gen. S. Tiushkevich published an article in *Politicheskoe Samoobrazovanie* that seemed to anticipate the line of the XXVII Party Congress. Although he still maintained that "imperialist forces are capable of, and may, create such a situation in which world war appears as a realistic possibility," in general his tone was more in line with the leadership's views, particularly his approval of the formula that Soviet defense priorities are clear: "Everything necessary for defense and nothing more." Tiushkevich's article is a mixed bag; his acceptance of Gorbachev's formulations is followed by warnings about the major military topic in 1986—the dangers (and likelihood) of surprise attack. See S. Tiushkevich, "Odna iz vazhneishikh funktsii obshchenarodnogo gosudarstva," *Politicheskoe Samoobrazovanie* 1 (1986), pp. 34, 35. In late 1991, Tiushkevich participated in a conference on military service and democracy in Moscow. While he had reservations about a complete divorce between the military and politics, it was evident that he had reconsidered his earlier positions from the mid-1980s.

[80] D. A. Volkogonov, "Zashchitit' i uprochit' mir—istoricheskaia missiia sotsializma," *Partiinaia Zhizn'* 10 (May 1986), p. 76.

tic forces are capable, as attested to by the events of past years, of creating a situation where world war appears as a possible, menacing reality."[81] This one passage perhaps said more about Volkogonov's view of Gorbachev's policies than any amount of ritualistic repetition of the congress formulas. These statements, and others, revealed Volkogonov's basic disagreement with Gorbachev's view of the world.

During 1986, Volkogonov was preparing a major book for release in early 1987. Publication data indicate that it was written after the congress; this is important, for in it, he scorned the idea of diplomatic dominance in security affairs (a point fellow officers would again raise in 1987), and he directly challenged the Gorbachevian idea of reasoning with "that great nation," the United States:

> Just what has restrained those who prepare for a [nuclear] war? Why have the people at the helm of power in Washington—despite their own declarations of readiness to "conquer socialism"—not decided on nuclear adventure, not taken that last, fateful step?
>
> Of course, it has nothing to do with being "peace-loving," which they love to talk about in the NATO capitals, nor with the "historic responsibility" of those who sit in the bunkers of the Pentagon and model ever newer and newer scenarios for nuclear war. Our political resolve to meet an encroachment on the security of the Soviet nation and its allies with a shattering retaliatory strike is what restrains them from taking that last militaristic step. Only our resoluteness, multiplied by defensive might, deters those who have not learned the lessons of past wars.[82]

Volkogonov then went on to quote Gorbachev's own words (cited in the epigraph of this chapter) from the XXVII Party Congress, in which the general secretary mentioned that he could say "with all responsibility" that the armed forces were up to the job of keeping the peace. "The responsibility," Volkogonov then added (as though explaining it to Gorbachev as well as to the reader) "is to the future, it is a responsibility *for life.*"[83]

Volkogonov and Nuclear Victory

Volkogonov's criticisms were even more pronounced on the touchier subject of nuclear victory in October 1986, at a conference on the

---

[81] Ibid., p. 77.

[82] D. Volkogonov, *Sovetskii soldat* (Moscow: Voenizdat, 1987), p. 7. The book was apparently completed in late 1985, but held back until after revisions could be made after the 27th Party Congress.

[83] Ibid., p. 12, original emphasis.

role of social scientists in relation to the XXVII Party Congress, a gathering one might be tempted to dismiss as typical in the wake of a party congress. But Volkogonov's remarks became decidedly untypical when he took the offensive against what he saw as the serious dangers of moral relativism and irresoluteness. After repeating his earlier warning that the imperialists were in a position to launch a war they cannot win, Volkogonov noted that "in the Party program, a clear-cut problem was formulated" and put before the armed forces. How, he asks, can the Soviet Armed Forces can be asked to "smash any aggressor," while "at the same time, it is asserted in one of our journals that the wisdom of Soviet military doctrine lies in [the fact] that the word 'victory' has disappeared from it. I think," he added, "that we cannot agree with this interpretation."[84]

At least publicly, the issue of nuclear victory had been a closed topic in Soviet civil-military discussions since approximately 1980. This is not to say that Volkogonov was arguing for a Soviet theory of victory in nuclear war (a theory that no doubt already existed), but rather to point out that he was willing to risk a major break with established protocol in order to criticize what he viewed as the pernicious pacifism inherent in the New Thinking. Since Volkogonov was the nation's top officer charged specifically with indoctrination of the troops, these remarks had to be viewed with concern in the Kremlin.

Volkogonov's anger was evident as well in his other remarks at the October 1986 conference. At one point, Volkogonov scoffed at a "respected," although unnamed, Soviet author who had written that the New Thinking will be realized "when we can reeducate and change the minds of those across the ocean." This reliance on the goodwill of the enemy was too much for Volkogonov, who then took the author to task: "I emphasize—'change the minds and reeducate' those on the other side of the barricade. I think the most important problem with such an interpretation is not simply that it is naive, but harmful. And there are, regrettably, not a few pronouncements such as this, or similar in essence."[85]

Actually, this protest was linked to a larger conceptual criticism.

---

[84] Volkogonov did not name the offending journal, nor did he elaborate on whether "our" meant "Soviet," "Party," or "military." *XXVII S"ezd KPSS i zadachi kafedr obshchestvennykh nauk* (Moscow: Politizdat, 1987), p. 130. The conference, entitled "The All-Union Conference of Directors of Cadres of Social Science of Higher Educational Establishments," was held in Moscow, October 1–3, 1986. The proceedings were published in early 1987, with a printing run of 100,000. See also Thomas Nichols, "Volkogonov and Nuclear Victory," *Sovset News* 3, 10 (September 8, 1987).

[85] Volkogonov, *XXVII S"ezd KPSS i zadachi*, pp. 129–130.

Volkogonov argued (correctly) that the New Thinking makes war, in the abstract, the enemy. But according to Volkogonov, "Lenin said that there are 'wars' and then there are 'wars.' We cannot discuss all wars in general."[86] Rather, Volkogonov (like Serebriannikov and others) insisted on identification of the moral dimensions and the reasons behind particular conflicts, and on assigning blame for them. Again, there is an undertone of a warning against being infected by one's own propaganda and losing the stolid moral perspective that is, in the eyes of the Soviet officer, the very foundation of defense policy.

It is especially ironic that Volkogonov reopened the issue of nuclear victory even as Gorbachev was preparing for the Reykjavik summit in Iceland later in October 1986. Col. Alekseev also returned to the pages of the military press the same month with a detailed two-part examination of NATO planning, and it seemed that the military was determined that Gorbachev understand the limits on his position before he left.[87] The now-legendary collapse of the summit can just as easily be blamed on the poor preparation of the American team as it can on Gorbachev's intransigent insistence that nuclear arms reductions be tied to limits on SDI research.[88] What remains unclear is the degree to which that position had been forced upon Gorbachev by the General Staff. Given previous episodes of military obstructionism on arms control it is not hard to imagine that the SDI-INF linkage was a military concoction, especially since the condition was finally dropped in time for the INF Treaty a year later—after a shakeup of the high command. Besides, Gorbachev apparently did not believe that SDI would work, and he revealed a certain nonchalance about it later. "I think you're wasting your money," he told Reagan with regard to SDI the day after the INF agreement was inked. "But if that's what you want to do, go ahead."[89] The marshals were probably not so complacent.

REVIEW, 1985–1986: THE ARMY HOLDS ITS OWN

Gorbachev's first two years, at least with regard to defense policy, must be considered a disappointment for him. The 1985–86 period

---

[86] Ibid., p. 130.

[87] See V. Alekseev, "'Obychnye' voiny i formy ikh vedeniia," *Krasnaia Zvezda*, October 3, 1986, p. 3 (part I) and October 4, 1986, p. 5 (part II); Alekseev fired again on the same subject in "Stavka na vnezapnosti," *Krasnaia Zvezda*, April 2, 1987, p. 3.

[88] See Newhouse, *War and Peace in the Nuclear Age*, pp. 394–397.

[89] Ibid., p. 404.

saw the reemergence of a generalized civil-military split on basic questions of defense policy, a process begun during Brezhnev's last-ditch attempts to stifle Ogarkov and the alarmists in 1981. And although such a division was to be expected in the wake of Gorbachev's arms control plans, there was more to the events of these two years than mere policy disagreements.

First, the Party leadership under Gorbachev failed to regain control of defense policy in 1985 and 1986 despite the guidelines put forward at the April Plenum of the Central Committee and the XXVII Party Congress. The military not only ignored the tone set at the congress (so much for Party discipline), but actually defended a world view whose implied policy prescriptions were in direct opposition to the positions taken by Gorbachev in statements on foreign and defense policies. Moreover, there is no evidence to suggest that Gorbachev's call for changes in military affairs had much of an impact either on military cadres or within the General Staff; to the contrary, it was Gorbachev who was warned off, not vice versa. "I began to receive information," Gorbachev said in looking back on his first years in office, "that the Defense Council and its Chairman [i.e., Gorbachev] were moving too sharply and the Marshals requested me to bear this comment in mind."[90] Indeed, as will be seen in the next two chapters, the staff and the MPA willfully resisted the New Thinking and the changes in military doctrine it entailed—acts of direct insubordination.

As a result, the civil-military confrontation once more, as in the days of Khrushchev, began to involve the prestige of the military and the authority of the general secretary himself, and once more the stage was set for a civilian attempt at a strengthening of subjective control. Gorbachev could not stand by and allow the military to remain in splendid isolation; after all, the general secretary's prestige and personal authority were now on the line, and the rest of the Soviet bureaucracy could hardly be expected to suffer the contortions and convolutions of dramatic reform while the high command circled the wagons and kept *perestroika* at bay. "Perestroika means revolution," Gorbachev warned, and the military (and the military budget) would have to be part of that revolution or the whole enterprise was doomed to failure.[91]

More threatening for both sides was that the debate now threat-

---

[90] Paul Quinn-Judge, "Gorbachev Hints at Troubles in the Military," p.1.
[91] See M. Gorbachev's *Perestroika i novoe myshlenie dlia nashei strany i dlia vsego mira* (Moscow: Politicheskoi literatury, 1987).

ened to expand beyond the narrower issues of national security. The agenda at the end of 1980s began to shift to the question of the role of the Soviet Armed Forces in a society turned against the military and against itself. On this front, the military would fight even more passionately than they had over military doctrine. For the leadership, the issue became one of basic legitimacy: who rules the USSR? Party leaders or braided "napoleonchiki"? Although there was yet no open rift between the soldiers and the civilians, the situation through 1986 became inherently unstable. The Soviet Union could not afford, in figurative or literal terms, to continue the stalemate.

By 1987 the time had come for action. Gorbachev's thrust to gain control of defense policy in his first two years had been badly blunted. The New Thinking and *perestroika* both had become equally irrelevant in the eyes of the military. The civilian counterattack would come at the January and June 1987 plenums of the Central Committee, but once again the military would manage to hold its own, at least for the time being.

[6]

Abandoning Pretenses:
Gorbachev and the Military, 1987–1988

It should be noted . . . that a considerable number of people
never enter the Army, they never serve, never in their whole
lives. Forgive me for the expression, they have never worn a
pair of military pants. There is such a category of people.
—Col. Gen. D. A. Volkogonov, January 1988

Between a man with arms and a man without them there is no
proportion at all. It is not reasonable to expect an armed man to
obey one who is unarmed, nor an unarmed man to be safe
among armed servants; because, what with the contempt of the
former and the mistrust of the latter, there's no living together.
Thus a prince who knows nothing of warfare, apart from his
other troubles already described, can't hope for respect from his
soldiers or put any trust in them.
—Machiavelli, *The Prince*, XIV

FROM REFORM TO CONFUSION

By 1987 Soviet defense policy was adrift in confusion, torn between
the various and competing influences of a stagnating economy, a
reformist general secretary, and a powerful and stubborn military
establishment. Worse, the machinations over control of military affairs were now beginning to strain the social contract between the
Party and the military—one of many such strained contracts appearing in Soviet society in the 1980s—in which each side had made at
least the public effort to support the other, despite their arguments
behind closed doors. To be sure, the civilians were the first to breach
that contract openly by inviting popular criticism of the armed forces
in the name of *glasnost'*. But a contract implies that something is

gained for something given in return. The military, from the civilian viewpoint, had ceased to provide that consideration, digging in and stubbornly resisting to obey the duly promulgated line of the Party while still expecting to maintain their own social and material privileges.

Whatever sense of mutual benefit there had been in the civil-military relationship in previous years began eroding at an exponential rate. The deal was about to be called off.

The "Commissar Staff" and Perestroika

By 1987, the Soviet defense establishment was in disarray, and the civilian leadership's efforts to impose order took two tracks. The first was an attempt at an overall civilian redefinition of the security environment, with the New Thinkers taking the lead and attempting to portray the world as a safer and better place due to Gorbachev's international efforts. The second and related goal was to reestablish the Party leadership, and Gorbachev personally, as the unambiguous source of national security policy. Neither succeeded, and confusion continued to grow over the proper source and direction of defense policy. The Gorbachev group mounted a counteroffensive of sorts, using both the rhetoric of *perestroika* and the imposition of an official revision in Warsaw Pact politico-military doctrine.

Still, the political leadership was slow to oppose military heresy perhaps because they themselves had such difficulty establishing— or, more likely, deciding—exactly what was "heretical." The New Thinking had already been rejected in the senior ranks, although for a short time a few officers chanted the phrase, like a political mantra, in the Soviet press. Most simply refused to imitate their civilian masters. More problematical was the failure of *perestroika* in the military, primarily because it was not clear—again, perhaps not even to the Party leadership—what *perestroika* was supposed to mean in the armed forces.[1]

In early 1985 Gorbachev spoke on the subject to the senior military

---

[1] For a typical example of the vagueness of *perestroika* in relation to the armed forces, see P. Bobylev et al., *Sovetskie Vooruzhennye Sily: Voprosy i otvety* (Moscow: Politizdat, 1987), pp. 393–396. *Perestroika*, according to the authors, "does not concern separate questions, but rather the whole sphere of life and activity of the Armed Forces, and directed at the decisive raising of the level of combat readiness and discipline of soldiers and naval forces" (p. 393). If the average junior or middle-grade officer was confused about what this was supposed to mean for him and his men, one can hardly blame him.

in Minsk, but there are few references to the speech, and its content has not been published.[2] This sort of secrecy, hardly the formula for success in a political reform campaign, enabled the military to avoid public discussion of the issue. Marshal Sokolov, Ustinov's unremarkable replacement as defense minister, told a March 1987 party *aktiv* meeting that Gorbachev's Minsk remarks stressed that *perestroika* should lead step by step to a new level of combat ability, an evaluation drawn from one of the older bits of military boilerplate that could mean almost anything.[3] Whatever Gorbachev actually said—almost certainly there was a stern warning that the days of budgetary excess were at an end—it did not take root in any obvious way (unless, of course, it was an exhortation to continue along as before). In the absence of a detailed explanation of *perestroika*, the military supplied its own stale definition: in the Soviet military press *perestroika* came to mean such things as less waste, better discipline, more efficient training, and other benign values.

Such vagueness allowed the military to ignore *perestroika* rather than oppose it. (One military book reviewer, to take a glaring example, was forced to take the deputy chief of the MPA himself to task in 1986 for editing an entire book on the Soviet Armed Forces in which the word itself never appears.)[4] Here, the military was protected by the tactical advantage gained by choosing to hang together rather than to hang separately, particularly among the cadres of the MPA. As one frustrated reformist officer put it in early 1990:

> The breakdown in the work of top-level political organs at a crucial stage in social development is no accident. Perestroika has essentially had no impact on the Main Political Administration and the entire system of political organs. The "commissar staff" has no precise concept of perestroika, nor have any mechanisms for the conduct of party-political and

[2] One of the very rare references to this speech may be found in a 1986 *Voennyi Vestnik* piece by the Ground Forces CINC, who said it was given "pered rukovodiashchim sostavom" [before the leadership personnel] of the Army and Navy. No detailed clue was given as to what was said, other than the predictable exhortations to better readiness, conscientiousness, etc. See E. Ivanovskii, "Glavnoe v deiatel'nosti voisk— boevaia ucheba," *Voennyi Vestnik* 1 (January 1986), p. 3.

[3] B. Pokholenchuk, "Perestroika—delo kazhdogo," *Krasnaia Zvezda*, March 18, 1987, p. 2. For a more detailed analysis of Sokolov's remarks, see Melanie Russell, "'Restructuring' in the Armed Forces," *Radio Liberty Reports*, RL 118/87, March 23, 1987.

[4] The book was *The Soviet Armed Forces in Conditions of Developed Socialism*, edited by Admiral Sorokin. The reviewer was none other than MPA academy professor Lt. Gen. V. Serebriannikov. "Sovetskie Vooruzhennye Sily na novom etape," *Voenno-Istoricheskii Zhurnal* (July 1986), p. 82.

political education work been elaborated . . . the only change is the introduction into currency of the vocabulary of perestroika.[5]

Thus, if Gorbachev wished to criticize the military handling of *perestroika*, he was left only with the choice of criticizing the entire military establishment and admitting outright that *perestroika* in the armed forces was a complete failure.

These missteps on the part of the leadership were compounded by an explosion of antimilitary *glasnost'*. It is probably true that Gorbachev initially allowed some outbursts of antimilitary sentiment among the intelligentsia as means both of undercutting the unassailable social position of the military, as well as to tap some of the underlying resentment toward the armed forces in Soviet society at large as a means of support for his own program. What began as criticism in 1987 and 1988, however, turned into outright public attacks on servicemen, including physical assaults, by 1990. Forcing the military to join the ranks of society as one of many institutions open to criticism and improvement was a canny move; allowing such criticism to spiral out of control, to the point of political warfare, was a foolish mistake. In 1989 and 1990 Gorbachev would face the repercussions of that loss of control.

In 1987, however, Eastern Europe was still intact, and at home in the USSR political victory over the military still seemed to be within reach. The Party leadership took steps to impose order on the military in 1987 at two major events: the January 1987 Plenum of the Central Committee, after which a renewed effort to force military acceptance of the Party line was made, and the May 1987 Warsaw Pact Political Consultative Committee (PCC) meeting, at which Gorbachev's New Thinking was made law. In these efforts, the leadership received the unlikely help of a young West German in a Cessna who made an unscheduled layover in Red Square.

THE JANUARY 1987 PLENUM

The official title of the January 1987 Plenum of the Central Committee was "On Perestroika and Party Cadre Policy."[6] The plenum was

[5] "General Assails Lack of Perestroika in Army Body," FBIS-SOV-90–089, May 8, 1990, pp. 56–57.
[6] *Materialy Plenuma Tsentral'nogo Komiteta KPSS, 27–28 ianvaria 1987 goda* (Moscow: Politizdat, 1987), p. 3.

called to discuss the slow progress of *perestroika* within Party organizations; it also brought Gorbachev ally Aleksandr Iakovlev, a key figure in the construction of the New Thinking, into the Politburo as a candidate member.

While Gorbachev spoke at length about problems in the Party's regional and administrative bodies, there is rather little that pertains to the military in the official record. However, events after January 1987 confirm that the leadership attempted to confront the military problem in some way at the plenum. Unfortunately, the Soviet record is of little help in deciphering what exactly happened between civilian and military leaders there, and the actual events of January 1987 may join Gorbachev's 1985 Minsk speech in the shadow of Soviet confidentiality.

This lack of detailed reference to the armed forces is itself interesting. Gorbachev mentioned the military, once, in his opening remarks to the plenum:

> And, finally, about the problems of military cadres. The Party is not for a minute weakening its efforts to raise further the defense capability of the country, and it assigns military cadres a special role in solving this vitally important task. And this as well defines their huge responsibility before the people. The Soviet Armed Forces likewise are restructuring [*takzhe zhivut perestroikoi*]. They are reliably guaranteeing the peaceful labor and security of the country, and fulfilling with honor their international duty.
>
> The Central Committee firmly counts on army cadres and the Soviet officer corps in the solving of the tasks of strengthening the defense capability of the state, confident that in the present complex international conditions communists, all cadres of the army and navy, will act with the greatest responsibility. . . . The Soviet people, and our Party, rely on their Armed Forces.[7]

This bland appraisal does not hint at the serious criticisms leveled at the military after the plenum (and again, at another plenum in June), nor does it explain the sudden attempt to defend and revitalize the New Thinking among the military in early 1987. Indeed, one wonders what Marshals Sokolov and Kulikov were talking about a month later when they noted in separate accounts the "high evaluation" given the armed forces at the plenum.[8]

[7] Ibid., pp. 62–66. This speech is also reproduced in vol. 4 of M. S. Gorbachev's *Izbrannye rechi i stat'i* (Moscow: Politicheskoi literatury, 1987), pp. 351–352.

[8] S. Sokolov, "Na strazhe mira i bezopasnosti Rodiny," *Pravda*, February 23, 1987, p. 2, and V. Kulikov, "Moguchii strazh mira," *Trud*, February 22, 1987, p. 3.

The Push for Perestroika

However bland the public pronouncements, it is nonetheless evident that something happened at or near the plenum. A public campaign of military support for the ideals of both *perestroika* and the New Thinking got under way, in force, almost immediately after the January meeting. On February 1, the front page of *Krasnaia Zvezda* was occupied by a reprint of *Pravda's* announcement about the work of the plenum, as is standard practice—although the military press managed to overlook Gorbachev's warning to the plenum of "crisis phenomena" in their accounts of the meeting.[9] Less than a week later, Strategic Rocket Forces CINC Iurii Maksimov authored an article on *perestroika* in which he made a point of affirming that he himself had taken part in the work of the plenum, a contrast with later such meetings at which the military would claim that it had been silenced.[10] *Krasnaia Zvezda* followed up with a major article on how to conduct political study of the plenum materials, in which it was recommended that propagandists emphasize—in a line dating back through Brezhnev to Khrushchev—the relationship between national security and a healthy economy.[11]

In the first weeks of February, editorials and articles pushed hard on the issue of *perestroika*, culminating in Sokolov's February 24 piece cited earlier.[12] Meetings in military units at all levels proliferated rapidly; between January and June, to take but one example, the Frunze Academy held no fewer than four major conferences on topics related to the plenum and *perestroika*.[13] In March, *Krasnaia Zvezda* gave a prominent review to a recently published anthology by several senior officers on party-political work and *perestroika*. The book, like the review, is fairly unremarkable, but it nonetheless served to make the point.[14]

[9] "Perestroika i kadry," *Krasnaia Zvezda*, February 1, 1987, p. 1; on the issue of selective military reportage, see Bruce Parrott, "Political Change and Civil-Military Relations," in Timothy Colton and Thane Gustafson, eds., *Soldiers and the Soviet State* (Princeton: Princeton University Press, 1990), p. 84.

[10] Iu. Maksimov, "Perestroika eksamenuet kazhdogo," *Krasnaia Zvezda*, February 5, 1987, p. 2.

[11] "Perestroika i kadrovaia politika partii," *Krasnaia Zvezda*, February 6, 1987, pp. 2–3.

[12] Examples include Col. Gen. V. Lobov, "Nachinaetsia c komandira," *Krasnaia Zvezda*, February 3, 1987, p. 2; "Kriterii zrelosti," *Krasnaia Zvezda*, February 13, 1987, p. 2; "Vysokoe prizvanie," *Krasnaia Zvezda*, February 7, 1987, p. 1, among others.

[13] *Voennaia akademiia imeni M. V. Frunze* (Moscow: Voenizdat, 1988), pp. 290–291.

[14] The book is part of the "Kursom XXVII s"ezda KPSS," *Na putiiakh perestroiki* (Moscow: Voenizdat, 1987). The review of the book was by a certain "N. Vasil'ev" (perhaps a pseudonym?), "Na putiiakh perestroiki," *Krasnaia Zvezda*, March 7, 1987, p. 2.

While the attempt to accelerate *perestroika* in the armed forces was not surprising in itself, it was noteworthy in two other respects. First, it had not been clear from the plenum, nor from Gorbachev's remarks, that a campaign in the military was in the offing.[15] This effort to broaden *perestroika* was either unexpected or left unpublicized, despite the fact that it was pursued quickly and repetitively. The second unusual aspect of the postplenum infusion of *perestroika* in the military is that the concept itself remained, as before, nebulous. The same formulas—that officers should be upright examples, efficient, honorable, and so on—reappeared with increasing frequency, but without consequent elucidation.[16]

Like previous efforts, the postplenum campaign did little to pinpoint exactly what the leadership expected "perestroika" to mean in the military. One possibility is that *perestroika* was a convenient rationalization for civilian action against recalcitrant and inefficient officers. In other words, military *perestroika* may simply have been a method of extending general oversight in the armed forces, rather than representing any well-defined set of policy implications. One piece of evidence that supports this interpretation appeared in the report of a March 1987 party *aktiv* meeting at the Ministry of Defense, ostensibly called as a result of the January plenum, which reported on "shortcomings in cadre policy." But somehow these cadre problems were responsible for broader predicaments: the Air Force and the Air Defense Forces came under serious fire for organizational problems, and the Navy was scored for what was only referred to the "disruption of important plans." This was more than pro forma criticism, since "a series of generals and officers of command rank were relieved of duty and subjected to service and party punishment."[17] It is, of course, possible that the foul-ups were of sufficient magnitude that these dismissals were inevitable, and that *perestroika* was only the rationale rather than the cause. No specifics of any kind were given

[15] In at least two cases, there is evidence that military books were pulled at the last minute to accommodate references to the January plenum. One, Babakov's *Vooruzhennye Sily posle voiny* (cited in chap. 3) was sent to press in September 1986, even though it includes references to the January Plenum (p. 271). Another, *Na putiiakh perestroiki* (Moscow: Voenizdat, 1987) was sent to press in December 1986, yet pulled soon thereafter to include references to the plenum.

[16] Radio Liberty analyst Melanie Russell, in her analysis of Sokolov's remarks to the same *aktiv* (reported in the Pokholenchuk article cited earlier), concurs that "it is difficult to visualize what 'restructuring' would entail in concrete terms" for the military. Russell, " 'Restructuring' in the Armed Forces."

[17] Pokholenchuk, "Perestroika—delo kazhdogo," p. 2.

on the transgressions involved or on exactly how *perestroika* was supposed to be put into action.

Within a year, the campaign for military *perestroika* was an acknowledged failure, even by the deputy chief of the MPA, Admiral Sorokin:

> Changes for the better [in cadre work], regrettably, are taking place slower than might be desired. *Zastoi*-like manifestations have not only accumulated in the most diverse areas of the life and activity of the troops and naval forces, but have even turned out to be highly tenacious. . . .
>
> The paramount question is the improvement of work with military cadres in accordance with the demands of the XXVII Party Congress and the January plenum of the Central Committee of the CPSU.[18]

In companion pieces in the same volume, Deputy Defense Minister Peter Lushev and military cadres chief D. S. Sukhorukhov both made similar reference (with detailed criticism for some military districts) to the military failure to comply with both the January plenum and the spirit of *perestroika* in general. None gave very specific advice on what should constitute better adherence to the policy beyond the usual rhetoric. (Volkogonov's interpretation, predictably, was that the exhortation to better cadre work meant improving the ideological indoctrination of appropriate "worldviews.")[19]

The New Thinking Resurrected and Attacked

The sound and fury, signifying little, surrounding *perestroika* in the military press obscured the serious polarization that was occurring in civil-military tussles over defense issues. Still, the reemergence of the New Thinking after the January 1987 plenum was so forceful that it seemed for a time to signal the beginning of the end of the doctrinal chaos that had characterized the Soviet civil-military defense debate since 1985. The postplenum defense of Gorbachev's foreign policy philosophy was far more striking than the *perestroika* campaign, and the statements of some senior officers hinted at the scale of opposition it must have encountered. After the plenum, it seemed that Gorbachev had enforced some sort of discipline, or managed some sort of an accommodation, with regard to security affairs. As 1987

---

[18] A. Sorokin, "Vremiia konkretnykh del," *Perestroika: Opyt, problemy, poisk* (Moscow: Voenizdat, 1988), pp. 12–13.

[19] D. Volkogonov, "Povyshat' rol' chelovecheskogo faktora," *Ideinaia zakalka voennykh kadrov*, 3d ed. (Moscow: Voenizdat, 1988), p. 13.

wore on it became evident that this was not the case, but all indicators before the summer of that year pointed to the imminent end of the debate on terms more favorable to Gorbachev.

One possible explanation for this renewed offensive on behalf of the New Thinking is that Gorbachev was bracing for military reaction to his imminent attempt to salvage the work done at Reykjavik. In March 1987, Gorbachev would cut the SDI-INF knot and offer to negotiate a separate pact on nuclear missiles in Europe. The Politburo, Gorbachev said in *Pravda* on March 1, had decided to take yet another "great step" along the path set forward in his January 1986 address in which he called for a nuclear-free world by 2000, and to separate INF from "the block of questions" now obstructing progress.[20] There was no specific mention of SDI.

Apparently, Gorbachev had managed to gain the backing for this move from Marshal Akhromeev (although the position of the General Staff overall remained unclear). The most visible sign of the resurrection of New Thinking was Akhromeev's early 1987 editorial on the front page of *Sovetskaia Rossiia*. This article, over which the shadow of the general secretary loomed large, marked the beginning of the Gorbachev-Akhromeev modus vivendi that was to last until Akhromeev's resignation in protest in 1988. Akhromeev's change of heart, of course, was not complete, as his resignation showed. But the General Staff chief may have thought it better to acquiesce on the issue of nuclear arms—inexpensive weapons unlikely to be used—and establish himself as a Gorbachev insider, positioning himself for the eventual fight over the conventional reductions that would later mean sudden joblessness for thousands of Soviet officers and their men.

Akhromeev's act of public fealty began with the acknowledgment that the plenum, Gorbachev's February 16 peace conference speech, and Gorbachev's recent foreign policy initiatives all pointed up the objective—that powerful word—realities upon which the New Thinking is based: "In the modern nuclear-cosmic age," Akhromeev wrote, "the guaranteeing of security appears ever more to be a political problem. It can never be guaranteed through military-technical means, even through the creation of the most powerful offensive or defensive forces, including a 'cosmic shield.'"[21] This was an endorsement, word for word, of Gorbachev's statements at the XXVII Party

---

[20] Gorbachev, *Izbrannye rechi*, 4:445.
[21] S. Akhromeev, "Slava i gordost' sovetskogo naroda," *Sovetskaia Rossiia*, February 21, 1987, p. 1.

Congress. It was probably meant to dampen the more dire predictions made about SDI and to rebalance the definition of military doctrine in favor of the social-political, rather than military-technical, side. Moreover, Akhromeev explicitly bowed to civilian supremacy: resolution of these pressing security problems, he said, "can and should" be done through political means. The *Sovetskaia Rossiia* piece also served as a preview of the new military doctrine that would be unveiled in May: "Soviet military doctrine," Akhromeev wrote, "is created and develops in accordance with the policy of the CPSU, and the principles of the new political thinking." Indeed, Akhromeev noted that the XXVII Party Congress "confirmed the defensive trend of Soviet military doctrine," in particular by approving a policy of no first use of nuclear weapons, thereby implying that the General Staff had actually taken the lead in the transition to a defensive doctrine.

As Gorbachev was later to discover, the military leadership had taken no such initiative, and in fact would manage to stonewall changes in defense policy for at least another year, as will be discussed in the next chapter. Even in the short term, resistance to the New Thinking was apparent before and after both the plenum and Akhromeev's act of public support. Marshal Sokolov made almost no mention of the New Thinking in his February speech, choosing instead to emphasize the growth of the Western threat and the strengthening of imperialist aggressiveness. (It must have grated on Gorbachev and his advisers to see the chief of the General Staff, a smart and respected soldier, explicitly adopting the Gorbachev line, while a stolid but colorless caretaker like Sokolov refused to follow suit.)

Marshal Kulikov, for his part, had no intention of becoming caretaker to the Warsaw Pact. He told a *Trud* interviewer in February 1987 that "today, Europe is the most explosively dangerous place on Earth." The choice of alternatives, for him, is no choice at all, and he invoked both Lenin and "objective necessity" to drive home the point: "We have been objectively presented with the necessity to provide a fitting response to the dangerous efforts of imperialism. Lenin emphasized that 'there is nothing you can do to disturb [those efforts], except the strengthening of defense capability.' Toward this end a series of major measures have been adopted. One of the most important is the strengthening of the combat potential of the Soviet Armed Forces."[22] But what about the alternative of arms control, the route mandated by the Gorbachev line? Kulikov suggested that the

[22] "Moguchii strazh mira," *Trud*, February 22, 1987, p. 3.

arms control implications of the New Thinking were both naive and toothless: "Regrettably, the voice of reason does not reach everyone. We propose peace to them, they propose war to us . . . our Armed Forces restrain the imperialists from the wish to set us up in a test of forces." Little wonder that these comments (made in observance of Army-Navy Day) were relegated to *Trud* rather than *Pravda*, as might otherwise have been expected.

Army Gen. Valentin Varennikov, a longtime deputy chief of the General Staff (and later CINC of the Ground Forces), was preparing an even more dedicated attack on the New Thinking even as Kulikov was giving his interview.[23] Varennikov, one of the most visible saber-rattlers during the 1990 Lithuanian rebellion, later made clear his distaste for Gorbachev's leadership: he is considered to have been a pivotal military supporter of the August 1991 coup and is now awaiting trial.

Varennikov took issue in particular with Gorbachev's view of the United States and of the superpower relationship. While Gorbachev was clearly unhappy with the outcome of the Reykjavik summit and critical of the Reagan administration's actions, his evaluation of it was generally cool-headed, and seemed to show some awareness that there was a relationship between Reagan's behavior and American domestic politics.[24] Varennikov's explanation of American behavior was more simple and direct: "Reactionary forces [are] forming the policy of the USA." He followed this comment with a listing of American military programs, noting, in an echo of Ogarkov and others in the early 1980s, that these new weapons were tools of the kind of conceptual work that "has always been, and remains, characteristic of any aggressor" (an understandable charge from a military viewpoint, especially where such programs as the MX and the Trident D-5 missile were concerned).[25] He finished with what sounded like an admonition to the leadership: "We have not forgotten the lessons of history, and we remember that imperialism is an insidious and relentless enemy. If it senses weakness, it will then stop at nothing."[26]

[23] V. Varennikov, "Na strazhe i bezopasnosti narodov," *Partiinaia Zhizn'* 5 (March 1987), pp. 9–10. For a different interpretation of Varennikov's piece, see Eugene Rumer, "Military Follows Party Lead on Arms Control," *Radio Liberty Reports*, RL 494/87, November 30, 1987, in which he asserts that Varennikov was "assuring the Party leaders of the military's unwavering loyalty."

[24] For the text of Gorbachev's television address to the Soviet people in the wake of the Reykjavik summit see *Pravda*, October 23, 1986, pp. 1–2, or Gorbachev, *Izbrannye rechi*, 4:168–180.

[25] Varennikov, "Na strazhe i bezopasnosti narodov," p. 11.

[26] Ibid., p. 12.

Until the January plenum, the high command had been content to leave the New Thinking alone, totemistically repeating it in form and ignoring it in substance. After the plenum, it apparently became clear that New Thinking was not just another slogan, and the general secretary just might be serious about coexisting with the West and slashing military budgets—both anathema to the military establishment. Worse, Gorbachev had somehow reached an understanding with a respected chief of the General Staff. Kulikov, Varennikov, and others soon made it plain that if Gorbachev was serious, so were they. The military and the Gorbachev leadership were now head to head.

Lizichev Steps In

By this point, the political leadership must have felt that the bounds of acceptable debate had been seriously transgressed. The initial response to the military critics fell, as it should have, to the chief of the MPA, Gen. A. D. Lizichev. Like Akhromeev, Lizichev took the idea of Party supremacy over the military seriously, and he too initially tried to play the role of the "good soldier" willing to follow the Party line. (And like Akhromeev, he would defect in 1988 from Gorbachev's cause when he found it too extreme.) The reward for his loyalty was an assignment that can only be considered as a rearguard defense of the New Thinking in a seminal article in the pages of *Kommunist* in March; this task forced him to cope with Gorbachev's critics even as Gorbachev was backtracking on the linkage between SDI and INF that had been adhered to so strictly, and to such mixed effect, at Reykjavik.

If nothing else, the Lizichev article represented one of the first official acknowledgments of the serious breach between the Party and the military since the XXVII Party Congress.[27] At last, the opposition to the New Thinking in defense circles was out in the open, and Lizichev responded directly: "To any sensible person it is clear that peace-loving initiatives, coming from a powerful state, are not evidence of weakness but rather are a manifestation of the necessity in the modern era for new political thinking," a defense that indicated the presence of such charges.[28] (SRF CINC Maksimov backed this

---

[27] For a detailed analysis of the article itself, see Thomas Nichols, "The Military and the New Political Thinking: Lizichev on Leninism and Defense," *Radio Liberty Reports*, RL 80/87, February 26, 1987.

[28] A. Lizichev, "Oktiabr' i leninskoe uchenie o zashchite revoliutsii," *Kommunist* 3 (March 1987), p. 85.

position with a similar statement on Soviet television.)[29] And although Lizichev acknowledged his military colleagues' arguments that the world was still "explosively dangerous," he added that insofar as that evaluation was correct it made obedience to the Party's demands on the military even more paramount.[30]

One of those demands was budget discipline, and for good reason: the Soviet budget deficit had tripled from 1985 to 1986 (to some 48 billion rubles) and would only get worse.[31] Noting that military expenditures are always dictated by defense needs, Lizichev said that "expenditures on defense, the number of personnel in the Army and Navy, the quantity and quality of weapons and military equipment are defined exclusively by the demands of the Fatherland and the collective defense of the gains of socialism. In our country, nothing more is being done than is necessary."[32] And while Lizichev agreed with the warnings of Volkogonov and others that there is danger in carelessness, complacency and "naive pacifism," he dismissed those who would nonetheless overestimate the "potentialities" of imperialism's aggressive circles.[33] This message in particular didn't take root, at least not to judge by comments made less than a year later by army Gen. V. Shabanov, armaments chief, who dwelt at length in *Ekonomicheskaia Gazeta* on the importance the huge efforts that went into the Soviet military industry before the Second World War.[34] Defense spending went on to rise for the third year in a row in 1988 (at least 3 percent in constant rubles), fueled primarily by weapons acquisition.[35]

Lizichev's article was a solid effort, but he was outclassed by his more fulminatory opponents, officers more experienced and senior than he. Indeed, it is revelatory that so major a defense of New Thinking fell to Lizichev, despite his position as head of the MPA; relatively recent in his post, he was neither prominent nor particularly well spoken.

More Trouble from the Main Political Administration

Perhaps most disturbing to the Party leadership was that the mechanism by which their wishes were to be transmitted to the troops, the

[29] Quoted in JPRS *USSR Report*, Military Affairs UMA-87–002, January 9, 1987, p. 38.
[30] Lizichev, "Oktiabr'i leninskoe uchenie o zashchite revoliutsii," pp. 86–87.
[31] See Marshall Goldman, "Gorbachev the Economist," *Foreign Affairs* (Spring 1990).
[32] Lizichev, "Oktiabr'i leniskoe uchenie o zashchite revoliutsii," pp. 87–88.
[33] Ibid., p. 88.
[34] V. Shabanov, "Shchit Rodiny," *Ekonomicheskaia Gazeta* 8 (February 1988), p. 18.
[35] Paul Mann, "U.S. Predicts Further Cuts in Soviet Defense Spending," *Aviation Week and Space Technology*, May 7, 1990, p. 69.

Main Political Administration of the Soviet Army and Navy, was actually working against them. Indeed, the most dedicated and eloquent opponents of the Gorbachev line were not to be found in the field (where the average commander was generally busy keeping his charges fed and housed), but rather in the rarefied atmosphere of the MPA institutes and academies; in other words, among the most able and elite—such as Volkogonov—of the Party's ideological watchdogs over the armed forces. The quiet revolt in the MPA underscored the problem of an ideologized military: what happens when the Party ideologists are no longer pure enough of heart for the military ideologists? Who shall watch the armed watchers?

In February 1987, even as Lizichev was slogging his way through his obligatory *Kommunist* article, Lt. Gen. Serebriannikov of the Lenin Military-Political Academy undermined this effort with a simultaneous appearance in *Kommunist Vooruzhennykh Sil*. Serebriannikov was a member of the group of authors who penned the 1978 version of the textbook *Party-Political Work in the Soviet Armed Forces* and subsequently dropped from the Party-ordered rewrite committee in 1982.[36] Despite his de rigueur opening in support of New Thinking, Serebriannikov revealed his doubts and disagreements even as he genuflected to the Gorbachev line.[37]

Serebriannikov did not directly attack Gorbachev's line about the need to abandon unilateral attempts at security. Asserting, like Maxim Litvinov at the League of Nations years before, that "peace is indivisible," Serebriannikov feinted at a defense of Gorbachev's socioeconomic approach to the problem of peace.[38] But this in turn set up Serebriannikov's most difficult problem: Does the aversion to violence mean that the Soviet Union will withdraw from the world competition, or sit in mute embarrassment in the face of aggressive Western challenges? Clearly not: "Imperialism has not renounced war as an instrument of policy . . . [and] this has principal significance for the defense of socialism," and that the "fact of possible aggression" made necessary "the use of military force in the just goal of defense from attack."[39] However, Serebriannikov then attempted to accommodate two conflicting points in a rhetorical maneuver that later became a standard position among Gorbachev's critics. The answer to the prob-

[36] See also V. Serebriannikov, "Imperializm: Usilenie agressivnosti," *Krasnaia Zvezda*, May 30, 1985, pp. 2–3, for a sense of some of Serebriannikov's pre-New Thinking writing.

[37] V. Serebriannikov, "S uchetom realnosti iadernogo veka," *Kommunist Vooruzhennykh Sil* 3 (February 1987), p. 9.

[38] Ibid., p. 13.

[39] Ibid., pp. 13–14.

lem *at this point*, he wrote, has been military "responding measures," and they have worked. The answer *in the future* will be politics, but that is not yet possible.

Serebriannikov's article foreshadowed several controversial issues, and raised more questions than it answered. For one, what are the "decisive actions" he says will be taken in retaliation to aggression? What constitutes aggression or "defensiveness" in the era of modern technology? Serebriannikov realized the polarizing military and political consequences of New Thinking, and he ended his article by calling for more attention to these questions on the part of military social scientists, *and* better coordination with civilian institutes working on the same problem, an arrangement that never materialized.[40] (This may indicate that Serebriannikov was aware of Volkogonov's comments at the October 1986 social-science conference in Moscow; given Serebriannikov's position, he may even have been present.)

The January 1987 Plenum: Concluding Thoughts

We may never know exactly what transpired between military and civilian elites at the January 1987 plenum. From the timing of events and articles that followed, it seems that there was an attempt to diffuse the general Gorbachev domestic and foreign programs of *perestroika* and the New Thinking throughout the military. Neither fared well.

After the plenum, *perestroika* became a serious issue in the military, if seriousness is to be judged by press attention and references by military elites. With the exception of the punishment of certain unnamed command-rank officers, however, it remains murky just what or whom was being "restructured." While the military was repetitive in its support of *perestroika*, it was also candid enough to admit that *perestroika* did not exactly take the armed forces by storm: reports of *aktiv* meetings in the summer of 1987, for example, were filled with references to the "sharp criticism" leveled because of "shortcomings" among military personnel that continued to "hinder the process of perestroika."[41] In any event, the failures of *perestroika*, however fascinating, pale in comparison to the failure of the New Thinking.

---

[40] This sort of call was relatively new. A good contrast is a late 1967 military-theoretical piece on the work of the Lenin Military-Political Academy, in which the author called for rectification of previous—that is, Khrushchevian—mistakes by greater interaction among "party historians, military historians, philosophers, economists and military specialists." V. Koniukhovskii, "V. I. Lenin and the Soviet Armed Forces," *Voennaia Mysl'* 1 (1968), Library of Congress microform, Washington, D.C., p. 79.

[41] See *Krasnaia Zvezda*, July 28, 1987, p. 2.

The immediate postplenum atmosphere suggested that Gorbachev was attempting to put his foot down about the New Thinking. This campaign, however, fizzled out even faster than the rediscovery of *perestroika*. The attempt to rehabilitate the New Thinking among military professionals never got off of its defensive footing, suggesting that at this stage the New Thinking campaign may have had only the negative goal of preventing even more discrediting of the idea, rather than the positive goal of broadening its support. Whichever the intention, it failed on both counts, and the resulting atmosphere was one in which views on foreign policy and defense issues became increasingly polarized.

Indeed, only a month after the plenum, one of the clearest indications of the failure to establish Gorbachev as the source of military leadership appeared. For the first time in modern Soviet politics, a general secretary found it necessary to remind his fellow citizens, personally and in public, that he himself occupied one of the most exalted positions in the Soviet defense hierarchy: the chairmanship of the ultra-secret Defense Council.[42] The top Party leader has long been understood to be a member of this shadowy body, but references to it are rare and its functioning has never been clear. Gorbachev, by contrast, announced his occupation of the post in a way that suggested his perceived need to establish his defense credentials, even if (as he was later to admit) the council itself was at the time essentially moribund. It did not produce obvious results, especially if it was meant to persuade the most conservative officers to moderate their views.

One final detail about the January plenum is worth noting. In all the eventual finger-pointing about *perestroika* and cadres, it was easy to miss the appearance of a little-known field officer, brought to Moscow from his former Far East field command. General, later Marshal and minister of defense, and now prison inmate Dmitrii Yazov was first identified by Western "funerologists" (those who deduce, quite accurately, rank from positioning at official funerals) as having replaced the elderly I. N. Shkadov as deputy minister of Defense for Cadres in February 1987.[43]

---

[42] For a history of the Defense Council and its missions and membership, see Ellen Jones, "The Defense Council in Soviet Leadership Decisionmaking," *Kennan Institute Occasional Papers*, no. 188, 1984.

[43] Astute and sharp-eyed followers of Kremlin obituary protocols—notably Peter Almquist—spotted Yazov in the February 10, 1987, obit for the venerable P. A. Zhilin. (Zhilin, ironically, was the officer who made the remark about the "Latin roots" of the word *doctrine* in the 1961 disputes.) Shkadov was shunted off to the Ministry of Defense Inspectorate, and died in early 1991.

A "NEW MILITARY DOCTRINE": THE BERLIN DECLARATION

The Party campaign to regain the high ground in the defense debate that took place in the first three months of 1987 was in large part only the prelude to the *coup de main* that Gorbachev was about to attempt in May: the capture of Soviet military doctrine.

On May 28–29, 1987, the Political Consultative Committee of the Warsaw Treaty Organization met in East Berlin to discuss military doctrine. The PCC meeting produced a document, simply titled "On Military Doctrine" in the Soviet press. Although the communiqué outlined the "new" Warsaw Pact doctrine only in broad strokes, it was nonetheless unusual for the PCC to adopt publicly a document specifically relating to "doctrine," and the choice of terminology reflected the authority with which Gorbachev wanted to imbue the proceedings.[44]

The Soviet delegation was led, of course, by Gorbachev. Other participants listed as official members of the Soviet mission were Gromyko, N. Ryzhkov, Shevardnadze, Sokolov, and CC secretary Vadim Medvedev (then a Gorbachev appointee in charge of Soviet-East bloc Party relations, promoted directly to full Politburo member status in 1988). Of these, only Gromyko and Sokolov were obvious opponents of the new doctrine, and their positions, weakened since 1985 (Gromyko had been promoted to president in 1985, at that time a ceremonial function, and Sokolov had been denied full Politburo membership), guaranteed that they could not significantly harden the final document. Ryzhkov, for his part, had only the month before supported the New Thinking explicitly, and with none of the conservative prodefense attitudes exhibited at times by Ligachev.[45]

Ligachev himself, at the time still holding the ideology portfolio in the Politburo, was absent. This was not in itself symbolic; Ligachev held no position that would have mandated his presence, and as the second-ranking member of the Politburo one might expect that he would stay behind and attend to matters of state while Gorbachev traveled. Not that their paths weren't already diverging by this time: Ligachev, whose doubts about *glasnost'* began to surface at the Janu-

---

[44] For examples of more typical PCC terminology (and a truly stupefying immersion in the rhetoric of Warsaw Pact communiqués), see the documentary history of the Warsaw Treaty Organization, *Organizatsiia Varshavskogo Dogovora, 1955–1985, Dokumenty i materialy* (Moscow: Politicheskoi literatury, 1986).

[45] See N. Ryzhkov, *Leninizm—osnova teorii i politiki perestroiki* (Moscow: Politizdat, 1987). Ryzhkov's speech, given on Lenin's birthday, was published in *Izvestiia* on April 23, 1987, pp. 1–3.

ary plenum, would spur the publishing of the notorious Nina Andreeva letter (a stark criticism of Gorbachev published in the open press) less than a year later while Gorbachev was again away on foreign business.[46] Also absent was the commander of the Western Theater, Marshal Nikolai Ogarkov, Brezhnev's old nemesis. It is possible that Ogarkov's name was left unpublished due to what the Soviets perceived as the sensitive (and officially secret) nature of his post. If he was indeed excluded from the PCC work on doctrine, however, this would be all the more evidence of Gorbachev's dedicated efforts to seize control of the issue.

Notably present, however, was Marshal Kulikov, who could hardly have been enthusiastic about the goals of the meeting. Kulikov, however, was not listed as a member of the Soviet delegation; rather, he is mentioned at the end of the participant list (just ahead of East German diplomat Herbert Krolikowski, the nominal general secretary of the PCC) as "also taking part in the work of the meeting."[47] If this brief mention is indication of an abbreviated role at the meeting, it should not be unexpected in light of Kulikov's attitudes to Gorbachev and the New Thinking. From an organizational standpoint, of course, more prominent mention of the Warsaw Pact CINC (a first deputy minister of defense and Central Committee member as well) might have been expected.

The Berlin Declaration appeared in the Soviet press on May 31, 1987, and contained six major proposals:[48]

1. A moratorium on nuclear testing (a sore point with the military back home in the USSR), later moratoria on development and production, and finally to liquidation, of all nuclear weapons, and consequently for a halt to SDI.
2. Liquidation of all chemical weapons "and other types of weapons of mass annihilation," presumably meaning conventional as well as nuclear systems.
3. Reduction of forces in Europe to levels at which neither side can successfully execute a surprise attack, "or [start] offensive operations in general."
4. Creation of a workable arms control regime, including verification both through national technical means as well as on-site inspection

[46] See Baruch Hazan, *Gorbachev and His Enemies* (Boulder, Colo.: Westview, 1990), pp. 14–39.
[47] "Documents of the Meeting of the Political Consultative Committee of the Warsaw Treaty Member States," Novosti Press Agency, 1987, p. 6.
[48] "O voennoi doktrine," *Izvestiia*, May 31, 1987, p. 1, and "Documents," pp. 17–20.

by international bodies (and not, it should be noted, by U.S. or Soviet teams).

5. Creation of nuclear and chemical-free trust-building zones on land and at sea, disbanding of bases on foreign soil, withdrawal of troops to national borders, and the mutual renunciation of force as an instrument.

6. Eventual liquidation of the Warsaw Pact and NATO, as an extension of the view that the "continuing division of Europe into opposing military blocs is abnormal," and supplanting them with an "all-embracing system of international security." (Few of the delegates probably realized how soon half of that demand would be realized.)

It was not difficult to find Mikhail Gorbachev's fingerprints all over the Berlin Declaration, and it reflected his efforts, in addition to his Western overtures, to go outside the domestic Soviet civil-military arena to create supports for his own program. While the tenets of the Berlin Declaration seemed at the time like standard Soviet rhetoric of the type milled by the PCC since the 1960s, it was in fact part of a genuine program to which Gorbachev intended to commit the Soviet Union and its allies. And although some in Europe and the United States were no doubt tempted to dismiss it as merely the latest Warsaw Pact posturing, the Soviet military knew that the general secretary was in earnest. They reacted accordingly.

Reactions to the Berlin Declaration

The Berlin Declaration immediately raised questions among military critics similar to those posed by Kulikov two months earlier.[49] One military observer asked in July 1987 why the West had not yet responded to the new doctrine, joining Kulikov in the assertion that the West was simply unprepared for a defense-dominant world. Answering his own question, the writer claimed that the West realized what would result from a comparison of doctrines: "The military doctrine of the NATO nations has a far from defensive character; its key element—'flexible response'—pursues offensive, aggressive goals."[50] More troubling for the Party leadership, MPA opposition rose another notch: it took the military press almost *four months*, an

---

[49] V. Serebriannikov, "Sootnoshenie politicheskikh i voennykh sredstv v zashchite sotsializma," *Kommunist Vooruzhennykh Sil* 18 (September 1987).
[50] V. Markushin, "Dve politiki—dve doktriny," *Krasnaia Zvezda*, July 14, 1987, p. 3.

unusually long delay, to publish even a short article on educating the troops about the new doctrine. That article did not carry a signature, nor identification as an MPA piece.[51]

In fact, the lack of an MPA push in the press to disseminate the new line was due to more than apathy; it represented a rejection of the new doctrine among key intellectual cadres within the MPA, a natural progression and extension of their general obstructionism in 1986 and 1987. In late 1987, several months after the emergence of the New Doctrine, MPA officer V. F. Khalipov published a major work entitled *The Military Policy of the CPSU*. Despite its authoritative title, Khalipov's volume indicated the depth of military opposition to the New Thinking; only 4 out of 270 pages discussed military doctrine, and even those pages glossed over the Berlin Declaration with boilerplate praise.[52] In place of Gorbachev's military doctrine, the stated task of which was to prevent war, Khalipov substituted military "policy," designed instead for the prevention of "imperialist aggression, and, if necessary—the decisive and utter destruction of any aggressor."[53]

If the MPA was opposed to it, then the new military doctrine was destined for trouble. Gorbachev certainly had to be aware of this opposition, and taken in the context of military rhetoric in 1986 and 1987, the Berlin Declaration in retrospect now seems more a defensive maneuver by Gorbachev, rather than a bold new stroke. (It may also have represented Gorbachev's attempt to cope with the first rumblings of the earthquake that was to destroy Eastern European socialism and consequently the Warsaw Pact itself in 1989.) The idea of the "defensive" character of Soviet military doctrine, after all, had been emphasized long before the XXVII Congress, and the opposition to it on the part of the military was clear right up to the May meeting itself. Indeed, looking back, one wonders why Gorbachev waited until late May to hold the PCC meeting, since such timing gave the military repeated chances to make their case in the press on V-E Day, May 9.

Marshal Kulikov realized this, for he seized the opportunity afforded by the national military holiday to argue directly against the Berlin Declaration. Kulikov was especially careful to point out that the United States had still not provided "a constructive answer" to the last PCC overture, a unremarkable resolution approved at a 1986

---

[51] "Doktrina zashchity mira i sotsializma," *Krasnaia Zvezda*, September 10, 1987, p. 2.
[52] V. F. Khalipov, *Voennaia politika KPSS* (Moscow: Voenizdat, 1988), pp. 156–160.
[53] Ibid., p. 15.

meeting in Budapest.[54] In Kulikov's view, this was hardly the time to try to reason with the West:

> The problem of saving ourselves, of saving our future, now stands before mankind in its full magnitude. Never before has the [situation] been so close to that dangerous borderline, across which is the destruction of everything alive, as today. And blame for this totally and fully rests with imperialism. Its policy is the policy of the most reactionary, militaristic, aggressive forces of modern times.[55]

Kulikov was more restrained in his interview in *Izvestiia* on Victory Day, but he used the opportunity to reemphasize the dangers of being duped by arms control rhetoric. (Maksimov, as usual, was somewhat more supportive of the general secretary in his comments the same day in *Sel'skaia Zhizn*.)[56] After praising Soviet arms initiatives, Kulikov warned that "the ruling circles of the United States and the imperialist states continue their material preparation for [nuclear war]. Dreams of world hegemony hypnotize the leading figures of the USA."[57] Virtually nothing had changed since the March interview in *Trud*; knowing of the impending PCC meeting, Kulikov was either criticizing it or attempting to derail it.

Once the Berlin Declaration was out, Kulikov turned up the heat through an interview in Bulgaria. "NATO's threat to the socialist countries is completely real," he said, citing President Reagan's June 1987 West Berlin speech ("Mr. Gorbachev, tear down this wall!") as proof. Then: "I shall stress that this [speech by Reagan] was explicitly made after the allied socialist countries declared at the Berlin meeting of the Political Consultative Committee that they will never and under no circumstances begin military actions against any state or al-

[54] V. Kulikov, "Edinyi kurs, edinye tseli," *Kommunist Vooruzhennykh Sil* 9 (May 1987), p. 28.

[55] Ibid., p. 27.

[56] Maksimov assured the readers of *Sel'skaia Zhizn* that socialism could never be destroyed by force, and he voiced brief support for Gorbachev's initiatives. "General Maksimov Interviewed on Victory Jubilee," JPRS-UMA-87-035, June 17, 1987, pp. 25–27.

[57] "Radi mira na zemle," *Izvestiia*, May 8, 1987, p. 2. No one can accuse Kulikov of refusing to present a united front to the West, however. His late 1987 interview with the Norwegian paper *Arbiederbladet* was full of his firm beliefs that a nuclear-free Europe was possible, if conventional force levels were reduced, if the Baltic were cleared of nuclear arms, and so on. See "Kulikov Interviewed on Nordic Nuclear-Free Zone," FBIS-SOV-87-229, November 30, 1987, p. 6. Needless to say, the tone of these remarks (appearing in a country long-targeted by the Soviet "nuclear-free-zone" proposals) were out of step with the mass of Kulikov's Soviet writings, and there is probably little in them that likely reflects any of his actual views on the subject.

liance first, providing that they are not themselves the target of an armed attack."[58] In other words: Gorbachev has played into American hands, by asking for peace while allowing himself to be threatened with war. Kulikov then went on to rail against the Rogers Plan (discussed in Chapter 4), a concept temporarily lost in the recent tussles over doctrine, but soon to reemerge, not least in the fulminations of Kulikov's own loyal chief of staff, Gen. A. I. Gribkov (who later, like Kulikov, was sacked).[59]

Kulikov's final salvo appeared shortly before he was fired and reassigned to the Inspectorate in 1988. As if he needed to make his dissatisfaction any more plain, he went ahead in early 1988 with the publication of a short book, *A Doctrine of Defending Peace and Socialism*. It was a direct polemic against the New Thinking, improved arms control efforts, any positive reassessment of the West, and the spirit of the Berlin Declaration.[60] The book could have as easily been written in 1978 as 1988: Kulikov's discussion of military doctrine is phrased entirely in terms of Marxist ideology, his reference to the INF Treaty is a passing one, and his discussion of the New Thinking is almost nonexistent. It would be the marshal's last such volley.

Had opposition to the New Thinking remained confined to some of the retrograde marshals such as Kulikov and a few like-minded officers, the political damage to Gorbachev's authority in foreign policy might have been easier to contain. Disturbing signs began to appear elsewhere, however, which indicated that Kulikov's criticism may have been only the tip of an iceberg. While Kulikov was painting an unsubtle portrait of the general secretary as a military dunce, even Marshal Akhromeev was beginning to express reservations. Akhromeev's Victory Day declaration was far more supportive of Gorbachev, in part because Akhromeev's overall style is more nuanced and his outlook is more progressive than Kulikov's. How-

[58] "Kulikov on NATO Threat to Pact States," FBIS-SOV-87-200, October 16, 1987, p. 3.

[59] See "Doktrina sokhraneniia mira," *Krasnaia Zvezda*, September 25, 1987, pp. 2–3; that same month, Gribkov warned that there "is not a day that doesn't bring yet new evidence of the strengthened preparation for war on the part of imperialist reaction and its leader the USA. . . . today, as never before, the threat to peace, the threat to socialism, is great." See "Doktrina zashchity mira i sotsializma" [roundtable], *Sovetskii Voin* 18 (September 1987), p. 30.

[60] V. Kulikov, *Doktrina zashchity sotsializma i mira* (Moscow: Voenizdat, 1988). The booklet, as of early 1989, was impossible to find in any of the military bookstores in Moscow, Leningrad, or Kiev (copies were available at the Leningrad officer's club); whether this was by design, accident, or popularity is hard to say, although it had a printing run of 30,000.

ever, this more polished style did not conceal his fears: "Reactionary forces in the USA and some of its allies are trying not to curb the arms race. . . . the perfecting of nuclear weapons is absurd and criminal. . . . However, influential imperialist circles do not wish to understand this, and are trying to attain world supremacy."[61] The obvious difference between Kulikov and Akhromeev was that Akhromeev saw the potential for negotiation with the reasonable elements in the West; Kulikov, by contrast, was explicitly arguing that in the West the inmates were now running the asylum and that hopes for dialogue were based more on wishes than reality.

It took little time after the Berlin Declaration for the leadership to recognize that it was not making headway. Sensitive to a possible image problem, an anonymous "high-ranking Soviet" (almost certainly one of the academic "institutchiki") indicated to *Frankfurter Allegemeine* while on a visit to Western Europe that all was not going smoothly back in Moscow. "We are no longer talking about winning the war . . . but about how to prevent it," to which end a doctrine of "sufficiency" was being developed, he said. But he added that it had not been easy to do: Gorbachev's call for changes in doctrine, said the unnamed Soviet, "does not sit well with many people [*Das behagt vielen Leuten nicht*]."[62] The *"viele Leute"* remained unnamed, but the message to the West was clear: change was under way, despite the obvious signs of struggle.

These mixed reactions to the Berlin Declaration, including the growing unease of the chief of the General Staff, revealed the extent to which the broader civil-military agenda was spiraling out of control. Given the atmosphere and tone of Soviet civil-military exchanges in the spring and summer of 1987, General Secretary Gorbachev can hardly be faulted for announcing his new doctrine from the relative safety of Berlin.

Meanwhile, Back in Red Square . . .

Actually, Berlin was not the worst place Gorbachev could have been on May 28, 1987. He could have been running for cover in Red Square, watching a nineteen-year-old West German named Matthias

---

[61] S. Akhromeev, "Velikaia pobeda," *Krasnaia Zvezda*, May 9, 1987, pp. 1–2.

[62] Jan Reifenberg, "Wir reden nicht mehr davon, wie der Krieg zu gewinnen ist," *Frankfurter Allegemeine*, July 4, 1987, p. 5. This anonymous analyst may have been Daniel Proektor, who said similar things while stumping for the New Thinking in Vienna in October 1987. See FBIS-SOV-87-200, October 16, 1987, pp. 3–4. If not Proektor, it was no doubt someone in a similar post at IMEMO, the international economics institute, or the USA/Canada Institute.

Rust land a Cessna there (in an area Muscovites later smirkingly referred to as "Sheremetevo Three") after buzzing Lenin's tomb. As it turns out, this weird incident allowed Gorbachev to sack Marshal Sokolov, who was probably soon to leave anyway, along with a number of Air Defense Forces officers including Chief Marshal of Aviation Aleksandr Koldunov. The importance of the Rust affair lies not in the actual event, but rather in the changes that followed it. Specifically, it allowed Dmitrii Yazov—brought into the Ministry of Defense around the time of the January plenum—to assume the post of minister of defense.

The most important aspect of the Rust scandal is that it provided an opportunity for almost any civilian leader to make credible charges of military malpractice. While Gorbachev even then was not the weakest of leaders, by any definition the grievous nature of the security breach revealed by Rust's landing prevents any estimation of the power necessary for Gorbachev to oust Sokolov and the others. However, it does raise questions about the more lasting aspect of the post-Rust affair firings—namely, the replacements.

Gorbachev knew that he was in the midst of a struggle with the military, and he may have thought that Yazov's reputation as a disciplinarian without any political pretensions would be helpful. Also, if Yazov was placed in the job, it would bring a field officer with recent (although brief) experience in cadres to the ministry, and one who owed his entire rise to Gorbachev. In this respect, Yazov's lesser intellectual stature (in comparison with the the more expected choice, P. G. Lushev) may have worked in his favor.[63] After all, it has been axiomatic among aspiring rulers (as Aristotle noted so pointedly in the *Politics*): if you want to consolidate your rule, promote mediocrity rather than excellence.

Another noteworthy aspect of the Rust scandal is that it "accelerated" normal processes of turnover. Until this point, Gorbachev had not forced turnover among senior military positions with the same vengeance he had visited on civilian administrative elites (which approached 50 percent in many areas).[64] Military turnover was a relative fraction of overall turnover, and most of that consisted of rotations

[63] For a brief summary of Lushev's fast-track career, see George Weickhardt, "General P. G. Lushev: 'The Very Model of a Modern [Soviet] General,'" *Radio Liberty Reports*, RL 423/87, October 27, 1987. Yazov's pre-1985 writings are few, uniformly dull and uncontroversial, and deal with practical matters such as discipline.

[64] Dawn Mann has commented that the turnover among domestic elites took on the scope of a bloodless purge. Military turnover has been slight by comparison, especially in the Central Committee. See Dale Herspring, "The Soviet Military in the Aftermath of the 27th Party Congress," *Orbis* 30, no. 2 (Summer 1986). I am grateful to Mann for her insights on the subject.

based on military factors (the upgraded status of military districts, for one) rather than any clear attempt at overall reform. This was an early sign of Gorbachev's impatience, foreshadowing the frustration that would reappear in the March 1989 political purge of the high command.

Gorbachev's impatience with the military was matched by the growing impatience of the military with Gorbachev. In 1987, civil-military disagreement became more than a matter of controlling defense policy, as Gorbachev allowed open criticism of the military. The ante had been upped as the military found itself, for the first time since the Great Purge, having to defend itself in Soviet society. This was, in military eyes, far beyond the pale of acceptable debate. Arguments over defense and arms control were one thing: criticism from woolly intellectuals who practically advocated pacifism and draft dodging was another entirely. The tone of civil-military dialogue was soon to change from tense to shrill.

Yazov's Defense of Socialism and Peace

In the end, the man responsible for stepping in and ensuring order in the Soviet Armed Forces was, naturally, the minister of defense. In late 1987 (about the same time Kulikov's parting shot was being readied for release) Defense Minister Yazov produced a booklet in which he weighed in on almost every major issue raised between 1986 and 1988. The booklet, *In Defense of Socialism and Peace*, has several interesting points, although midway through Yazov turned to the more routine subject of cadre policy. In the first half, however, he attempted to mediate the civil-military debate without forcing a surrender on the part of the soldiers. Yazov appeared in *Defense of Socialism* to be torn between the political aspects of his job as the minister of defense and his loyalties as a professional combat officer. Since the book is at least half devoted to cadre policy, it seems that Yazov took some political chances; he could have stuck to what he knew best and written on *perestroika*, readiness, or military democratization, rather than jumping in on a number of controversies. As a result, the book has a confused tone about it, Gorbachevian one page and warlike the next.

The book is especially useful here, in that a review of its major points also outlines the continuing issues of civil-military conflict in late 1987 and early 1988, a period in which the military debate was marked by voluminous writing and little guidance. Yazov's thoughts on various issues provide a compact framework for the events in the defense debate over in 1987 and 1988, and the major themes of *In Defense of Socialism* will serve as introductions to other military writings in the same area.

The Party and Doctrine

On the major issue of Party authority, *In Defense of Socialism* provided a mixed message. On one hand, Yazov made only the standard pitch about military doctrine and defensiveness. But Yazov's loyalties become questionable in a key passage where he defines doctrine as "based on a system of scientific knowledge about war and the army, on the experience of the defense of the socialist Fatherland, and the practice of Soviet military construction."[65] This was not in line with the intentions of New Thinking, since Yazov resorted to the traditional definition of doctrine, not as a system of disembodied political views, but *based on science*, meaning, of course, military science. This is a subtle but politically important distinction, primarily because such a definition would leave the chief responsibility for formulating doctrine with the military. (It was also an uncomfortable throwback to the days of Ogarkov's rantings about "objective" demands for defense.) Later, Yazov writes that doctrine is "*a system of fundamental views on the prevention of war, on military construction, preparation of the nation and the Armed Forces for the repulsion of aggression and means of the conduct of armed struggle in the defense of socialism.*"[66] This is an amalgam of Gorbachevian thought and traditionalism, adding "the prevention of war" to the definition while retaining the traditional military phraseology about the repulsion of aggression.

Yazov's discussion was complimented in 1987 statements by Col. Gen. Gareev of the General Staff. Gareev's writings on military doctrine indicated that he was less irresolute than Yazov about excluding the leadership from doctrinal formulation. "*The political side of socialist military doctrine,*" Gareev wrote in a 1987 pamphlet, "is based on Marxist-Leninist teachings on war and the army, socialist military science and the entire system of military-theoretical knowledge."[67] Military science was clearly understood in the USSR as the responsibility of the professional military, and Gareev's basing of military doctrine on military *science* was another way of saying that military

---

[65] D. T. Yazov, *Na strazhe mira i sotsializma* (Moscow: Voenizdat, 1987), p. 26.

[66] Ibid., p. 28, emphasis in original.

[67] M. A. Gareev, *Sovetskaia voennaia nauka* (Moscow: Znanie, 1987) [Series: Zashchita Otechestva, no. 11], p. 15, emphasis in original.

[187]

doctrine could only be grounded on the work of military theorists in the General Staff like himself.[68] This expansion on the usual terminology moves doctrine from the realm of science to the realm of military science, and thus provides a distinct argument for a heavy military influence on doctrine.

This interpretation was not adopted by, of all people, Volkogonov, Gareev's erstwhile traveling companion on the lecture circuit. Perhaps, due to his rigorous training as an ideologist, Volkogonov understood that the Gareev formulation was, even for him, too direct a contradiction of Marxism-Leninism. But rather than joining Yazov in the traditional definition, or supporting Gareev's more parochial description, Volkogonov found a middle way, one which, after the Berlin Declaration, would have pleased even Gorbachev. "In the military doctrine of the Warsaw Treaty member-states," he said, "basic goals are laid out, the achievement of which serve to block the arising of wars. The very character of these goals demonstrates in relief [our] doctrine as a *state conception of the prevention of war*."[69] However, Volkogonov left a loophole (like Serebriannikov before him), arguing that for doctrine to be considered in this way, three things were necessary: liquidation of the material bases of nuclear war, creation of political mechanisms of international security, and a change in the world ideological atmosphere. The first and third conditions seemed in 1987 a long way off, and Volkogonov stressed repeatedly that the second— necessarily the responsibility of the leadership—has not been attained.

One outright rejection of Gareev's implications came from Rear Admiral G. Kostev, a military professor and relatively recent participant in the debate. In an article apparently commissioned to bring the New Thinkers' viewpoint to bear in this debate, Kostev turned Gareev's formula around, and asserted that "military doctrine conditions the development of military science" rather than vice versa. "Therefore, changes introduced in our military doctrine in accordance with the new political thinking objectively demand refinements in the theory of military art [strategy, operations art, and tactics] as well."[70] Following Kostev's line of reasoning, the General Staff should react to

[68] See the entry for "Voennaia nauka" in the *Voenno-Entsiklopedicheskii Slovar'* (Moscow: Voenizdat, 1986), pp. 135–137.

[69] D. A. Volkogonov, "Doktrina antivoiny," *Novoe Vremia* 25 (June 19, 1987), p. 15, emphasis in original.

[70] G. Kostev, "Nasha voennaia doktrina v svete novogo politicheskoe myshleniia," *Kommunist Vooruzhennykh Sil* 17 (September 1987), p. 13.

the leadership's changes in policy, rather than expecting the leadership to react to the political judgments of the military.

Surprise Attack, War, and Victory

Another issue on which Yazov's positions reflected the general confusion in the military is nuclear war. At the outset of *In Defense of Socialism*, Yazov says: "World war, and especially nuclear war, would have catastrophic consequences not only for the nations immediately involved in it, but also for life on Earth itself." War "should once and for all be excluded from the political arsenal. This is a reality of our day that it is impossible not to see." This is the Gorbachev line, of course. But having said this, Yazov warns: "However, reactionary imperialist circles, above all in the USA and NATO stubbornly continue to ignore [this reality]." He then accuses the United States of preparing for war: "Simultaneous with the accumulation and perfection of the means of war in the attempt to achieve unilateral advantage the United States is working out 'rational variants' *for the unleashing and conduct of war, in the first place nuclear, and is counting on the attainment of victory in it.*"[71] This is clearly not the preferred Gorbachevian rhetoric, but it does seem to be the kind that would satisfy concern among the war planners. Moreover, it reaffirms the idea that the enemy is convinced of the possibility of nuclear victory, itself an oblique argument for maintaining a similar stance.

These are, of course, themes important to Volkogonov in particular, who cautioned in the spring of 1987 that "peace is possible, but war is also probable," although he did not press the point about nuclear victory, as he had in 1986.[72] However, he did reemphasize Washington's readiness and conceptual preparedness for war, even as he was supporting other aspects of the Berlin Declaration.

Meanwhile, Yazov continued to harp on the danger of surprise attack in Europe. On this issue it was especially surprising to see Yazov so bellicose, at a time when Gorbachev was trying to keep a steady course of stability in European relations. "*The preparation of the NATO armed forces* is oriented toward the unleashing and conduct of conventional, as well as nuclear, war," he wrote. "Exercises are reg-

---

[71] Yazov, *Na strazhe mira i sotsializma*, p. 3.

[72] Volkogonov, "Doktrina antivoiny," p. 15. This is not a new idea for Volkogonov; in his May 22 *Krasnaia Zvezda* piece, he referred to the lack of monuments to peace, and the plethora of monuments to war, as indicative of what a rare "guest" peace is on earth.

ularly conducted near the borders of the socialist states, which are—by their scope, the composition of their forces and means, their organization and direction, in essence—repetitions of aggression."[73] By any definition, this is challenging rhetoric and serves little purpose other than allowing the Soviets to renounce attacking first while still maintaining their offensive posture, a posture to which the General Staff and even Akhromeev were committed. This left Yazov in a strange position, defending the pacifist Gorbachev line while making a threat about NATO exercises that almost sounded like a prelude to war.

Other officers returned to the threat of surprise in 1987, both before and after Yazov. One, of course, was the indefatigable Colonel V. Alekseev, who had made similarly heavy-handed charges in April 1987.[74] Another was Col. L. Levadov, who implied that the Rogers Plan envisioned an attack on Soviet conventional forces on Soviet soil, a very serious charge. Levadov, however, was not quite as alarmist as Alekseev, and he candidly admitted that these plans "had opponents even among [NATO's] leading figures."[75]

Sufficiency and Reliable Defense

Yazov's "reliable defense" definition came in his military doctrine chapter, and it was fairly content-free: "Thanks to the concern of the party and of the entire Soviet people, the combat might of the Armed Forces is supported at the level necessary for the reliable defense of the peaceful labor of the Soviet people and the successful solving of all tasks by the army and the navy which follow from the principle tenets of Soviet military doctrine."[76]

Was this military code for bigger budgets or civilian code for smaller budgets? Probably neither; it was a formulation that cost Yazov nothing to repeat, since he did not choose to elaborate on it. On reflection, simple repetition was the best course for Yazov, in that both soldiers and civilians would be gratified as long as Yazov did not proceed to define what he meant.

The most important development in the "reliable defense" question

---

[73] Ibid., pp. 16–17, emphasis in original.

[74] V. Alekseev, "Stavka na vnezapnosti," *Krasnaia Zvezda*, April 2, 1987, p. 3.

[75] L. Levadov, "Stavka na agressiiu," *Krasnaia Zvezda*, August 4, 1987, p. 3. Later, Levadov returned on Rocket Forces Day (on which Yazov made reference to the existing danger of nuclear war) to warn that NATO aggressiveness posed "a serious danger to the cause of peace of Earth." L. Levadov, "Eshche odna repetitsiia," *Krasnaia Zvezda*, November 19, 1987, p. 3.

[76] Yazov, *Na strazhe mira i sotsializma*, p. 26.

was the issue of whether it should reflect internal or external criteria. At first, the military seemed prepared to accept, or at least not to challenge, the civilian concept that "sufficient" should be considered in subjective terms, in relation to the needs and position of each country. As Gareev said in June 1987, "The military doctrine of the socialist states has the goal of guaranteeing sufficiency for defense, to deter the aggressor," and his 1987 pamphlet did not significantly stray from this simple conceptualization.[77]

By 1988, however, the military flirtation with the Gorbachev formulation was over, and discussions of "reasonable" sufficiency became descriptions of "defensive" sufficiency. The editors of *Voennaia Mysl'*, after a ritualistic bow to the XXVII Congress (in which Gorbachev was mentioned but once) took to task the idea of asymmetric reductions in January 1988:

> It is well known that, even though the military-political leadership of the USA and the NATO bloc contend that nuclear war can never be won, they nonetheless consider the threat to unleash it as a real instrument to achieve their own military-political goals. . . .
>
> The everyday activities of the armed forces of the USA and NATO assume a dangerous character. It is difficult to distinguish training and maneuvers carried out every year in Europe, the Atlantic, and in other strategically important areas, from real deployments of forces for the conduct of war. . . .
>
> In the conditions of the continued military threat which has been created by the military preparations of imperialism, defensive sufficiency cannot be interpreted one-sidedly . . . its limits are set not by us, but by the real actions of the USA and NATO.[78]

This was the most support that could be mustered for the Party defense program in the lead editorial in the premier military journal in the first issue of the new year, and it portended trouble in the year ahead. One of the strongest underpinnings of the Gorbachev approach to defense was about to come under attack from the military, and from the very top of the military leadership.

Marshal Akhromeev himself penned a stingingly anti-NATO piece in March 1988, in which he explicitly linked the ideas of defense and sufficiency to the level of external threat, exactly the kind of tradition-

---

[77] This comment occurred during a Foreign Ministry press conference. "Doktrina predotvrashcheniia voiny," *Krasnaia Zvezda*, June 23, 1987, p. 3. See also Gareev, *Sovetskuiu voennuiu nauku*, p. 16.

[78] "Oboronitel'nyi kharakter sovetskoi voennoi doktriny," *Voennaia Mysl'* (January 1988), p. 5.

[191]

al action-reaction dynamic that Gorbachev's New Thinking rejected. "The Soviet Union is guided by the principle of sufficiency for defense, for the repulsion of possible aggression," Akhromeev wrote. "And the boundaries of sufficiency are limited not by us, but by the actions of the USA and NATO." Criticizing NATO's "asymmetric" demands, Akhromeev also moved back toward a less flexible line in arms control. "In reality [i.e., despite NATO claims], there is an approximate parity [*paritet*] between the [Warsaw Pact] and NATO in the area of armed forces and conventional weapons."[79] Note that he did not use the usual word, *ravnovesie* ("equilibrium"), choosing instead the cognate for parity, with its more strictly numerical connotations.

When Akhromeev's polemic appeared, Gorbachev was nine months away from his UN announcement of unilateral cuts, a move that had to have been discussed with Akhromeev earlier. The article was clearly a warning: our agreement, the chief was saying, does not cover conventional forces.

Eventually, even Yazov would abandon any pretense of support for the Gorbachev position, and it soon became clear that Gorbachev could find no support for his plans either before or after the fact. Later admissions by Akhromeev's successor, Gen. Moiseev, suggest that the Soviet president was, in the end, trying to conduct military policy by political brinkmanship, committing the Soviets to actions in public, and then forcing fulfillment of those promises on his return to Moscow.

The overturning of the asymmetric Gorbachev position did not come without warning; in 1987 *Kommunist Vooruzhennykh Sil* carried an article by military academic P. Skorodenko that presented Akhromeev's themes in even more decisive rhetoric. Skorodenko reappeared in 1988 to reinforce the Akhromeev stance.[80] Ground Forces CINC Ivanovskii followed suit in February 1988:

> To have armed forces as large as is necessary for defense against an attack from without—this is the clear-cut position. The personnel of the Armed Forces and the quantity and quality of the means of armed struggle *are strictly commensurate with the level of the military threat, and the character and intensity of imperialism's military preparations*, and are defined by the requirements of guaranteeing the security of the Warsaw Treaty countries and the repulsion of aggression.[81]

[79] S. Akhromeev, "Chto kroetsia za briussel'skim zaiavleniem NATO," *Krasnaia Zvezda*, March 20, 1988, p. 2.

[80] P. Skorodenko, "Voennyi paritet i printsip razumnoi dostatochnosti," *Kommunist Vooruzhennykh Sil* 10 (May 1987); "Voenno-strategicheskii paritet kak faktor nedopushcheniia voiny," *Kommunist Vooruzhennykh Sil* 12 (June 1988).

[81] "My—armiia naroda," *Izvestiia*, February 7, 1988, p. 3, emphasis added.

This shifts the argument, of course, from internal squabbles over weapons and numbers to the higher ground of threat definition—an endeavor usually associated with the social-political side of doctrine. (Kulikov—of course—made a similar statement in early February.)[82]

The Danger of War and Western Intentions

In general, despite the thaw in Soviet-American relations (and especially in Kremlin-White House relations), Soviet military figures never returned to the optimistic assessments of the world situation that could be seen from time to time in 1985. However, neither was there a return to the extremely tough rhetoric of 1986, and Yazov and others paid at least nominal tribute to the improvement in East-West tensions. Still, Yazov used *Defense of Socialism* to put forward a hawkish assessment of the international situation, in statements jarringly out of step with the Gorbachev program. For example, after Yazov discussed the unthinkability of war and the defensiveness of the Warsaw Pact, he continued:

> However, we cannot close our eyes to the fact that the aggressive circles of imperialism, in spite of everything, continue to prepare a new war. The possibility of the unleashing of aggression by imperialism against the USSR and other socialist countries exists. This is a bleak reality, which demands that we build a system of our own defense readiness in such a way as to stop the aggressor, to frustrate his criminal plans, and, should aggression be unleashed all the same, give him a destructive rebuff.[83]

This material argument is reinforced on the very next page, when Yazov warns that the next war will exact huge losses, even greater than those of World War II. This, according to Yazov, is because many conventional systems "approach the destructive power of nuclear weapons of lesser yield."[84]

Yazov was not alone: Navy CINC Chernavin made a similar argument during an interview in the pages of *Komsomol'skaia Pravda*. When the interviewer pointed out the huge efforts and "sizable resources" that have gone into equipping the Soviet military, Chernavin interrupted: "But there is no other way out. Many of us military men dream of the time when the arms race will finally end and when there will be no need for new, unprecedented tanks or missile complexes.

---

[82] V. Kulikov, "Strazh mira i sotsializma," *Krasnaia Zvezda*, February 21, 1988, pp. 2–3.
[83] Yazov, *Na strazhe mira i sotsializma*, p. 30.
[84] Ibid., p. 31.

But dreams are dreams and reality dictates its own laws." Chernavin also warned that the desire of "U.S. strategists" for military superiority "has not slackened," but he was also sure to emphasize military support for the INF Treaty.[85]

In any case, Yazov maintained this pessimistic view throughout the year. In July 1987, Yazov made a major speech on military doctrine in which he credited the Soviet approach in general and the Berlin Declaration in particular with sober realism and humanitarianism. However, he added, "this conclusion has not been reached by the U.S. Administration. It has not suspended its policy of hegemonism, it has not given up its hopes of social *revanche*. . . . All of this creates a military threat and dangerous tension in the world."[86] Later, in his November *prikaz* (order) for Rocket Forces Day, Yazov referred to the "complex foreign policy situation, [and] the existing threat of nuclear war" created by "reactionary imperialist circles who are ignoring the lessons of history."[87]

Yazov later began to moderate his rhetoric, although he was still far more wary than the general secretary. In his Armed Forces Seventieth Anniversary *prikaz* in 1988, Yazov remarked that the international situation "has really begun to improve." But he followed this immediately by noting that "the danger of war persists, however, and social *revanche* remains the core of the West's strategy and militarist programs."[88] He elaborated in his speech at the festivities: "The changes for the better taking place in the international situation today cannot fail to gladden one. However, anxiety is aroused by the attempt by reactionary imperialist circles to negate the results of the Washington [summit]. With this aim, various actions are being undertaken in a militaristic style, from propaganda fabrications to direct provocations on our frontiers."[89] Yazov's alternating views were probably the result of his recognition of the political need to say something positive in the wake of the INF Treaty and the Washington summit three months earlier, despite his previous concerns.

Marshal Kulikov apparently felt no such obligation. Two days before the anniversary celebration, he appeared in *Krasnaia Zvezda*, re-

---

[85] "Chernavin on Anniversary, 'Defensive' Doctrine," FBIS-SOV-88–037, February 25, 1988, p. 71.

[86] D. Yazov, "Voennaia doktrina Varshavskogo Dogovora—doktrina zashchity mira i sotsializma," *Krasnaia Zvezda*, July 28, 1987, p. 2. The speech appeared in other Soviet newspapers as well.

[87] "Prikaz ministra oborony SSSR," *Krasnaia Zvezda*, November 19, 1987, p. 1.

[88] "Yazov Congratulates Servicemen," FBIS-SOV-88–036, February 24, 1988, p. 65.

[89] "Doklad ministra oborony SSSR generala armii D. T. Yazova," *Krasnaia Zvezda*, February 23, 1988, p. 3.

calling the difficult history of East-West relations: the 1918 intervention, World War II, and the Cold War. Hailing the INF Treaty—briefly—as a "historic breakthrough," he immediately moved into a criticism of NATO "compensatory" measures under current consideration. This, he said, was part of "the existing threat of the unleashing of a new war by imperialism."[90] It is evidence of the military's power that Kulikov got away with this kind of talk for as long as he did. Although he would be removed in March 1989, at the Seventieth Anniversary ceremonies he received the Order of Lenin, along with Lushev (his eventual successor) and Lizichev. Maksimov and Air Force CINC Y. Efimov received Orders of the October Revolution.[91]

Offense and Defense

One of the most direct challenges to Gorbachev's idea of "defensiveness" was written even before Gorbachev managed to have his conceptions codified by the PCC in Berlin. Col. G. Lukava, one of the more dire alarmists of 1986, tackled the problem of defensive politics in a 1987 anthology entitled *The Military-Theoretical Heritage of V. I. Lenin and Problems of Modern War*. The title was convenient, for Lukava invoked Lenin's name in making his point:

V.I. Lenin turned his attention to the mutual link of the *offense and defense*. . . .

Extremely important in this connection is the Leninist instruction that the socialist state conducts and only conduct *defensive* wars. However, these wars are defensive in *political goals* and not in their means of conduct. . . . The offensive is the fundamental type of military action, and its goal is the full and utter destruction of the opponent. Making war, Lenin said, "must not 'dislodge' but rather *destroy*," the opponent.[92]

When applied to questions of strategic nuclear weapons, this means that retaliation and preemption may be synonymous:

The very long range of missiles allows for the concentration of their strikes even when the launch sites are widely separated. Powerful, simultaneous, surprise strikes permit the destruction of the opponent's

---

[90] Kulikov, "Strazh mira i sotsializma," p. 2.

[91] *Krusnuiu Zvezda*, February 23, 1988, p. 1.

[92] A. S. Milovidov, ed., *Voenno-Teoreticheskii Nasledie V. I. Lenina i problemy sovremmenoi voiny* (Moscow: Voenizdat, 1987), p. 251, original emphasis.

vital forces and equipment over significantly broader areas than in the past. . . .

In modern times, the correlation of offense and defense has become deeper and more complex. Defense in large measure includes retaliatory strikes, often using means also used by offensive forces.[93]

Of course, Lukava is correct; an accurate ICBM can be a disarming weapon, or an instrument of revenge, and neither is inherent in the design (although highly accurate weapons such as MX and the SS-18 understandably raise first-strike concerns). Lukava's intention was clearly to leave little doubt as to the necessity of a vigilant, even preemptive, strategic posture.

Yazov's *Defense of Socialism* at one point attempted to structure the offense-defense problem. But Yazov did not rebut Lukava's argument that defensive political goals do not negate the importance of an offensive military strategy, including strategic preemption. Instead, he straddled the problem, arguing that "Soviet military doctrine considers the basic type of military action for the repulsion of aggression to be the *defense*. It should be reliable and firm, unyielding and active and should count on stopping the offensive of the enemy, bleeding him white, not allowing losses of territory, and securing the utter crushing of the encroaching enemy groups." This might have been Gorbachev's reply to the offense-enthusiasts, although it is hard to believe that Lukava would have been satisfied with it. There is no need to guess at Yazov's opinion, however, because he soon turned to a support of tradition, abandoning his defense of Gorbachev's defensiveness. Since "the defense alone cannot utterly crush [*razgromit'*] the aggressor," he wrote, "therefore, after the repulsion of the attack the troops and naval forces should be able to conduct a *decisive offensive*. Transition to this would be in the form of counterattack, which would be conducted in a complex and tense situation of opposing struggle with a well-armed opponent."[94] If Yazov was trying to tone down military rhetoric about offensive operations, he failed. Not only is this a confused answer, but also it says nothing about strategic preemption, which was probably the really grievous sin of the Lukava chapter.

The Intermediate-Range Nuclear Forces Treaty

Yazov approached the INF Treaty very cautiously in his book, largely because it had not yet been signed.

---

[93] Milovidov, ed., *Voenno-Teoreticheskii Nasledie V. I. Lenina*, pp. 249–252.
[94] Yazov, *Na Strazhe*, pp. 32–33, original emphases.

The USSR has demonstrated its good will, having divided out the problem of medium-range rockets from the block of questions of nuclear disarmament which were proposed by M. S. Gorbachev in Reykjavik. He made concrete proposals. . . . The achievement of an agreement on this problem has huge political and military significance, in that it would lead to the liquidation of two classes of US and Soviet nuclear weapons, and the destruction of all of the nuclear warheads, including those for the West German "Pershing-1A" rockets. It would stabilize the situation, and lower the danger of the arising of nuclear war.[95]

Even though the agreement was only pending, this is still only a lukewarm endorsement, notable more for its brevity than its content. The INF agreement must have been a touchy subject, since Yazov skips over it so quickly. After all, the INF Treaty was at least a public success for Gorbachev, but Yazov does not seem eager to dwell upon it.

In general, the Soviet military press was supportive of the treaty at first, although there were some early indications that the idea required a certain amount of defending before the military public.[96] One surprising supporter of the treaty was L. Semeiko, one of the more conservative voices of the 1979–80 period. Identified in 1988 as the "deputy chairman for disarmament of the Soviet Committee for the Defense of Peace," Semeiko appeared in *Izvestiia* to defend the agreement as a "balance of [Soviet and American] political and military interests."[97] A similar, sober assessment was made by a *Krasnaia Zvezda* reviewer, who pointed out that the treaty had been hard-won "through the obstacles of confrontation and the ice fields of mutual suspicion."[98] As will be seen in the next chapter, this sanguine military assessment would soon pass and the INF Treaty would emerge in military rhetoric as a NATO stratagem to hoodwink the USSR.

The Expanding Agenda

Yazov's book framed the strictly military questions yet unresolved in the civil-military dialogue. But the civil-military agenda was expanding beyond issues of national security even as Yazov was making

[95] Ibid., p. 22.

[96] See, for example, editorials before and after the signing: "Politika posledovatel'naia, printsipal'naia," *Krasnaia Zvezda*, December 1, 1987, p. 1, and "Na puti k bez"iadernomu miru," *Krasnaia Zvezda*, December 20, 1987, p. 1.

[97] L. Semeiko, "Ne prosto arifmetika," *Izvestiia*, March 2, 1988, p. 5. Of course, Semeiko's support took three months to appear in public, but that does not detract from his apparent turnaround—perhaps linked to his seat on the Peace Committee and the fact the he was speaking to a civilian readership.

[98] "Golts Ponders Summit Prospects," FBIS-SOV-87–225, December 8, 1987, p. 19.

this confused effort to impose order. The social attack on the military as an institution, led by many of the Soviet Union's ablest intellectuals, served to move the debate away from military concepts to the much larger and explosive issue of the role of the armed forces in Soviet society.

THE PATRIOTISM OFFENSIVE

The views on which "New Thinking" and the "New Doctrine" were predicated combined in 1987 with *glasnost'* to bring about vocal criticism of the military and military thinking from leading Soviet social and cultural intellectual circles. Civilian criticism raised fears among officers about the pernicious effects of the New Thinking on Soviet society, and the military's own standing in that society. The patriotism debate has revealed the extent to which military prestige and civilian authority had become entangled in the disputes that began over narrower defense issues such as military doctrine and the New Thinking. This debate continued until the last days of the USSR itself.

The military-intellectual dialogue became raucous, as an angry military establishment went on an outright offensive on the issue of patriotism and military-patriotic education. It was evident from the writings of Volkogonov and others that many senior officers feared a weakening of Soviet security would arise from too much emphasis on what they saw as the pacifism inherent in the New Thinking, either by denying the armed forces actual access to young men, or by providing them with young draftees of questionable fortitude. The patriotism debate also served to provide the military an arena in which they could open fire on the New Thinking without appearing to criticize Gorbachev himself, particularly on the question of the ethics of defensiveness.

The charge was led in 1987 and 1988 by Volkogonov, for the understandable reason that the pacifistic trend was a threat to the requirements of his job as agitprop chief, the MPA officer responsible for indoctrination and morale among military cadres. He proved to be an able opponent when he fired one of the early volleys in this battle in the pages of *Literaturnaia Gazeta*. Addressing unhealthy pacifism among some Soviet authors, Volkogonov argued that "in literature, as in politics, it is important to take into account that pacifism and the struggle for peace are not one and the same thing." Volkogonov, whose concerns for the morale of the missile forces have already been noted, related a specific incident involving a certain "very respected author" (Belorussian writer Ales' Adamovich later admitted to being the culprit) that led to his later comments on missileer morale:

> A writer, in his words, visited the commander of a Soviet atomic submarine (an anonymous one; I think that such a commander of a Soviet atomic submarine doesn't exist). The essence of the dialogue went something like this. The writer asked the officer: imagine that our country has been turned into an asphalt desert as the result of an American first strike, as even their doctrine envisages. But you have managed to get the signal, the order, to carry out a retaliatory strike. Would you make that strike? The sub commander thought a bit, and asked the author: how about you? Would you push the button? The writer categorically and repeatedly said: "No." Then, in the writer's words, the sub commander likewise showed doubts, but did not give a definite answer.[99]

From here, Volkogonov launched into a harangue about the "conscience of a writer" and the missileers on watch, and so on, which became the basis of a scathing article in *Krasnaia Zvezda* two weeks later.

In that later piece, the full scope of Volkogonov's fears was revealed. He warned that too open a debate over the morality of deterrence would dangerously affect the morale of the guardians of Soviet military security—the missileers of the Strategic Rocket Forces. Of course, these problems are not unique to the Soviets: the United States Air Force has similar concerns about its own missile personnel.[100] Volkogonov apparently shared a fear with his American counterparts about what might happen should the men tasked with the promise of revenge become pacifists. His remarks on this are worth quoting here at length:

> If the authors of "massive retaliation," "deterrence," "flexible response," and "Star Wars" were one day to cross the Rubicon dividing war and peace . . . the Soviet soldiers and officers controlling strategic might would be forced to fulfill their duty to the end. That is what the tenets of our military doctrine order.
>
> Regrettably, certain authors are in doubt as to the legitimacy of this conception. For example, [one] writer considers this approach absurd and ridiculous.

[99] "Vystuplenie D. A. Volkogonov," *Literaturnaia Gazeta*, May 6, 1987, p. 3. For Adamovich's retort, see page 7 of the same issue.

[100] One is reminded, for example, of the attempts to quash publicity surrounding the cashiering of a U.S. Air Force major who was dismissed during the Carter administration for questioning the chain of command that would lead to a launch order.

Ordinarily, Volkogonov would agree that a writer's judgments are "a matter of his conscience."

> It must not be overlooked, however, that in doing so a writer is in fact casting doubt on the advisability of Soviet soldiers fulfilling their military duty. And this is not merely a harmless rhetorical exercise.
>
> Every day, thousands of Soviet soldiers are on watch at missile complexes. They are directly attached to missions of strategic, I would even say, fateful, significance. We all hope and believe that none of them will ever have to fulfill the command to launch against real targets. But their *readiness* to do so, as the highest expression of their military and civic duty, remains an awesome deterring factor.[101]

Volkogonov did not deny the weight of political dominance in solving security problems (a key aspect of the New Thinking), only the present feasibility of that dominance. Being prepared for war, he argued, will remain crucial "as long as political mechanisms for blocking war have not been created." This article, it should be noted, was a marked turn toward intolerance for Volkogonov. In 1985, he was willing to accept that those who would assign equal blame for the arms race to both sides were at least honorable people; by 1987, he had nothing but contempt for such a view, and for its proponents.[102]

In both pieces, Volkogonov suggested that New Thinking was being taken too far by excitable intellectuals. New Thinking "is not a new worldview, but rather a new facet" of good Leninist sense on the defense of the Fatherland, and Volkogonov criticizes those (yet again) who only view such questions through the "prism of apocalypse."[103]

A week after Volkogonov's diatribe against Adamovich, the intellectuals returned fire when *Literaturnaia Gazeta* carried the proceedings of an academic roundtable discussion. The entire debate need not be of concern here; suffice it to say that the tone of the discussion was set by claims that the drafting of college students meant that good minds were going to waste in the military. This was and is an explosive issue with the high command, who saw draft dodging as a

---

[101] D. A. Volkogonov, "Imperativy iadernogo veka," *Krasnaia Zvezda*, May 22, 1987, pp. 2–3, emphasis in original. This article was part of an ongoing feud with pacifistic Belorussian writer Ales' Adamovich. For details of this feud, see Stephen Foye, "Intellectuals Attack the Military," *Sovset News* 3, no. 9 (July 30, 1987), and Thomas Nichols, "'Intellectual Pacifists' Criticized by Military Officer," *Radio Liberty Reports*, RL 308/87, July 28, 1987.

[102] Volkogonov's 1985 piece was "Voina i mir v 'iadernyi vek,'" *Pravda*, August 30, 1985, pp. 3–4.

[103] Volkogonov, "Voina i mir," p. 3.

rejection of the multinational cohesion of the USSR, an insult to the military itself, and a dire threat to Soviet security. (In 1989, the spring call-up was suspended due to massive draft evasion, which rose six-fold between 1988 and 1989, reaching 70 percent of eligible men in some areas and tens of thousands throughout the Union.)[104] In response, Gareev rose to the challenge from the academics and made it clear that the professional soldiers (many of whom hold advanced degrees) were mightily and personally annoyed, as well as concerned about the image of military service more broadly.[105]

Yazov joined in the attacks on other authors, which turned from criticism to outrage. In December 1987, he appeared on the Soviet television program "I Serve the Soviet Union" with—there should be no surprise—Volkogonov, and the two joined forces in excoriating the Soviet version of the "liberal media." In fact, Yazov seemed to defer to Volkogonov early on. Volkogonov's remarks were predictable: "When no political mechanism exists for curbing war is available, we, in reality, have no other option but to resort to the military mechanism. I would like our esteemed authors to understand this better as well."[106] Yazov, however, was surprising in his own vitriolic response:

> Imperialists dream of a situation where our country has no [heroes]. . . . they are deeply insulted when our young men fight, if need be, to the last man in Afghanistan.
>
> Some journals attempt to bite the Soviet Army whenever they can. Here is an issue of *Ogonek*. [Yazov points to an issue of *Ogonek* and then begins criticizing a story carried in it about a private named Kolya.] "Here is to . . . "—a habitual toast of an alcoholic. What obscenity! Why was it necessary to connect this alcoholic to a general? "Here is to the shoulder-boards of a general." . . .
>
> What has all this got to do with an alcoholic and a general? Is there an *Ogonek* representative present? Are you ashamed? I think that the *Ogonek* people, if present . . . [Yazov is interrupted by applause][107]

Nor did *Literaturnaia Gazeta* escape Yazov's anger. "Look at the way *Literaturnaia Gazeta* burst forth," he said, mimicking the journal. "Oh

[104] See "Trouble among Soviet Troops," *Los Angeles Times*, May 10, 1990, p. B6, and Michael Dobbs, "Draft-Dodging Season," *Washington Post*, May 6, 1990, p. 1.

[105] For the details of the offending article by the academics and the response it generated from Gareev, see Stephen Foye's analysis in "Intellectuals Attack the Military," in *Sovset News*, and *Radio Liberty Reports*, RL 221/87, Stephen Foye, "Soviet General Staff Theorist Defends the Military," June 9, 1987.

[106] FBIS-SOV-88–014, January 22, 1988, p. 65.

[107] Ibid., p. 69.

my God, if one is to serve as a soldier, he will never be a mathematician!" The threat inherent in all this? It is nothing less, says Yazov, than aiding imperialist propagandists in weakening Soviet morale and "tearing off the laurels of our victory" in World War II.[108]

More was at stake here than the egos of a few senior officers. A debate was under way over draft deferments for college students, an important issue for the military. Men are a scare commodity in the USSR, and the military believed, quite correctly, that it was competing with the civilian economy for capable people. This battle was eventually won by the civilians: a December 1987 announcement in *Literaturnaia Gazeta* indicated that such deferments were to be reinstated, after being generally suspended since 1982.[109] The question of the limits, and dangers, of military *glasnost'*, of course, remained, no doubt linked to the concerns voiced by such officers as Ivanovskii about the "immaturity" of today's Soviet soldier in comparison to his 1941 counterpart, the general unwillingness of Soviet boys to shoulder even the more mundane responsibilities of the nation's defense.[110]

An interesting footnote: Volkogonov reappeared in 1991 as a convert to the Gorbachev cause, despite the fact that his candor and vitriol initially cost him his job in the Main Political Administration in the spring of 1988, when he was moved from the MPA to the Military History Institute.[111] He now chairs the commission within the Ministry of Defense charged with overseeing the removal of Party organizations and the overall "de-ideologizing" of the Soviet Armed Forces, presumably exactly the event he feared most as an MPA officer.[112] Although Volkogonov has yet to comment explicitly on his turn toward Gorbachev, in my view it was probably the result of two aspects of Volkogonov's career. First, in 1989, Volkogonov completed an astonishing four-volume biography of Stalin, for which he was granted unprecedented access to Soviet archives, and he clearly convinced himself of the awful legacy of the Stalinist burden on the very structure of Soviet power itself. While denying that the Stalinist experience discredited socialism "in general," he called for a "new conception of

[108] Ibid.

[109] See Sergei Voronitsyn, "Deferment of Military Service for Students Again Extended," *Radio Liberty Reports*, RL 12/88, January 13, 1988.

[110] See "My—armiia naroda," p. 3, and Boris Leonov, "Glasnost' bez chuzhikh standartov," *Krasnaia Zvezda*, February 7, 1988, p. 4.

[111] "Istina prevyshe vsego," *Izvestiia*, May 4, 1988, p. 6.

[112] I am grateful to Volkogonov's colleague, Professor Nikita Chaldymov, for his enlightening comments on the work of these and other postcoup commissions.

socialism."[113] Certainly, he came away from the project with a new understanding of the horrors of the 1930s. Reflecting on the lessons of the past in the concluding chapter of *Triumph and Tragedy*, he wrote, "Some may say that the author of this book has, in painting this portrait, limited his palette to the dark and dismal shades. I had no special prejudices about [Stalin]. But ten years ago, when I started to collect materials for a book, I could not then imagine the kind of depths of the human spirit and immorality that I would come across." "There is no alternative to freedom," he concludes. "I believe that now more than I ever have."[114]

More broadly, the accelerating decay of the Soviet Union, and the Party's inability as an institution to deal with it, may have brought Volkogonov to the realization that his duty as an officer was to support the legitimate holders of state power, whoever they may be, who were now left to contend with the fallout of Communist rule. In other words, by abandoning his loyalties to dogma and swearing a new allegiance to the state, Volkogonov may have been among the first of his brethren to take the final step from Marxist officer to professional officer.

The Unresolved Agenda

By late 1988, the civil-military situation was mired in confusion. If national security was part of the unresolved agenda of 1986, by 1988 that agenda had expanded to include arms control, Soviet-American relations, military prestige, draft issues, *glasnost'*, and in the end, the authority of the Party itself. Efforts by the chief of the MPA were half-hearted and ineffectual; Lizichev and some of the political chiefs of the services seemed, by 1988, only partly willing to defend the Party line, while the intellectuals in the MPA academies openly criticized Gorbachev's plans as well as his general attitude toward the Soviet Armed Forces. The participation of the minister of defense in this debate only added to the confusion, as he vacillated between the hard-line rhetoric of a field commander and the more obedient tone of a political appointee.

The year ended with a watershed event for both Soviet foreign policy and Soviet civil-military relations, as Mikhail Gorbachev appeared before the United Nations in December 1988 and offered uni-

---

[113] D. Volkogonov, *Triumf i tragediia* (Moscow: Novosti, 1989), vol. 2, book 2, p. 249.
[114] Ibid., pp. 250–252.

lateral conventional force reductions. It would precipitate another round of criticism, and another round of personnel changes. It was to be the first real showdown, without pretense and for high stakes, between Gorbachev and his critics in the high command. In the immediate future, he would win and they would lose, for Gorbachev had one trump card that he was until early 1989 unwilling to use against several members of the senior military: he could fire them. In March 1989, he played that card.

[7]

The End of an Era: The Soviet Armed Forces and the "Political Struggle"

Yes, . . . tensions in the world have lessened. This has a place.
. . . But, you know, a lessening—this doesn't mean a full liquidation, and the military danger for us and our allies still remains. And so then it is objectively necessary for us to have
Armed Forces of corresponding quality. This must be sensibly
evaluated and recognized.
                                    —Marshal Akhromeev, July 1989

What a beautiful fix we are in now; peace has been declared.
          —Napoleon Bonaparte at the Treaty of Amiens, 1802

"WHEN WILL THE DENIGRATION END?"

Until 1989, the civil-military agenda had been a relatively specialized one, centered specifically on control of Soviet defense policy.
The 1990s, however, found the Soviet military in a new kind of struggle, in which nothing could be taken for granted. The "political struggle," as Soviet officers called it, became at times a physical battle as
Soviet servicemen were literally assaulted in the streets. Gen. Mikhail
Moiseev spoke for many when he revealed his dissatisfaction with the
results of the February 1990 Plenum of the Central Committee:

True, it cannot be denied that the Party and the government show tre-
mendous concern for the Armed Forces. But we also cannot close our
eyes to the fact that in the public consciousness today, the army's role is
belittled, and attempts are being made to drive a wedge between the
army and the people. *This is, I am convinced, a direct failure of our party and
soviet organs.*
  We are prepared to fulfill any order of the Motherland for the defense

[205]

of the Soviet people. But together we must do everything to ensure that the people do not lose faith in the army.[1]

Maj. Gen. Nikolai Kuznetsov of Moscow put it more plainly when he called in to a radio question-and-answer session with Marshal Akhromeev in April 1990: "Comrade Marshal of the Soviet Union, when will the denigration of our country and everything that we hold sacred end?"[2]

The beginning of the "denigration" can be traced back to December 1988, when Gorbachev abandoned the search for civil-military consensus and turned to the more dramatic and reliable methods of subjective control: unilateral reductions in the military and political sackings within the high command in particular. These actions, the final blow to the civil-military contract, would strip Gorbachev of his last military supporters and open a dangerous breach between the political leadership and the senior officers of the Soviet military that persisted until the mass firings of those officers in the wake of the August 1991 coup.

December 1988: The End of an Era

Gorbachev's 1988 United Nations speech, committing the USSR to unilateral arms reductions, was the beginning of the end of an era in Soviet civil-military affairs. Within three months, several high-ranking officers would either resign or be fired, and the civilian leadership would make a dedicated effort to wrest control of the defense agenda from the professional military once and for all, even if it meant taking unilateral arms measures and committing the Soviet Union to them publicly. The Khrushchev pattern had come full circle, with Gorbachev announcing plans that, as would be revealed later, did not carry the imprimatur of the General Staff or the approval of the high command.

One of the most important results of Gorbachev's UN appearance was the departure of Sergei Akhromeev, the widely respected chief of the General Staff. Akhromeev was thought to be a crucial Gorbachev supporter as well as an expert arms negotiator, and Westerners were concerned about the obvious protest signaled by the timing of his resignation. Of more concern, as it turns out, was his replacement,

---

[1] "Zadachi u nas odni," *Krasnaia Zvezda*, February 10, 1990, p. 1, emphasis added.
[2] Highlights of the radio program were reported in *Krasnaia Zvezda*, April 24, 1990, p. 1.

Mikhail Moiseev. Moiseev, although a loyal and smart officer, was hardly more amenable to Gorbachev's plans than was Akhromeev. The chief is instrumental in setting the tone of the relationship of the high command to the leadership, and this unusual turnover apparently caused more problems than it was supposed to solve.[3] The more important question concerns the similarity of views between Moiseev and Akhromeev, and the inability to replace Akhromeev with a more agreeable officer, for it suggests that Gorbachev in 1990 finally ran out of supporters for his plans within the military.

There was one other sign of Gorbachev's desperation in 1990. In an ostentatious attempt to sooth bruised military pride and to imbue the minister of defense with authority he might otherwise have lacked, Dmitrii Yazov was promoted to Marshal of the Soviet Union, four years after Gorbachev had made it clear that the rank was never again to be conferred in peacetime. Although dismissed at the time by some analysts as a "gold watch" for impending retirement, the granting of a marshal's star to a mediocrity like Yazov in contravention of Gorbachev's own policy was actually a sign of the decay of the civil-military relationship; it also represented the degree to which Gorbachev, in his frustration, was willing to accede to the methods of subjective control. The appointment was not only a political surprise, but it was surrounded as well by the type of fawning, almost embarrassing, Soviet rhetoric rarely seen in the days of *glasnost'*: the Marshal, according to TASS, is "a tall, well-built Siberian known for his practical gumption and rare capacity for work," who never forgets a detail and "intersperses his speech with quotes, including poetry."[4]

Whatever the reasons for the promotion of the now-jailed Marshal Yazov, in 1989 Gorbachev had another marshal to contend with: S. F. Akhromeev, soon to be former chief of the General Staff.

Exit Akhromeev

In July 1988, Chief of the General Staff Akhromeev, long thought to be a firm Gorbachev ally, visited the United States. In his meetings with senior American military leaders, he balanced promises of Soviet flexibility on arms control with assertions that Soviet offensive conventional capabilities were purely counteroffensive, and not nearly as

---

[3] Dale Herspring has documented the relationship of the chief of the General Staff to the political leadership in *The Soviet High Command, 1967–1989* (Princeton: Princeton University Press, 1990).

[4] The comments were made on TASS radio. "Yazov Named Marshal of Soviet Union," FBIS-SOV-90-083, April 30, 1990, pp. 82–83.

overwhelming as they had been described in the West. The same day Akhromeev made these statements, the Soviet Foreign Ministry reaffirmed that there would be no unilateral cuts in Soviet forces in the near future.[5] All in all, a smooth visit and promising developments for all concerned.

Five months later, Mikhail Gorbachev (in the wake of earlier moves making himself president of the Soviet government in addition to his previous post as general secretary of the Communist Party) announced unilateral cuts before the United Nations.[6] Akhromeev, as Gorbachev was speaking, resigned. Less than a month later, the first reports emerged from Moscow that Warsaw Pact chief Marshal Kulikov was also being retired.[7]

Akhromeev's resignation was a direct result of Gorbachev's commitment to unilateral action, to which Akhromeev had been opposed for some time. In January 1988, he wrote that "in conditions of the constant military threat being created by the active military preparations of imperialism, defense sufficiency cannot be interpreted one-sidedly, without regard to the developing correlation of forces. It would be even more of a mistake to understand it as unilateral disarmament, a unilateral lessening of our defense efforts." Furthermore, "the limits of defense sufficiency are not set by us, but by the practical actions of the United States and the NATO bloc and their attempts to have a military capability that would ensure military superiority over us."[8] He delivered a very similar speech to a Party *aktiv* meeting at the General Staff in August 1988, which set the tone for statements from several other Soviet officers.[9]

The day before his resignation, Akhromeev told the Bulgarian press:

> Errors in evaluating the likely nature of aggression and in forecasting the possible results of such an aggression are always dangerous and,

[5] Walter Pincus, "Soviet Pledges Military Changes," and "Soviets: No Unilateral Cuts," both from the *Washington Post*, July 13, 1988, p. A16.

[6] Gorbachev had made himself chairman of the Presidium of the Supreme Soviet after Gromyko's death, at that time the office of the official Soviet head of state. Later that office would be superseded by "President of the USSR," a post elected by the Congress of Peoples' Deputies.

[7] Bill Keller, "Soviets Seen Retiring Warsaw Pact Chief," *New York Times*, January 12, 1989, p. A3.

[8] "Warsaw Pact Military Doctrine Described," FBIS-SOV-88–001, January 4, 1988, p. 1.

[9] "Perestroika trebuet del," *Krasnaia Zvezda*, August 13, 1988, p. 2. Among those to follow suit was air force political chief Col. Gen. Batekhin, who supported Akhromeev's conclusion that "the desire for peace does not mean unilateral disarmament." "Za bar'erom zvuka," *Izvestiia*, August 21, 1988, p. 3.

especially given the defensive nature of our strategy, may entail serious consequences. . . . Certain influential circles in the West are now more realistic in evaluating the situation in the Soviet Union and within its Armed Forces, as well as the disastrous consequences which the arms race may produce for world peace. *Other, no less influential circles, however, are relying, as in the past, on the "position of strength" as regards the Soviet Union, are trying to frighten our country and to extort one-sided actions from us.*[10]

The timing of his resignation eliminates any remaining doubt as to Akhromeev's position; it is inconceivable that the chief of the General Staff could be so oblivious to the impact of such a move.

Akhromeev's resignation represented the defection of a previously willing participant in Gorbachev's plans for foreign policy reform. Paul Nitze, for example, described Akhromeev as a solid and flexible partner in arms negotiations who, after the collapse of the Reykjavik summit, put an arm around Nitze's shoulder and said "This was not my fault."[11] Gorbachev's unilateralism was the last straw, however, and when Gorbachev ignored repeated warnings not to do what he was apparently bent on doing in New York, Akhromeev resigned and left the President without a real source of capable support in the military high command except for the unexceptional Dmitrii Yazov.

For a time, Akhromeev was described as an "adviser" to the president of the Soviet Union and a member of the Ministry of Defense Inspectorate, the traditional dumping ground of the Soviet high command. There was some disagreement in Western circles about what this meant, but all evidence pointed to the strong possibility that Akhromeev was out of the foreign policy loop. In a July 1989 interview, Akhromeev described his duties and his working environment: a staff of two, and an office in the Kremlin where he "prepares materials on military-political issues."[12] He claimed he was chosen for the post because of "experience," although this likely meant that his knowledge of the arms control process was too valuable to waste immediately. American officials who attended a high-level May 1990 meeting in Moscow noted that Gorbachev "noticeably ignored [Akhromeev] and went out of his way to give the representative of

---

[10] "Marshal Akhromeev on Military Restructuring," FBIS-SOV-88–237, December 9, 1988, p. 1, my emphasis. The original appeared in Bulgaria's *Rabotnichesko Delo* on December 6.

[11] John Newhouse, *War and Peace in the Nuclear Age* (New York: Knopf, 1989), pp. 395–397.

[12] "Sovetnik predsedatel'ia verkhovnogo soveta," *Krasnaia Zvezda*, July 2, 1989, p. 2.

the armed forces [at this meeting, Col. Gen. B. Omelichev] his say."[13] Another indication of Akhromeev's demotion and ensuing pessimism was the souring of his well-known friendship with the former U.S. Joint Chiefs of Staff head, Admiral William Crowe, who was reportedly "concerned" by changes in the Soviet military after a March 1990 meeting with Akhromeev.[14]

In any event, retirement gave Akhromeev even more latitude to voice his opposition to current trends. In the July 1989 interview, he expressed his growing exasperation this way:

> I'm giving only my personal, and maybe, arguable, point of view. It disturbs me that not all of the people's deputies at present fully understand the objective necessity that our army and navy be at the appropriate qualitative level and to reliably guarantee the nation from aggression. . . .
>
> Like many other servicemen, I think that now there are declarations that hurt military people, for they are unfair and without substance, and sometimes insulting to the uniform. They are not a help to the strengthening of [our] defense capability. In part they arise out of a mistaken evaluation of the military-political situation in the world, that now we have come to such a time when the army has become unnecessary. This opinion is fundamentally mistaken.

Akhromeev continued to be a popular spokesman for the social and political interests of the Soviet military, making the rounds of talk shows and media commentary, and even debating USA/Canada Institute analyst Georgii Arbatov and *Ogonek* editor Vitalii Korotich over the course of months, an exchange which reached the level of heated and personal attacks from both sides.[15] This should not be underestimated, for Akhromeev was a well-respected figure both in the military, where he was thought of as a "soldier's soldier," and in Soviet society at large.

[13] Thomas Friedman, "Gorbachev's Military: A Bigger Role?" *New York Times*, May 21, 1990, p. 14.

[14] David Lynch, "Sour Mood Colors Crowe-Akhromeev Talks," *Defense Week*, April 23, 1990, p. 1.

[15] "Sovetnik predsedatel'ia verkhovnogo soveta," p. 2. The debate has been extensively covered in both the Soviet and the Western media. An example of Akhromeev's point of view can be found in "Za prodolzhenie obsuzhdeniia problemy," *Krasnaia Zvezda*, December 26, 1989, p. 4. Eventually *Ogonek* refused to print follow-up letters from Akhromeev, and he took his case once again to the pages of *Krasnaia Zvezda*; see "Napadki na vooruzhennye sily SSSR. Pochemu?" *Krasnaia Zvezda*, April 8, 1990, pp. 1, 4. For an overview of the debate, see David Remnick, "Kremlin's America Expert Attacks Gorbachev's Chief Military Adviser," *Washington Post*, May 26, 1990, p. 18.

One of the last tangles between Akhromeev and the media found great resonance among many in the USSR, and revealed the depths of Akhromeev's disillusionment. As Akhromeev himself put it during an early 1990 radio interview, "A political struggle is under way, a real conflict between philosophies. We must fight for the truth, for humane, democratic socialism—there is simply no other way." One of the program's callers, a retired colonel, agreed, and in one short outburst expressed the deep ideological and social frustration felt by many Soviet officers: "I read your rebuke to *Ogonek*'s editor-in-chief with great interest," he said, "and share its views completely, like many of my comrades. You gave that reproof with great sincerity, like a real crusader and Communist. We lack true crusaders today. They make themselves scarce when we need to hold a united stance."[16] "Thank you," Akhromeev replied simply, "Then we must fight together."

A few days after the failed coup against Gorbachev, Western media reported that officials of the Procurator's Office went to Akhromeev's apartment to question him about his possible role in the matter. He was found hanged, a suicide note nearby supposedly indicating that he could not go on in the wake of the collapse of the USSR. These, and reports about his complicity in the coup, remain unverified at this writing. Given Akhromeev's growing disillusionment throughout 1989 and 1990, however, it is not hard to accept that he was a co-conspirator, or that he would take his own life when the end of the Soviet Union itself was at hand.

If Akhromeev resigned in protest, it stands to reason that the leadership would have hoped for a more pliable replacement. But Mikhail Moiseev, an able officer and winner of the Gold Medal during his years at the General Staff Academy, proved to be more difficult than Akhromeev.

Enter Moiseev

The new Chief, Col. Gen. Mikhail Moiseev, when appointed was a relatively young (fifty) field commander, two steps lower in rank than Akhromeev and several steps down the ladder of seniority in Moscow, with a solid but unremarkable professional record. His connection to Moscow was almost certainly Yazov, the man he replaced

---

[16] "Akhromeev Answers Soldiers' Phone Questions," FBIS-SOV-90-081, April 26, 1990, p. 78. For other responses to Akhromeev's performance as well as similar appearances by Aleksandr Iakovlev, see "Kuda smotrit Politburo?" *Krasnaia Zvezda*, June 14, 1990, p. 1.

as commander of the Far Eastern Military District when Yazov was made a deputy minister of defense. Two *Radio Liberty* observers were probably correct when they suggested that Gorbachev "did not want a military genius; all he needed was a young unconnected military organizer whose major quality would be loyalty."[17] But Moiseev, like Yazov, was a career field officer, and he had his own views about the direction of Soviet defense policy. many of them highly critical of efforts to restructure the work of the General Staff. At times his rhetoric was more blistering than Akhromeev's, and it is indicative of the Gorbachev leadership's eventual lack of options that they accepted Yazov's recommendation of this tough-talking, headstrong officer.[18]

Still, Moiseev was willing to defend the unilateral cuts that led Akhromeev to resign. He confronted this problem head-on in a 1989 article, in which he acknowledged that "our unilateral initiatives have raised an understandable anxiety in many Soviet people about the reliable guaranteeing of our national security." He nonetheless defended the reductions as a stabilizing influence on the East-West relationship.[19] Although later comments have revealed that Moiseev probably shared that anxiety, he did loyal service in allaying public fears as best he could.

One of the most complete examples of such a defense took place in mid-1989, in a response to a letter to *Kommunist Vooruzhennykh Sil* from attorney Nina Koldaeva, who asked if the "incredible hastiness" of the reductions was not endangering Soviet security. Moiseev replied by making clearly uncomplimentary reference to the Khrushchev reductions of 1960, "when we were in the 'Cold War'"; the current reductions, he said, are in no way comparable. "Yes, it is a bold step of the Soviet government. Yes, it is a far from simple decision which, naturally, does not make us stronger. But neither does it make us weaker." More interesting, and more honestly, he told Koldaeva that "he would be committing a great sin against the truth" if he tried to tell her that questions concerning reorganization of the Armed Forces were discussed "with full unanimity."[20]

---

[17] Milan Hauer and Alexander Rahr, "New Chief of Soviet General Staff Appointed," *Radio Liberty Reports*, RL 546/88, December 16, 1988, p. 3. One Soviet official connected to foreign policy told me in 1989 that Moiseev's appointment was part of a dedicated political decision to promote "mediocrity" in the Soviet military.

[18] After the coup, Gorbachev suggested Moiseev as interim defense minister, no doubt a desperate and confused move which was quickly quashed by Yeltsin.

[19] M. Moiseev, "Sokrashchenie vooruzhennykh sil i vooruzhenii—garantiia bezopasnosti," *Mezhdunarodnaia Zhizn* (August 1989), p. 9.

[20] M. Moiseev, "Eshche raz o prestizhe armii," *Kommunist Vooruzhennykh Sil* 10 (May 1989), p. 7.

Although less hostile to Gorbachev's troop reductions ("we need to economize even in defense") than was his predecessor, this is little consolation in light of Moiseev's other views.[21] He began his tenure as Chief, for example, with a warning that "it is impossible also not to see the resistance of reactionary imperialist circles," and that Soviet arms overtures do not "signify an underestimation of the level of the military danger that exists to this day, [as well as its] scale and character." Even when praising Gorbachev's achievements in East-West relations, Moiseev struck a pessimistic note, adding that despite the thaw in East-West relations, "the radical turning point in international relations has not taken place, [and] military construction in the NATO states as before is realized in the course of aggressive doctrines." The usual military phraseology is to point out that positive processes are "not irreversible"; Moiseev went a step further by hinting that those processes were not yet all that positive. He followed this statement with a recounting of NATO's conventional strength (3.6 million men), and a repetition of Navy CINC Chernavin's oft-stated complaints about the provocative nature of American naval maneuvers in the Pacific that are conducted too close to the shores of the Soviet Far East.

More surprising was Moiseev's adoption of a definitively non-Gorbachevian line, in which, like Akhromeev before him, he argued for a symmetrical response to the American threat.

> Precipitousness in any matter is dangerous. And this is all the more so when we are talking about the preservation of peace and the defense of the nation. Here it is especially important, as they say, "not to lose touch with the earth." The reality is that the USA, for example, has not given up, and is not thinking of giving up, even one of its military-technical programs. Moreover, they are talking about equipping their armed forces with the kind of weapons systems for which the search for countermeasures will demand many times more time and resources from the Soviet Union. Thus the issue here is not some sort of "imaginary military threat" to our country invented, as some think, by military men, but in the urgent necessity of a search for new ways to guarantee the reliable defense of the peaceful labor of the Soviet people.[22]

Moiseev was attempting to support two essentially conflicting arguments: one that accepts limits on military growth, the other that

[21] M. Moiseev, "S pozitsii oboronitel'noi doktriny," *Krasnaia Zvezda*, February 10, 1989, p. 2.
[22] Ibid.

warns of a harsh "reality" in which the West will quickly outpace the USSR in the race for military-technical superiority. Meanwhile, Gorbachev's statements repeatedly downplayed the dominance of technology in military affairs, and it is doubtful that Moiseev was unaware of the implications of his statement.

Whatever Moiseev's views on defense policy, one thing was certain: he would not accept the reformation of the armed forces from the outside—that is, initiated by civilians. Twice in February 1989 he made it clear that the "dozens" of proposals sent to the General Staff on restructuring the armed forces were "absolutely unrealistic."[23] Why? Because the proposals were not thoroughly grounded in military science (that term again) and because they did not take into account the continuing NATO threat.[24] Like Gareev and Volkogonov, Moiseev believed that threat to be real, despite the fact that "some [Soviet] authors in our publications try to cast doubt on the reality of the military threat and on the rectitude of defense measures that have been adopted." As he told Nina Koldaeva, such measures are off-limits for consideration by civilians: "On strictly military questions, only professional military men can give a competent answer to the leaders of the party and state, to whom the people have entrusted their defense."[25] (Or as Yazov angrily put it, why should the Soviet Armed Forces ask "some old lady in a shop" what kind of army she wants?)[26]

TROUBLE IN THE GENERAL STAFF

Even before the UN speech, there were signs of trouble in the General Staff, including comments by Gareev, who sounded off in June 1988 during an interview with *Argumenty i Fakty*. "In all branches of activity of the Armed Forces many new and complex questions arise. A fundamental question is about the reality of the military threat to us from the imperialist states. Certain press organs have begun to cast doubt on the presence of such a threat, and conse-

[23] Ibid.
[24] M. Moiseev, "Na strazhe mira i sotsializma," *Krasnaia Zvezda*, February 23, 1989, p. 2.
[25] Moiseev, "Eshche raz," p. 7.
[26] "Well," Yazov continued, "what does she know about what kind of army we should have?" The comment was made in a December 1989 television interview. See "Yazov Interviewed at Moscow Officers' Meeting," FBIS-SOV-89–241, December 18, 1989, p. 121.

quently, on the necessity of defense measures, of the defense of the Fatherland." Positive international changes, he added, must also be considered along with "military preparations of the imperialist states," which continue to constitute "a real military threat." In Gareev's view, Soviet doctrine was indeed defensive, but apparently only during the initial repulsion of aggression, after which offensive means must ensure the destruction of the aggressor. In any event, Gareev asserted, NATO simply was not ready to deal with the USSR in good faith.[27] (This latter point was picked up by a *Krasnaia Zvezda* reviewer in September 1988, who said that "realistic tendencies" in NATO military policy are not yet "dominant.")[28]

Gareev's comments reflected a more pervasive opposition within the General Staff itself. A report of the December 1988 party *aktiv* meeting in the General Staff indicated that the Central Committee was aware of this opposition, and the report reiterated Party criticisms of the General Staff that were left unpublished in the materials of the June 1987 Plenum of the Central Committee:

> A subject of special concern in the current period was the work of the General Staff and all of its *podrazdelenii* [subordinate units] and party organizations on the elimination of shortcomings noted by the Central Committee in June 1987. And in the report as well as in the speeches it was noted that the work conducted has been great. But this is only a part of the matter. Approaches have changed principally not only in the organization of duty and service in the troops, including the solving of extraordinary problems in peacetime, but also in the theoretical bases of a whole series of standing conceptions.
>
> In consideration of the defensive military doctrine, plans are being reworked, and documents and regulations are being defined more precisely and perfected; other work is being carried on as well.[29]

The report does not elaborate on these "shortcomings," nor does the report of the June 1987 plenum make detailed reference to such a critical evaluation. (Apparently, *glasnost'* notwithstanding, these sessions of the plenums were still secret.) Most likely the report was based on the poor results in the wake of the January 1987 plenum, discussed in the previous chapter, but it also foreshadowed admissions to be made by the new Chief later that General Staff cadres were unsupportive of the new defensive doctrine.

[27] "Vooruzhennye Sily v usloviiakh glasnosti," *Argumenty i Fakty* 39 (1988), p. 4.

[28] V. Markushin, "Inertsiia protivostoianiia," *Krasnaia Zvezda*, September 13, 1988, p. 3.

[29] "Kursom obnovleniia," *Krasnaia Zvezda*, December 28, 1988, p. 2.

This admission came during Moiseev's speech at the *aktiv* meeting. In the most unusual part of his statement, Moiseev admitted directly that the General Staff had consciously evaded the orders of the civilian leadership:

> One of the most complex problems of military science is the prevention of war. Such a task was never before put before our Armed Forces. . . . It has been put before us to generalize experience and realize in practice the tenets of a defensive military doctrine, and to work out unified views prevention of aggression. Together with this, *it must be noted that military-scientific organizations called upon to provide preliminary deep working through of these questions often lag behind.* In part, one of the questions that has been *insufficiently worked through is connected with the organization and conduct of combat actions of a defensive character.*[30]

The implications are considerable, since this is apparently a direct reference to disobedience in the General Staff. At the very least, it casts doubt on the assertion (made repeatedly by Akhromeev and others) that the new "defensive doctrine" had already been worked out in the General Staff even before it was adopted; it was also another indication that Gorbachev's announcement of the new doctrine in Berlin in 1987 may have taken the Staff by surprise.

Gareev was at the time in charge of military-scientific work in the General Staff, and he and several other officers were directly taken to task. According the report of the *aktiv*, "Communists B. Omelichev, M. Gareev, G. Krivosheev, K. Kobets and E. Evstigneev underwent meaningful criticism" for "shortcomings and negligence in work."[31] The June 1987 plenum took place a month after the publication of the Berlin Declaration, and this public criticism of the staff appeared shortly after Gorbachev's UN speech, all of which suggests that the staff had chosen simply to ignore their new orders and close ranks, an act of direct disobedience that could not go unchallenged by the Central Committee. However, there is no evidence that this passive opposition resulted in serious punishment for any significant number of officers in the high command.

Another episode that supports the possibility that the General Staff simply balked at Gorbachev's call for a defensive doctrine occurred at the 1989 Soviet war games in East Germany involving 18,000 Soviet troops. Western military observers said that the new doctrine had had

[30] Moiseev, "S pozitsii," emphasis added.
[31] "Kursom obnovleniia," p. 2.

no apparent impact on Soviet training. Indeed, the performance was an obvious sham:

> To the surprise of the [Western] officers watching through field glasses, the Soviets allowed their tanks to advance toward dug-in positions without putting infantry on the ground with them. . . .
> Soviet commanders called a halt to the battle just before it looked like the attacking column would win. Elements of the defending motorized rifle regiment launched a counterattack and were called victorious, to the surprise of military observers.[32]

Perhaps even more embarrassing to the Soviets was the response of a young tank driver to a Western reporter's question about his opinion of the change in doctrine. "What new doctrine?" the confused tanker asked.[33]

At the least, there was a sense among some in the General Staff that Gorbachev's unilateral measures should now elicit similar actions from the United States, in essence turning a unilateral offer into an opening bid. Maj. Gen. V. Kuklev, a recent arrival to the General Staff, challenged Western estimates of the European balance shortly after the Gorbachev speech, and he stressed that although the Soviet actions were unilateral, "We have the right to expect an adequately significant answer from the other side."[34] He was supported in this call by *Krasnaia Zvezda* reviewer Manki Ponomarev, who wrote that at NATO headquarters "talk was not about responding steps . . . but how to demand yet greater concessions from the USSR."[35]

Responses from other members of the General Staff were more muted, and some even tried to be supportive of Gorbachev's moves. First identified in the General Staff in spring 1987—the same time as both the Rust affair and the Berlin Declaration—Col. Gen. V. Lobov

[32] George Wilson, "Westerners Fault Soviet War Game," *Washington Post*, April 20, 1989, p. A36.

[33] Ibid. During a May 1989 discussion with General Staff representatives in Moscow, I asked about this particular exercise. The rather irritated response was that no conclusions could be drawn from the small part of the exercise witnessed by Western officers, and that the substantive change in battlefield training would appear in 1990 or 1991 exercises. This, of course, was before the collapse of the Warsaw Pact, and the military point is now moot. The political possibilities surrounding the 1989 exercises remain intriguing.

[34] V. Kuklev, "Po printsipu razumnoi dostatochnosti," *Krasnaia Zvezda*, December 28, 1988, p. 3.

[35] M. Ponomarev, "Realizm idei, smelost' podkhodov," *Krasnaia Zvezda*, December 11, 1988, p. 3.

was a consistent defender of the New Thinking, the new doctrine, and *perestroika*.[36] He also refrained from anti-American rhetoric; in a 1988 lead piece in *Voenno-Istoricheskii Zhurnal*, he did not make a single reference to the United States or to the present international situation, most unusual in a historical journal whose lead articles are notable for their discussions of the future rather than the past.[37] Perhaps the ultimate proof of Lobov's loyalty is that he was chosen chief of the General Staff after Moiseev was dismissed, at Boris Yeltsin's insistence, under a cloud of suspicion after the coup. (This appointment, as it turned out, only lasted until December 1991, but it was noteworthy under the circumstances.)

Even Lobov, however, joined the military call for a Western response to the cuts. In May 1989, he said that the reductions were carefully studied in light of world conditions and would not affect international stability or Soviet security, but that "such actions have their limits" and further progress would rely on U.S. moves.[38] Another of Kuklev's colleagues, Iu. Lebedev, also voiced his ire over the Western reaction to Gorbachev's proposal. The cuts, he argued, were not propaganda, nor did they injure Soviet security. Nonetheless, they were deeply significant and Lebedev was upset at any implication that they were not: "Judging from some statements in the West, their scale and depth are not yet acknowledged by everyone."[39] Yazov made the same point a week later in a speech to a party conference in the Group of Soviet Forces Germany (later renamed the Western Group of Forces), and repeated the warning that the processes of disarmament are not irreversible; he also took the opportunity to yet again criticize the slow pace of *perestroika* in the army.[40]

As far as many in the senior command were concerned, however, the December 7 reductions were a bad idea even before they were proposed. Air Defense chief Tret'iak used Khrushchev's 1960 cuts as an object lesson in the multifaceted dangers of unilateralism in an early 1988 complaint:

> We've already had sorry experiences of this kind. At the end of the 50s the USSR reduced its army unilaterally by 1.2 million men. The econo-

[36] "General Staff Officer on Impact of New Thinking," FBIS-SOV-88–064, April 4, 1988, p. 51. See also V. Lobov, "Nachinaetsia s komandirom," *Krasnaia Zvezda*, February 3, 1987, p. 2.

[37] V. Lobov, "Strategiia pobedy," *Voenno-Istoricheskii Zhurnal* (May 1988).

[38] "Nadezhnyi oplot mira," *Krasnaia Zvezda*, May 13, 1989, p. 5.

[39] "Sokrashchenie armii i oboronosposobnost'," *Krasnaia Zvezda*, December 16, 1988, p. 3.

[40] "Perestroika trebuet dela," *Krasnaia Zvezda*, December 25, 1988, p. 2.

mists estimated that this enabled us to set up ten house building plants. On the surface it looked rather convincing. But only on the surface. As a military man, I'll tell you that the step was a rash one, it dealt a terrible blow to our defense capacity, and at our officer personnel. The army lost prestige in the eyes of the people. To be honest, we are still feeling this. Therefore any changes in our army must be considered a thousand times over.[41]

Others have picked up on the Khrushchev comparison as well. "I well remember that time," the deputy chief of the Air Force general staff, Lt. Gen. A. Pozdniakov, said in early 1989. "Although I was a young pilot at the time, I saw perfectly well the thoughtlessness and haste of [those] actions. . . . Under no circumstances are the mistakes of the past being repeated."[42] Asked about the reduction of 800 Soviet aircraft, Pozdniakov pointedly remarked that 800 planes would equal the air forces of France and Belgium taken together, or somewhat more than all of Britain's air force.

Gorbachev and the Navy

Some of the most vehement criticism of the unilateral reductions came from the Soviet Navy, probably because the Navy realized that it was due to bear—as it had under Khrushchev—the brunt of Gorbachev's plans for economizing in the military.

The Soviet Navy reacted almost instantaneously to the Gorbachev speech. As Gorbachev was giving his speech to the UN, Navy CINC Chernavin was complaining about American naval activities in that day's issue of *Krasnaia Zvezda*. Declaring in the title that "Restraint should be mutual," Chernavin pointed out that the Soviet Navy has already taken its share of reductions in accordance with the defensive doctrine. Besides, he said, the arms control ball was now in NATO's court, a direct contradiction of the spirit of the UN speech. Chernavin even went so far as to suggest that "if the naval activities of the USSR in the Asian-Pacific region are evaluated objectively . . . then it is not difficult to see that the Soviet Pacific fleet is designated, first and foremost, for the coastal defense of the Soviet Far East."[43]

Chernavin was being deceptive: this is a complaint, not a defense. The Navy's true desires were perhaps better expressed in June 1987

---

[41] "Reliable Defense First and Foremost," *Moscow News*, February 21, 1988, p. 12.

[42] A. Pozdniakov, "800 samoletov," *Krasnaia Zvezda*, January 18, 1988, p. 2.

[43] V. Chernavin, "Problemy Tikhogo okeana: Sderzhannost' dolzhna byt' vzaimnoi," *Krasnaia Zvezda*, December 7, 1988, p. 3.

by Adm. K. Makarov, chief of the naval staff, who managed to link even the Strategic Defense Initiative to naval power:

> Our country is a great naval power. It sails the waters of fourteen seas and three oceans. The defense of the Fatherland from an aggressor's attack coming from the seas or oceans is a vital necessity, all the more so now when the international situation is so highly alarming and explosively dangerous, when the forces of imperialism and reaction are bringing forth plans for a new world war.
>
> The Washington administration does not want to abandon its program of "Star Wars," and continues the arms race. . . . It is not accidental that the Pacific ocean is being turned into an arena of future aggression against the USSR and its friends and allies. To frustrate these sinister plans is the duty of the soldiers of the Armed Forces, and above all the Navy.[44]

"Above all" the Navy? So much for coastal defense.

Others in the Navy were upset as well. In June 1988, Capt. 3d Rank A. Petrov, the senior assistant commander of the cruiser *Aleksandr Nevskii*, charged that questions of defense and patriotic education had heretofore been dealt with an "insufficiently precise" way. Furthermore, he warned, "we do not have the right to allow the loss of the military parity with the West that was so hard to attain." Petrov claimed to speak for many on his ship, and his letter is all the more interesting because of the front page, lead-off position it got in *Krasnaia Zvezda*, in the space usually reserved for editorials.[45]

Captain Petrov and his men had good examples to follow among their superiors. In February 1988, as Yazov and the others at the Seventieth Anniversary celebration were praising the improvements in the international situation, Chernavin wrote in *Morskoi Sbornik:*

> The Leninist conclusion about the source of military danger has been supported by history. The civil war and the intervention. . . . Armed provocations on the eastern and western borders of the USSR in the 20s and 30s. . . . The Great Patriotic War. . . .
>
> And today global imperialism has not rejected its aggressive aspirations. The core of the West's strategy and militarist programs, as before, remains social revanche, the attempt to guarantee military superiority in space, on land and at sea, and the igniting of military conflicts in various parts of the world.[46]

---

[44] K. V. Makarov, "Na strazhe morskikh rubezhei," *Sovetskii Voin* 13 (June 1987), p. 2.
[45] "Sokhranit' paritet," *Krasnaia Zvezda*, June 4, 1988, p. 1.
[46] V. Chernavin, "Vysokaia bditel'nost' i boevaia gotovnost'—velenie vremeni," *Morskoi Sbornik* 2 (1988), p. 3.

Chernavin then went on to point out the specifically naval aspect of this multipronged American drive; this kind of pessimistic rhetoric is easily found throughout the naval literature. Like Chernavin, the naval writers are distinguished from their colleagues in other services by their constant interpretation of the threat in primarily naval terms.[47] This was also the case in a 1988 naval treatment of the Berlin Declaration.[48]

Some naval officers returned to the idea of preventive war, a threat that was as unlikely in 1988 and 1989 as it is now in post-Warsaw Pact Europe. Nonetheless, in June 1988 Capt. Iu. Varganov argued in *Morskoi Sbornik* that the idea of preventive war, "as shown by historical experience, was always in the arsenal of the aggressor."[49] He also made a veiled warning about the need to keep military resource allocations secure. "It must not be forgotten," he wrote, "that it is precisely on the reckoning of attaining the advantage in the military-technical area that imperialism is trying to gain military-strategic superiority over the USSR. The measures of the CPSU and the Soviet state for equipping the Armed Forces carried and carry a necessary and responding character."[50] Varganov even took a small shot at Brezhnev-bashers: formulations on the character of the armed forces, he says, were "first worked out at the 26th Congress" and further "creative development" was done at the XXVII thus implicitly giving Brezhnev credit—accurately—as an early influence on Gorbachev's thinking.

Perhaps Gorbachev assumed that the success of the INF Treaty would smooth the way for his other intentions in arms control. The reverse occurred, however, with opposition to unilateral reductions serving to open the INF Treaty itself to criticism. Doubts about the wisdom of the treaty were one more step in the general disintegration of the civil-military dialogue on national security.

The INF Treaty, "Compensation," and the Strategic Rocket Forces

The military frustration with Gorbachev's unilateralism was complimented by the appearance of criticisms and warnings about the INF

---

[47] See "Vernost' ideiam: dela velikogo Oktiabria," *Morskoi Sbornik* 11 (1985), esp. p. 4; "Istoriia uchit i preduprezhdaet," *Morskoi Sbornik* 8 (1985), p. 9, in particular regarding American Pacific intentions, "preparations that cannot but cause anxiety"; "Okeanskye vakhty Flota," *Morskoi Sbornik* 7 (1987), p. 4.

[48] V. Gulin and I. Kondyrev, "Oboronitel'naia napravlennost' sovetskoi voennoi doktriny," *Morskoi Sbornik* 2 (1988).

[49] Iu. Varganov, "Vozrastanie rokovodiashchei roli KPSS v voennom stroitel'stve," *Morskoi Sbornik* 6 (1988), p. 10.

[50] Ibid.

Treaty. The major complaint that surfaced among the Soviet military concerning the INF Treaty was that it has led to "compensation" or "rearming" by NATO, thus implying that the treaty was a kind of sucker's bet in which the USSR showed unilateral restraint. This criticism is pervasive among all the branches; Yazov himself on Revolution Day 1988 made the same accusation.[51] The July 1988 meeting of Warsaw Pact defense ministers, at which Yazov and Kulikov appeared without other Soviet civilians, also accused the West of compensatory measures in its communique.[52]

Others repeated the "compensation" argument in later months. General Staff officer G. V. Batenin, described as a "military expert of the Central Committee," scored NATO inertia, adding that "in the case of the reduction of one type of weapon it is necessary for the West to compensate with another."[53] And Air Defense Forces (PVO) chief Tret'iak put it more dramatically on Soviet television in April 1988:

> With feverish haste the NATO reactionary circles are developing plans for filling the nuclear breach in Western Europe which allegedly emerged after [the INF Treaty] was signed in Washington. The intensity of aircraft flights, exercises, and maneuvers conducted by capitalist countries in immediate proximity to our border is increasing. By their scale, duration, numerical strength, and the degree of saturation with military equipment they exceed reasonable limits by far, while their spearhead is still pointed against the Soviet Union and the Warsaw Pact member-countries.
>
> Let us get it straight: The new political thinking and the principle of sufficiency in defense have not yet won the minds of all Western politicians and military.[54]

The only thing missing from Tret'iak's diatribe is a direct insult to Gorbachev personally, for his statement is a clear rejection of everything Gorbachev had stood for in foreign affairs, delivered not to a closed military audience but over the open Soviet airwaves. Tret'iak may have been saddled with the PVO, but he obviously did not intend to play the part of a caretaker.[55] (After the coup, Tret'iak was

---

[51] "Rech' tovarishcha Yazova D. T.," *Krasnaia Zvezda*, November 8, 1988, p. 1.

[52] *Krasnaia Zvezda*, July 9, 1988, p. 1.

[53] G. V. Batenin [interview], "Evropa posle Varshavy," *Krasnaia Zvezda*, August 31, 1988, p. 1.

[54] "Tret'iak Marks Celebration," FBIS-SOV-88–069, April, 11, 1988, p. 85.

[55] The PVO commander was also a Warsaw Pact deputy commander for air defense, and Gorbachev's spring 1988 proposal to cut aircraft in Europe would necessarily do serious damage to Tret'iak's service.

dismissed, and the PVO was eliminated as a separate service after being absorbed by the Air Force and elements of a strategic defense force.[56])

The aging Air Force chief Marshal Efimov was one of the few supporters of the Gorbachev line on the INF Treaty. It is not surprising that the air force, generally the technological elite in every military, and with a fairly stable mission, was willing to be more supportive of reform than mass organizations slated for deep cuts such as the army. (After the coup, Yeltsin and Gorbachev would eventually reach into the air force for a loyal minister of defense: Efimov's successor, Colonel General—and later Marshal of Aviation—Evgenii Shaposhnikov.) In March 1988, Efimov was asked about parity, and Efimov answered that the INF Treaty did not disrupt overall parity when "political, military, moral and psychological factors" were taken into account. Efimov, who also pointed out that U.S. weapons are so deadly that their removal is worth it, finishing by saying that "I think we are on the right path and are doing everything to ensure that our army and navy are at the requisite level of readiness."[57]

Criticism of the INF Treaty was coupled with attempts to shore up the battered honor of the Strategic Rocket Forces. The attacks on the SRF that began in 1986 were designed to deemphasize the glory and preeminence that has accrued to this most particularistic of the Soviet services, and they were accompanied by the firing of both the SRF service chief and its top political officer, both of whom were service loyalists.[58] The new SRF CINC Iu. Maksimov kept a low profile; the 1988 article for Rocket Forces Day was written by political chief V. Rodin, who was at the time generally uncontroversial.[59] (In 1990, however, Rodin let slip one small insight into the Rocket Forces reaction to the INF Treaty: "Of course it's difficult for [missileers] to destroy that which they not so long ago cherished. In conversation,

[56] See John W. R. Lepingwell, "Gorbachev's Strategic Forces Initiative: Dissolving the Air Defense Forces," RFE/RL Reports, November 20, 1991.

[57] "Yefimov Recalls Past Service, Celebrates Holiday," FBIS-SOV-88–043, March 4, 1988, p. 59.

[58] For typical examples of SRF glorification, see "Vysokoi meroi boegotovnosti," *Kommunist Vooruzhennykh Sil* 10 (May 1985), and "Vsegda v boevoi gotovnosti," *Krasnaia Zvezda*, April 25, 1985, p. 2. This service particularism does not seem to be as pronounced in one of the subordinates passed over for the job of CINC, Col. Gen. Iashin. See Iu. Iashin, "Rezerv na vydvizhenie," *Krasnaia Zvezda*, February 15, 1986, p. 2. Iashin become a deputy minister of defense for electronics.

[59] V. Rodin [interview] "Zakon zhizni—boegotovnost'," *Krasnaia Zvezda*, November 19, 1988, p. 2. It should be noted that the appearance of Rodin was a trend that occurred in the other services as well, where articles to commemorate service holidays were written more often by political officers or chiefs of staff rather than service heads.

veterans even avoid the words 'destruction of the rocket.' In their lexicon, they are 'parting with the rocket.')[60]

The SRF propaganda response to Gorbachev's early attacks did not slow the steady deemphasis of the SRF's status. In his 1987 Rocket Forces Day *prikaz*, Yazov wrote:

> In conditions of the complex foreign policy situation in which the threat of nuclear war exists, and when the reactionary imperialist circles, ignoring the lessons of history, strive for military superiority over the USSR and the Warsaw Pact nations, the soldiers of the Rocket Forces and artillery persistently master modern military equipment and fulfill with honor the tasks set before them for the defense the great gains of socialism.[61]

Compare this with his *prikaz* a year later, where he leaves out an acknowledgment of the special role of the SRF, saying only that "the positive processes in world development have not yet become irreversible. Through the fault of imperialist reaction the threat of war exists."[62] Indeed, Yazov made a point of the absence of strategic weapons from Revolution Day parades in 1988, noting that it was "evidence of the new thinking, the triumph of which led to the signing of the historic INF Treaty."[63]

The SRF continued to fight on, as a January 1989 article by SRF Colonel A. Belousov made clear. After stressing approval of the INF Treaty, he then launched into this glorification of his colleagues while sneaking in a shot about NATO compensatory measures:

> How in general is our missile shield—hasn't a gaping hole appeared in it? . . . It's possible, of course, to give the impression that these questions simply do not exist. It's possible to pass over them in silence. But that doesn't make them any less sharp.
>
> This is something that our missileers—people of political maturity [who] understand the situation from the state perspective [*po-gosudarstvennomu*]—that we know well. But we also know something else: it is early to be complacent. The positive changes in world developments, alas, have not yet become irreversible. In the West there are not a few forces that long for the "good old days" of the arms race, and who cannot in principle accept the new political thinking. Even the less than five percent of the general quantity of nuclear weapons that composes

---

[60] "Esli podpishem dogovor," *Krasnaia Zvezda*, November 18, 1990, p. 1.

[61] "Prikaz ministra oborony SSSR," *Krasnaia Zvezda*, November 19, 1987, p. 1.

[62] "Prikaz ministra oborony SSSR," *Krasnaia Zvezda*, November 20, 1988, p. 1.

[63] "Rech' tovarishcha Yazova D. T.," *Krasnaia Zvezda*, November 8, 1988, p. 2.

the liquidated [INF] brings calls from them for "compensation" and "rearmament."

And lest anyone remain in doubt about the sacrifices demanded of the SRF missileers, Col. Belousov went on:

> They set themselves before the launcher and wait. They wait every second, by themselves, alone—for the command to launch. When the command is received, it means that someone's evil hand on the other side has already pressed the fateful button. And maybe "Minutemen," or maybe "Tridents," are already carrying their kilotons of death here. . . . Your mission now: only to succeed in launching your own missiles, before the seismological hurricane from the collapsing explosion hammers them flat in their silos or gets you yourself. Missileers have no other conception of a retaliatory strike.[64]

One can only wonder about the "other" concepts of retaliation that Belousov implicitly criticizes, or who represented those concepts.

The Demise of "Reasonable Sufficiency"

By 1989, the combination of cuts in conventional as well as nuclear arms had led to the nearly complete abandonment of Gorbachev's view of sufficiency by the military. Even Yazov jumped ship: in a 1989 speech to the Central Committee, he warned that West was making "intensive military preparations," and that this "obligates us to have not only sufficient, but unconditionally reliable defense, and combat-ready armed forces in our own country as well as in the Warsaw Pact as a whole."[65]

One sign of the opposition to reasonable sufficiency came in the leadership's effort to defend the concept in the pages of *Kommunist* in May 1989.[66] In a major article, USA/Canada Institute member L. Semeiko attempted to revive the Gorbachev vision of sufficiency while at the same time delivering a rebuke to officers—and Yazov by name—who were subverting the Party's plans.

Semeiko's defense began with the acknowledgment that "reasonable sufficiency" has no meaning, an admission which again raises doubts about the military claim that Soviet forces were already being

---

[64] A. Belousov, "Liudi u pul'tov," *Krasnaia Zvezda*, January 3, 1989, p. 2.

[65] D. Yazov, "Armiia druzhby i bratstva narodov," *Kommunist* 20 (October 1989), p. 5.

[66] L. Semeiko, "Razumnaia dostatochnost'—put' k nadezhnomu miru," *Kommunist* 7 (May 1989), pp. 112–127.

restructured along these lines.[67] If nobody knew what it meant, how was it serving as a blueprint? His central thesis concerned the relationship between parity and stability, and he pointedly attacked the definition of "nuclear parity" given in the *Military-Encyclopedic Dictionary* as too imprecise: "But just what kind of equality [*ravenstvo*] are we talking about, and according to which indicators of military potential?"[68] This was an attempt to cover ground lost by Gorbachev in 1986, for Semeiko was trying to set up the original line of Gorbachev's argument that the military (i.e., strictly quantitative) view of stability and parity is insufficient.

This leads to a surprising moment of direct criticism, in which Semeiko attacked Yazov's formulation of sufficiency. In earlier statements, Yazov had defined sufficiency in conventional arms as "the quantity and quality of armed forces capable of reliably guaranteeing the collective defense of the socialist commonwealth." Semeiko's retort was that Yazov's formulation "is sufficiently flexible and so does not fix any kind of concrete level of strength of conventional forces. This, strictly speaking, cannot be allowed, for [such a definition] will always depend upon the character of the military confrontation."[69] In other words: Yazov and the military were only using the terminology of reasonable sufficiency to serve their own ends. Shortly afterward, Yazov gave up trying to mask his preference for "defensive" sufficiency, rather than the Gorbachevian "reasonable" sufficiency.

There is a difference between these terms, and Semeiko knew it. There are several schools of thought marked by these terms, which range from "reliable defense" (the most hard-line military position), to "reasonable sufficiency" (the most liberal civilian formulation.)[70] At one point Semeiko dove into the terminological quandary surrounding the sufficiency debate and attempted to neutralize these differences by ignoring them. "Is there," he asked, "a difference between the general concepts of 'reasonable' and 'defensive' sufficiency?" Semeiko admitted that there are differing opinions on this, but his own inclination was to regard them as the two sides of the same question; namely, determining which forces were sufficient for defense at the lowest (and therefore most rational) level.[71]

[67] Ibid., p. 113.

[68] Ibid., p. 114.

[69] Ibid., p. 117.

[70] For a dissection of these various terms, see Thomas Nichols and Theodore Karasik, "The Impact of Reasonable Sufficiency on the Soviet Ministry of Defense," *U.S. Naval War College Review* (Autumn 1989).

[71] Semeiko, "Razumnaia dostatochnost'," p. 118.

Semeiko's counterattack was a game try, but by 1989 the debate had spun too far out of control, so there was little point in this attempt to redefine the issue along 1986 lines. Without support in the Ministry of Defense or the General Staff, "reasonable sufficiency" became a cottage industry for Soviet intellectuals, and only a slogan for Soviet officers. In neither case was it a viable source of planning concepts.

PROBLEMS AND DIVISIONS IN THE MAIN POLITICAL ADMINISTRATION

The Main Political Administration, the organization that was charged with ensuring military adherence to the Party line, remained divided, although its best and brightest were clear opponents of the New Thinking and its fallout. The main source of opposition was in the MPA academies, where MPA intellectual cadres had been steadfast in their harsh rhetoric and direct challenges to the ideas of the leadership. Other cadres, most notably chiefs of political work in the service branches, stayed relatively obedient to the Gorbachev line, but political differences in the field were harder to spot, since it was difficult to tell opponents of New Thinking apart from colleagues who were simply trying to instill a willingness for battle among their troops. As Col. Gen. N. Repin (then the chief of political work in the Moscow Military District) noted in 1985, it is possible to indoctrinate the troops about the class hatreds and mercilessness of the enemy without necessarily being specific about who that enemy is or exactly when and where he might arrive.[72]

In the main, however, opposition in the MPA was centered not among political officers in the field, but rather among the most intellectual, capable, and visible MPA academics. While it is natural to expect the MPA to concern itself particularly with problems such as preparing youth for military service, stamping out "vegetarian pacifism," and keeping soldiers on their moral and patriotic toes, MPA officers also weighed in with un-Gorbachevian rhetoric on most of the major issues in military affairs and foreign policy. The most vocal representative of the MPA without doubt was Volkogonov, reassigned after almost twenty years in the MPA as the head of the Military History Institute (and within a year to undergo a Damascene conversion to Gorbachev's cause). However, colleagues such as Lukava and Serebriannikov of the Lenin Political-Military Academy, a center of

[72] N. Repin, "Formirovanie moral'no-politicheskikh i boevikh kachestv u voinov," *Kommunist Vooruzhennykh Sil* 10 (May 1985).

conservative thought, continued to wave the bloody shirt even after Volkogonov's departure.

In May 1988 Serebriannikov strengthened earlier themes in his writing, returning again and again to the pessimistic view of international relations that Gorbachev was dedicated to quashing:

> It is perfectly obvious that, as long as imperialist policies are conceived in obsolete categories, as long as an effective mechanism for managing military-political processes in the world is not created, as long as the danger of war exists, and social revanche remains the core of the strategy and militaristic programs of the West's ruling circles, then military means will remain for us a most important factor in restraining the aggressor.[73]

Again, this is the clever end-run around the New Thinking, accepting that Gorbachev's principles are not wrong, but only too early. Nor did he moderate his rhetoric, as his 1988 book, *V. I. Lenin on the Aggressiveness of Imperialism*, showed:

> Imperialism, the cause of two world wars and many hundreds of local wars and conflicts, today creates the threat of a third world war with the use of weapons of huge destructive force. . . .
>   None of the aggressors of the past contemplated a war that could destroy humanity. But the American imperialists not only acknowledge the permissibility and expediency of such a war, but also do all they can to open up preparations for it.

"The war that the imperialists are readying," he concludes, "would be the most reactionary, regressive, unjust and criminal with respect to the interests of the entire international community and human progress."[74]

The notable exceptions to this hawkishness were the chief of the MPA and the heads of political work in the services. Lizichev at first glance seemed very much like the late Epishev, concerned almost entirely with Party-political work, organization, and patriotic education.[75] To some extent, this was to be expected. But it would also be

---

[73] V. Serebriannikov, "Bezopasnost' gosudarstva v iadernyi vek," *Kommunist Vooruzhennykh Sil* 9 (May 1988), p. 36.

[74] V. Serebriannikov, *V. I. Lenin ob agressivnosti imperializma* (Moscow: Voenizdat, 1988), pp. 1, 26.

[75] For examples of Lizichev's work, see *My—patrioty, internatsionalisty* (Sovetskii Obraz Zhizni), (Moscow: DOSAAF, 1985); "Boevoi gotovnosti voisk—partiinuiu zabotu," *Kommunist* 3 (March 1986); "Perestroike partiino-politicheskoi raboty—

expected that the head of the MPA might attempt to carry the struggle for the Party line to his own senior comrades; Epishev, after all, never had to contend with the outright and public disobedience in the officer corps allowed under *glasnost'*. Except for one brief moment in early 1987 when he joined other officers in a defense of the New Thinking, Lizichev never took the lead in restraining conservative opposition to Gorbachev, nor did he take the lead in the patriotism debate. This suggests that whatever tenuous control the leadership may have had over the MPA chief, there was really no firm mechanism for censoring the MPA's more aggressive (in both style and content) thinkers.[76] Lizichev's first deputy, Admiral A. Sorokin, likewise did little to stem the anti-Gorbachev forces.[77]

In general, the most prolific service MPA heads also seem to have been fairly dependable and obedient promulgators of the Gorbachev line.[78] Col. Gen. M. Popkov of the Ground Forces, for example, was most supportive, appearing regularly to comment on *perestroika* and military discipline, two relatively safe topics. He rarely mentioned the international situation.[79] The same may be said of the Air Force representative, Col. Gen. L. Batekhin, and the former PVO head, Col.

---

tseleustremlennost' i delovitost'," *Kommunist Vooruzhennykh Sil* 14 (July 1986); "Na perelomnom etape istorii," *Krasnaia Zvezda*, March 19, 1986, pp. 2–3. For a piece written during his days as top political officer in the Group of Soviet Forces Germany (GSFG), see "Byt' v avangarde—dolg kommunista," *Kommunist Vooruzhennykh Sil* 15 (August 1983). For a biography of Epishev, see A. I. Skril'nik, *General armii A. A. Epishev* (Moscow: Voenizdat, 1989).

76 Another writer of interest is Maj. Gen. M. Iasiukov (professor and Ph.D. in philosophy). See "Vo glave voennogo stroitel'stva," *Krasnaia Zvezda*, December 3, 1986, pp. 2–3; "Problemy voiny i mira—ostreishaia problema sovremennosti," *Kommunist Vooruzhennykh Sil* 10 (May 1986).

77 See A. Sorokin, "Partiia—nash polkovodets," *Kommunist Vooruzhennykh Sil* 9 (May 1985); "V tsentre partiinoi raboty—chelovek," *Na putiiakh perestroiki* (Moscow: Voenizdat, 1987); "Za vysokie rezul'taty partiinoi raboty," *Kommunist Vooruzhennykh Sil* 19 (October 1987); "70 let na zashchite zavoevanii velikogo oktiabria," *Voprosii Istorii KPSS* 2 (1988).

78 This is also true of other MPA chiefs. For a recent example, see Lt. Gen. A. I. Makunin (MPA head in the Southern Group of Forces since 1984), "Rukovodstvo KPSS—osnova osnov moguchestva Sovetskikh Vooruzhennykh Sil," *Voenno-Istoricheskii Zhurnal* (March 1988).

79 Popkov even stayed above the "war-scare" fray in the summer of 1986. See M. Popkov, "Partiinaia demokratiia i partiinaia distsiplina," *Kommunist Vooruzhennykh Sil* 16 (August 1986). Also: "Druzhba i bratstvo narodov SSSR—odin iz istochnikov Velikoi Pobedy," *Voenno-Istoricheskii Zhurnal* (March 1985); "Zabota obshchaia, gosudarstvennaia," *Krasnaia Zvezda*, May 7, 1987, pp. 1–2. For his comments on the XIX Party Conference prior to the event, see "Vremiia novykh podkhodov," *Krasnaia Zvezda*, March 17, 1988, p. 2; for a more general interview, "Budit' mysl', zvat' k deistviiu," *Krasnaia Zvezda*, May 5, 1988, p. 2.

Gen. S. A. Bobylev.[80] Indeed, Bobylev, appointed in 1975, held on to his job even through the rocky post-Rust affair personnel shake-out that claimed Sokolov and the chief of the Air Defense Forces himself, Koldunov. Bobylev was replaced in September 1987 by his own deputy, Col. Gen. V. Silakov, and there is little reason to be suspicious of political motives in his replacement.

It should be noted, however, that relative quiescence on the part of the service political chiefs did not mean that the leadership's policies had permeated the ranks. The MPA chiefs in the services were passively receptive of the Party line, rather than active propagandists for that line, perhaps a protest in itself. The reticence of MPA rank-and-file officers to promote New Thinking and *perestroika*, and the hostility of the MPA intellectuals to the leadership, are significant political failures indeed. Moreover, it is apparent that talk of "depoliticizing" the military—that is, removing the organs of Communist party control from military units—served to reunite the MPA, whatever their various opinions on international matters.[81]

CIVILIAN REACTIONS: WIDENING THE POLICY CIRCLE

In 1988 and 1989, Gorbachev seemed finally to accept that the military would not, and in some ways could never, support his foreign policy program. As an institution steeped in Marxist ideology, and bound by a strong group identification, everything about the Soviet Armed Forces worked against their participation in a program designed to de-ideologize the Soviet relationship with the West, to remove the nuclear underpinnings of Soviet superpower status, and to decrease radically the size of the military and thereby inflict severe deprivations on officers and their men alike.

The answer, then, was not to coopt the Soviet high command, but to expand pluralistic reform from the domestic to the foreign policy sector and thereby outnumber the military opposition. This strategy

[80] On L. Batekhin, see his "Povyshat' rezultativnost' partiinogo rukovodstva," *Kommunist Vooruzhennykh Sil* 16 (August 1985); "Nadezhnye kryl'ia Rodina," *Krasnaia Zvezda*, August 8, 1985, p. 2, and "Liudi i nebo," *Krasnaia Zvezda*, August 16, 1987, p. 2. On Bobylev, see "Polkovodets velikoi pobedy," *Vestnik PVO* 4 (1985); "Rabotat' po-novomu, otvetstvenno i initsiativno," *Vestnik PVO* 3 (1985); "S uchetom sovremennykh trebovanii," *Krasnaia Zvezda*, April 13, 1986, p. 2; "Utverzhdaia novye podkhody," *Krasnaia Zvezda*, April 12, 1987, p. 3.

[81] Not one senior officer supported depoliticization before the coup. For one of many examples of military comment on the idea, see "Obnovlennyi politorgan: Kakim emu byt'?," *Krasnaia Zvezda*, July 29, 1990, p. 1.

was alluded to at the XIX Party Conference in June 1988, when Gorbachev criticized previous foreign policymaking for being restricted to a "narrow circle" with a resultant "concentrat[ion] on the military aspect" of superpower relations.[82] Thus, in order to continue the positive changes brought about in the international order by the New Thinking, Gorbachev called for better information and the creation of a "fully empowered" constitutional organization [*konstitutsionno-polnomochnyi mekhanizm*] in the formulation of foreign policy.

Accordingly, Gorbachev sought to widen the circle of policymaking and to introduce more institutions of civilian oversight. This included a call for more civilian defense expertise to undermine the military stranglehold on specialized information, a legal reformulation of the Defense Council (stipulating that the president is ex officio chair), the creation of a secret committee within the Politburo for "military-technical" and arms control issues, a Presidential Council, and a national security council.[83]

His intention here was obviously to diffuse foreign and defense policymaking power, and consequently to marginalize the military in the political process. In the end, however, none of these organizational measures worked; that is, none of them succeeded in lifting civilian defense decision makers over their military counterparts. The reason for this failure is simple: none of these measures took the essential step of de-ideologizing the military and then removing them from political bodies, two of the most enduring aspects of the Soviet style of subjective control. Indeed, in some ways Gorbachev's maneuverings were yet another resort to subjective control, in that they were a means by which civilians were invited to become even more deeply involved with military issues as participants rather than as overseers. Thus, the military was allowed to defend its turf, to hold its own in the Supreme Soviet, to block requests for information, to lobby legislators: in short, to participate in the political process. The nature of the Stalinist heritage, and the system of subjective control it produced, meant that power over these issues had to rest either with the center, in the person of the General Secretary, or with the military.

[82] M. S. Gorbachev, *Izbrannye rechi i stat'i*, vol. 6 (Moscow: Politicheskoi literatury, 1987), p. 345.

[83] See Richard Starr, *Foreign Policies of the Soviet Union* (Stanford, Calif.: Hoover Institute Press, 1991), pp. 27–31; Theodore Karasik, "The Defense Council and Soviet Presidency," *Perspective* (December 1990), pp. 2–3; Thomas Nichols and Theodore Karasik, "Civil-Military Relations under Gorbachev: The Struggle over National Security," in T. Karasik and W. Green, eds. *Gorbachev and His Generals* (Boulder, Colo.: Westview, 1990), pp. 54–55.

Second-rank civilian figures, without expertise or standing, could hardly expect to fill the gulf between.

Only one innovation in this period held out some promise of a move toward objective control: the establishment in June 1989 of the Supreme Soviet Committee for Defense and State Security, which for a time looked as though it might develop an oversight function analogous to the U.S. Senate Armed Services Committee or similar institutions.[84] The problem, as before, was the membership on the committee of several senior officers (including Akhromeev), effectively disabling it as an independent oversight body, despite its mission. As one Soviet civilian analyst put it, "[The committee] was awful. It was just the military-industrial complex's lobby within the Supreme Soviet, rubber stamping all the demands of the Defense Ministry."[85] This, coupled with a slew of other problems (the committee didn't have office space, classified storage facilities, or even a staff in 1989) ensured that this small but promising start would come to nothing.

Gorbachev's strategy of pluralizing the defense policy process was a sound one, even if poorly executed, but time was running out. There was no sign of progress in the struggle with the military, and so far Gorbachev had managed to prevail issue by issue only through his unique ability, as head of state and Party, to act outside Soviet borders and to commit the Soviet Union publicly to dramatic internal changes in the name of arms control. But the larger argument was lost; the military never accepted the ideal of objective control (nor did the civilians give them any incentive to do so), refusing to subordinate themselves fully to the civil power. This recalcitrance left only one last avenue open to the political leadership.

The Return to the Personnel Weapon

By March 1989, every noncoercive method of controlling military dissent had failed. The New Political Thinking, rather than imposing order on the growing debate of the late Brezhnev period, actually touched off a storm of antimilitary pacifism and provided more grist for the military mill. The introduction of the New Doctrine in Berlin was ignored by the General Staff, and derided by everyone else. Finally, the introduction of unilateral measures was met with an outcry in the military echoed even by some of the Soviet citizenry.

Until early 1989, the high command had been spared the personnel

[84] See Nichols and Karasik, "Gorbachev and His Generals," pp. 54–55.
[85] David Shipler, "After the Coup," *New Yorker*, November 11, 1991, p. 72.

weapon except in grievous cases of stupidity or incompetence, probably due to Yazov's presence first as deputy minister for cadres and
later as minister of defense. Eventually, however, the axe fell, beginning with those who would under any circumstances deserve to be
fired. Gen. V. Altunin, for example, was sacked earlier as head of civil
defense (a position carrying deputy minister of defense rank) in connection with his poor handling of the early days of the Chernobyl
nuclear disaster cleanup; Marshals Koldunov and Sokolov were put to
pasture when Matthias Rust skidded to a stop in Red Square;
Akhromeev, of course, resigned. All of these men ended up in the
traditional "pasture" of the Soviet military, the Ministry of Defense
Inspectorate, where they joined Marshals Petrov and Tolubko (former
CINCs of the ground forces and SRF, respectively), and even Marshal
Ogarkov, who was finally removed as the commander of Western
Theater forces in 1988.

These disconnected firings were followed by a concerted round of
dismissals in early 1989. In March 1989, the Central Committee announced that several senior officers were removed from their posts
and transferred to the Inspectorate.[86]

The roster of the retired contained few surprises. Perhaps the most
obvious candidate for a quick dismissal was Marshal Kulikov, and the
only surprise here is that the bellicose Warsaw Pact chief, first appointed in 1977, held on for as long as he did. He was replaced by the
pliant Gen. Lushev, who was not given a marshal's rank (or, apparently, an army); within five months, Lushev was forced to stand by as
the Poles elected a Solidarity government. Three months after that,
the Berlin Wall fell. It is somewhat frightening to consider Kulikov's
reaction had he been on the scene as Warsaw Pact chief, and the
removal of Kulikov may well have been a necessary prerequisite to
Gorbachev's decision to stand aside as Eastern European communism
collapsed. In any event, it only made sense to sack as well Kulikov's
loyal subordinate and ideological coreligionist, General A. I. Gribkov.
Gribkov had served as the Warsaw Pact's chief of staff since 1976, and
his replacement, V. Lobov, followed Lushev's lead until the Pact was
disbanded.

Other casualties included the generals Mikhail Zaitsev and Ivan
Gerasimov, two officers who appeared to be on the fast track, appointed to newly created theater commands in 1985. While they have
not appeared in print with any detailed criticism, it is possible that
they were a source of opposition to the reorganization of the military

[86] *Izvestiia TsK* 2 (1989).

in general. Another possibility is that they were sacked as a first step in dismantling the large theater commands themselves. Age was probably not the issue; Zaitsev was only sixty-seven and Gerasimov sixty-eight (both sprightly by Soviet standards) when they were removed. Two older men, General Ivanovskii and Marshal Kurkotkin, both seventy-two, were removed as deputy ministers of defense. Ivanovskii had been Ground Forces CINC since 1985, the year the theater commands were created, and was replaced by Gen. Valentin Varennikov, an officer more conservative than Ivanovskii himself.[87] (Viewers of the Lithuanian crisis will recall television footage of Varennikov on the spot in Vilnius, a presence that continues to fuel speculation that he was the prime mover behind the saber-rattling that took place there during the 1990 secession crisis.)[88] Kurkotkin, for his part, was appointed chief of the Rear Services by Brezhnev in 1972, and this vestige of the era of *zastoi* was replaced with Gen. Boris Arkhipov, the former Moscow Military District commander. Arkhipov probably won Gorbachev's approval during the early 1987 *perestroika* push, in which he was a loyal participant. There was also a great deal of activity in the field as commanders were shuffled about in a consolidation and reorganization of the military districts.

Most of these men were members of the Central Committee, and so became "dead souls," active members of the Central Committee who lost the jobs that entitled them to Central Committee status in the first place. If Theodore Karasik is correct in his estimation of the number of dead souls by autumn 1989 at about forty-four, then in one month the percentage of military officers among the dead souls jumped from about 18 percent to almost 30 percent.[89] Like others in this position, it would have been only a matter of time before they were removed from the Central Committee as well, an event overtaken by the collapse of the Party. In the interim, they were still voting members, but their power, like that of all Central Committee members, was undermined by the national collapse of the CPSU and Gorbachev's strengthening of state authority. At the time, Kulikov and several

[87] One Moscow source said in 1989 that Varennikov was well connected in the Central Committee, and that this accounted for the appointment of an officer whose views were so diametrically opposed to Gorbachev's.

[88] "I am convinced," Varennikov told the Congress of People's Deputies in December 1989, "the people will not allow our nation to be plunged into chaos. On the contrary, they are bound to demand from us that we bring order." V. Varennikov, "Armiia— zerkalo obshchestva," *Krasnaia Zvezda*, December 26, 1989, p. 4.

[89] I am indebted to Theodore Karasik for several discussions on the "dead souls" and the figures cited.

other officers were members of the Congress of People's Deputies and the Supreme Soviet, but they were more a minority in these large bodies then in the smaller Central Committee.

"I Want the Armed Forces to Remain as They Are"

For the first three years of Gorbachev's tenure, the struggle for control of defense policy between the Soviet military and the new leadership was a familiar one, fought on territory and over issues well known to both sides. Moreover, the old rules of Kremlin politics— refraining from ad hominem attacks, direct mention of specific leaders, discussion of the Party in critical terms, and the like—were observed by all involved. Other things being equal, perhaps the civil-military relationship might have continued in this tense duet for some time.

But "other things," as is usually the case, did not remain equal. In 1989, the Soviet world, and along with it most norms of Soviet political life, exploded. The Baltic states went into revolt. The Party admitted its own hollowness as a social force. Ethnic violence became a daily occurrence. And, in the crowning blow to Soviet prestige, the Berlin Wall was dismantled in a matter of days by groups of dancing teenagers for whom the mighty East German and Soviet armies in East Berlin seemed only remnants from a comic-opera, irrelevant at best and annoying at worst. Of course, to the Europeans, the chief villains, the cause of so much distress, at home and abroad, were the men and officers of the Soviet military.

In the wake of these successive setbacks, the civil-military relationship disintegrated, which is to say that it ceased to be a coherent, if strained, dialogue between political leaders and senior officers. In its place, there arose an encirclement of the military by a hostile populace, many of whom had recently been elected to the new Congress of People's Deputies. Soon, government ministers, including Yazov, were being called on the carpet in front of angry neophyte legislators, while the Party simply turned its back, consumed with its own imminent demise. Those officers who themselves had joined the ranks of the new politicians were subjected not only to the scorn of their civilian colleagues, but also of their younger military comrades, the new corpus of junior officers and enlisted men who embraced radical change as legislators. It is little wonder that General Gromov, the highly regarded commander of Soviet forces in Afghanistan, when asked what he wanted for the military, said simply, "I want the armed forces to remain as they are."[90]

Despite Gromov's nostalgia, however, by 1990 there was no possibility that the army, the Party, or the Union of Soviet Socialist Republics itself could remain "as they are." (Gromov, in an ominous development, changed portfolios, joining the Interior Ministry in December 1990 as second in command to former KGB apparatchik and eventual coup leader Boris Pugo. His relation to the coup is unclear, although he did not actively participate.) The one constant is that the pattern of Soviet civil-military politics since Stalin remained unchanged: the professionalization of the Soviet officer corps was undermined by repeated civilian intrusions into military matters, including use of the personnel weapon against the high command. This civilian behavior invited reciprocal military behavior, and in 1990 the Soviet military viewed its increased political activism as a natural right rather than an aberration. In a Soviet Union at rest—or even, as it was in the 1970s, comatose—the weakness of civil-military borders might be a less urgent issue. But in a country torn by ethnic unrest, economic collapse, and outright counterrevolution, it is a paramount question.

In the following, concluding chapter, we will consider the evolution of the Soviet military, and prospects for the civil-military relationship, in the 1990s.

[90] Gromov made the comment in an interview in *Argumenty i fakty*, March 24, 1990, p. 1.

[8]

Rethinking Soviet Civil-Military Relations: Prospects for the 1990s

> Communists of the Army and the Navy are indignant at the inaction of the Central Committee and the Politburo and the government with regard to their defenders, with regard to those who persecute their soldiers and trample on patriotism and military duty, sacred concepts for any people.
> —Col. Gen. A. Makashov, June 1990

> Military reform began only in August of 1991, with the departyization of the Armed Forces and the abolition of the military-political organs; that is, when deideologizing [of the army] began to take place.
> —Col. Gen. D. A. Volkogonov, September 1991

LESSONS OF THE SOVIET CIVIL-MILITARY EXPERIENCE

The Soviet military remains adrift in the social chaos of the 1990s. Although steeped in Marxist dogma and Leninist discipline, there is no longer a Soviet Communist Party to which the officer corps can swear allegiance; their very raison d'être, the beliefs and the state for which they had pledged to give their lives, are both gone. Denied the legal-constitutional loyalties characteristic of their Western counterparts, there was only a vestige of central state authority they could support, for a time split between the president of the USSR and the president of Russia—the former an office they respected held by a man they distrust, the latter a weak office headed by a strong leader—and now resting in the fractious hands of the Commonwealth leaders.[1] In short, the Soviet Armed Forces have been left to determine their own loyalties and their own direction. Even now, in the wake of reforms brought on by the failed coup, the role of the military in the Commonwealth government and in the republics remains unclear.

This unstable and untenable situation is the legacy of seventy years of subjective control, in which civil authorities have sought to exercise control of the military through political means, and encroached upon traditionally military matters for political and practical reasons. The Bolsheviks sought to control the military through an institutional ideology; Stalin and Khrushchev, through personal and political coercion; Brezhnev, through bribery. Gorbachev in some measure tried all of these and found them—as in the end every leader must find systems of subjective control—to be wanting. The institutional ideology was captured by the military, who turned the tables on the Party and used Marxist orthodoxy as a means of criticizing Party policy rather than vice versa. The personalized totalitarian control characteristic of the Stalin period created a military that was physically and psychologically devastated; the price of Stalin's victory over the Red Army was a young, frightened and inexperienced military completely unprepared for war in 1941. Khrushchev wanted to acquire Stalin's powers without using Stalin's methods, resulting only in the first serious civil-military breach in modern Soviet history and a half-realized and incompetent military doctrine. This left Brezhnev with the choice of either carrying on Khrushchev's fight or seeking peace, which he did at a high material and political cost to himself and his successors.

In the end, Gorbachev bore the brunt of the mistakes of his predecessors, at a time in Soviet history when a reliable and subservient military might well have made a crucial difference in the success or failure of economic and political reform. When he needed Soviet foreign policy to speak with one voice, the military struck the dissonant chord. When he needed to regain control of a budget gone awry, the military fought to preserve their massive material privileges. And when he sought to renegotiate the status of the rapidly crumbling Union, the high command joined hands with the retrograde and primitive hard-liners in the KGB and the Interior Ministry who sought to turn back the Soviet clock by force in the August 1991 coup.

---

[1] In theory, all of the republic defense chiefs will now supposedly meet on a regular schedule as a unified ministerial council, but it remains unclear how often this group will gather, what powers it has, or what it is supposed to do. Moscow Central Television, evening news, November 6, 1991.

These are the failures of the past. What is perhaps more disturbing is that there has been, as yet, no indication that the new governments in the former Soviet Union have learned from the mistakes of their Bolshevik predecessors; although many commanders have been replaced, and steps are currently being taken to remove party bodies from military units, senior Soviet military officers are still part and parcel of the policymaking structures of the Commonwealth and of the Russian, Ukrainian, Kazakh, and other proto-states now emerging in Eurasia. The loyalties of these men are unknown, for now. But it is hard to imagine that all of their previous training and indoctrination ceased to be of relevance on August 19, 1991. Moreover, it seems that previous means of subjective control are being supplanted with new ones: is a Russian military that has sworn personal loyalty to Boris Yeltsin any more stable or professional than a Soviet military previously sworn to the Party? Abandoning a system of subjective control requires that civilian leaders overcome the temptations of that system. The new post-Soviet leaders seem to understand civil-military relations only as subjective control over the military through personal, ideological, or nationalist mechanisms of domination, and this does not raise hopes for civil-military stability in the immediate post-Soviet future.

In the introduction to this book, four major aspects of the civil-military relationship that contribute to the instability of military control were discussed. Three—the power of doctrine, the lack of a constitutional culture, and the dual role of the Soviet officer—flow from the first: the nature of a Marxist military. A review of the development of the civil-military relationship described in this book helps illuminate the path that has led the Soviet military to the present impasse.

THE ROOTS OF SUBJECTIVE CONTROL

The Marxist Military

As discussed in chapter 2, the Frunze-Trotsky debates of the 1920s resulted in the creation of a military that was to be, by design, pervaded by ideological dicta in the belief that an organic link between Party and Army would ensure military loyalty to the Soviet state. This insistence on an ideological foundation within the military was perhaps the single most important factor in the quick ascendance of subjective control. As Huntington pointed out in *The Soldier and the State*, subjective control means that the military is made the "mirror of the state" rather than a distinct professional class; for the founding fathers of the Red Army, however, making the military a mirror of the state was a goal to be achieved rather than a misfortune to be avoided.[2]

The unintended effect of insisting on military loyalty to a promulgated ideology was that it tied military loyalty to something higher than the state. Marxism is a teleological philosophy, oriented toward the eventual achievement of transnational goals loftier than the interest of an individual state. Thus, rather than seeing itself as the servant of the state, the Soviet military was encouraged to see itself as an agent of History itself, defending not only Soviet communism but the interests of a entire international class as well.

The political indoctrination of the officer corps in the USSR also served to weaken professionalism because Marxism itself is, in Huntington's words, an "antimilitary" ideology, in that it is predisposed toward suspicion of the military as an institution and disdainful in general of military values.[3] This observation was at the foundation of Kolkowicz's *The Soviet Military and the Communist Party*, which described the tension between "natural" military traits (such as nationalism and elitism) and the traits desired by the Party (such as internationalism and egalitarianism). But Kolkowicz's belief that the Soviet military was striving to become a "natural" military in opposition to the "ideological" Party was not quite accurate; rather, Huntington correctly noted that in societies dominated by "inherently antimilitary" ideologies, "the military acquire substantial political power only by sacrificing their professionalism and adhering to the values and attitudes dominant within the community."[4] In the Soviet case, the military adhered to Marxism first because it was thrust upon them, and later because successive generations of indoctrination produced officers who remained believers in what became the powerful legitimating mythology behind the armed forces.

This strange amalgam, in which the military embraced the antimilitary ideology of the Bolsheviks within the militarized society created by Stalin, resulted in a military organization that combined aspects of both Marxism and professionalism. The Soviet military is a study in paradoxes: schooled by Lenin but trained in World War II, it is both antiwar and aggressively militaristic; staffed by the sons of the working class but segregated from society, it is both proletarian and elitist; multiethnic but dominated by Russian culture and history, it is both

[2] Samuel Huntington, *The Soldier and the State* (Cambridge: Harvard University Press, 1957), p. 83.
[3] Ibid., pp. 92–93.
[4] Ibid., p. 94.

internationalist and chauvinistic. In sum, the result of the conflict between political indoctrination and military professionalism has been that the Soviet Armed Forces are *"military" in organization but Marxist in orientation.* While the Soviet military may be run like other large militaries, and adheres to traditional military values such as patriotism, discipline, and valor, as a political entity it is unmistakably Marxist, and its political activity—the views, policy prescriptions, even the style and imagery of its arguments—are products of that ideology. And it was this ideology, combined with what Kolkowicz refers to as "natural" military traits, that led the Soviet military to define its purpose, as it did in a typical 1968 description, as both messianic and defensive, fulfilling a "high patriotic *and* international-ist mission," while guarding both the "peaceful labor of the Soviet people," and "shoulder by shoulder with the other fraternal socialist armies," the interests of the "entire socialist commonwealth."[5]

The most important point to bear in mind about the indoctrination of the Soviet military is that it was a politicized military because the civilian leadership always chose to have it remain one. Indeed, Khrushchev had a golden opportunity in the 1950s to recast the armed forces in a more professional mold. Stalin's annihilation of the military and its political officers provided an opening for later Party leaders to depoliticize the armed forces. Just as the Nazis managed to destroy what was left of the Prussian military tradition in the creation of the *Wehrmacht*, so too did Stalin destroy the emerging cadre of Red officers in the purges of 1937–38.

But Khrushchev left the Marxist military in place, as Brezhnev and Gorbachev would in later years, in part because Soviet leaders have failed to understand that military Marxism is an impediment to con-trol, rather than an instrument of control. After Stalin's death, it became clear that this obsession with political indoctrination among the military was to cause more problems than it solved. In the 1950s and 1960s, the Soviet military became the voice of stolidly anti-Western Marxism; in the 1970s, they emerged as the avowed enemies of Brezhnev's détentist line; in the 1980s, they made a stand against the end of the empire abroad and the dissipation of Marxist values at home. Although Soviet Marxism-Leninism never recovered from its Stalinist destruction as a creative force, it is testimony to the en-durance of ideology in the officer corps, as well as to the endurance of civilian insistence on a politicized military, that the armed forces

---

[5] *Partiino-politicheskaia rabota v sovetskikh vooruzhennykh silakh,* 2d ed. (Moscow: Voenizdat, 1968), p. 3, emphasis added.

maintained their commitment to ideology even as Marxism-Leninism was becoming completely moribund in society at large.

While the civilian leaders never considered depoliticizing the military—as they were never able or willing to consider the depoliticizing of the society itself—they did attempt to circumscribe military influence over policymaking. In Stalin's case, of course, military authority and influence were circumscribed with bullets. Other leaders, however, chose, the standard maneuver of subjective control: the diminution of military power through the increase of relative civilian power over military issues. The primary vehicle for this enlargement of the civilian sphere of influence was military doctrine.

The Power of Doctrine

The creation of the concept of Soviet military doctrine was a direct result of the decision to create a Marxist military. Doctrine would flow from ideology, and military thought would always take place within the confines of that ideology, designed and approved by the Party leadership. In doctrine, the Bolsheviks thought they were creating the means by which the wisdom of the Party leaders would be translated into concrete guidance for the Soviet Armed Forces.

This was not to be, since Stalin's capture of the Kremlin, and the subsequent evisceration and taming of the Party, naturally led to the appropriation of military doctrine as the private preserve of the general secretary. By the time of the German invasion of 1941, Soviet military doctrine had little to do with Marxism, the Party, or military expertise of any kind. Instead, it simply came to be shorthand, as one Soviet officer put it, for "the habit . . . of being guided only by what [Stalin] had said."[6] The deputy commandant of the Frunze Military Academy reflected this intersection of personal power and military policy when he vetoed the introduction of a strategy course in 1935 with the exclamation, "What is this strategy course? Strategy is Comrade Stalin's personal occupation and it isn't any of our business."[7]

After Stalin's death, there was no clear heir to the doctrinal throne. In theory, only the Party had the right to define military doctrine, but Stalin drained the ideological essence from the concept when he absorbed it into his own cult of personality. And while the military might have laid claim to doctrine on the practical grounds of expertise, they had neither the substantive knowledge (that is, among

---

[6] I. A. Korotkov, "O razvitii sovetskoi voennoi teorii v poslevoennye gody," *Voenno-Istoricheskii Zhurnal* 4 (April 1964), pp. 40–41.

[7] Cited in William T. Lee and Richard Starr, *Soviet Military Policy since World War II* (Stanford, Calif.: Hoover Institute Press, 1986), p. 15.

those officers still alive in 1941) nor the political stature to press such a claim. Thus, Soviet military doctrine remained ideological in form but political in practice, much like the Soviet military itself.

Had Party and Army found a more rational division of labor between them, the conflicts of the Khrushchev era might have been avoided, but the very structure of doctrine worked against this more rational evolution. The nature of doctrine—as both the expression of the wisdom of the Party and the source of all military planning—is such that the Party's failure to lay claim to it would have been taken as an admission of impotence and invited de facto power sharing with the soldiers; moreover, the Party needed to control doctrine if it was to control fully and legitimately the resource base of the USSR. Khrushchev recognized both of these imperatives, and he acted on that recognition with vigor.

These structural imperatives inherent in military doctrine have been sufficiently strong to compel all Soviet leaders since Khrushchev to emulate Khrushchev to some degree or another—which is, in effect, to emulate Stalin. After all, why fight the military issue by issue, when the potential exists for exerting supreme and pervasive control of military issues simply by gaining control of a single concept? Even Brezhnev, despite his reticence about conflict with the military in the 1960s, eventually found himself making sweeping doctrinal pronouncements in the 1970s in an attempt to outflank his officers. And Gorbachev attempted nothing less than a complete revolution in military doctrine, aimed in large measure at overturning the influence of the military.

The structure of doctrine made civil-military conflict endemic in Soviet politics, for it created an arena in which civil and military elites necessarily interact on issues that cut across domestic and foreign policy. Moreover, the ideologically determined power of doctrine made it a tempting target for politicians and generals alike. But the civil-military relationship, had it centered only on doctrine, would have been more manageable were it not for the lack of clear boundaries on the competition for influence between the soldiers and the civilians. In Western polities, these boundaries are set both by custom and by constitutional decree; in the Soviet Union, the lack either of a firm constitution or a culture of constitutionalism provided the fertile ground in which subjective control flourishes.

The Constitutional Complication

Military loyalty to the Soviet state as a Marxist state also undermined the possibility of more constitutional or legal mechanisms of control. If the Party is the living expression of society (and the general secretary is the embodiment of the Party), then there is little role left for the constitution in Soviet life in general and among the military in particular. Indeed, it was the Bolsheviks' intention that the Soviet constitution would reflect the will of the Party, rather than vice versa; it is instructive to recall that Lenin accorded the constitution such limited significance that he did not even sit on the first Soviet constitutional commission.[8] In any event, the first two attempts at a basic document fell to the new, so-called Stalin Constitution in 1936 that made a mockery of the idea of constitutional supremacy in Soviet government.

The absence of a strong constitutional tradition in Russian and Soviet history hampered social development in many areas of the modern Soviet state, but nowhere was this absence sharper and more dangerous than in the civil-military relationship. More is at stake than this or that article of the Soviet constitution; without obedience to a constitution, military loyalty becomes a function of the legitimacy of the Party. The lack of constitutional norms complicates the already delicate balance between military obedience and Party legitimacy, a situation described more generally by Robert Tucker when he wrote, "Where [a political culture of] constitutionalism does not exist, even though a constitution may have been formally proclaimed, the authorities treat disagreement with the given government's or ruling party's policies, or disapproval of the government itself, as disloyalty to the state. In effect, they say, *L'etat, c'est nous.*"[9] Thus, in the absence of a constitutional tradition, the Party becomes the State. This is all the more true in the civil-military realm, where the definition of "disloyalty to the state" is not necessarily shared by Party and military elites. Because there is no firm legal or historical tradition embodied in a constitution to adjudicate disputes, the constitutional complication opens the possibility of an endless cycle of disagreement between conflicting notions of duty and patriotism.

The question remains whether constitutionalism can be learned. (Small steps appeared here and there: for example, references before the 1991 coup to the defense of the USSR as a soldier's "constitutional duty" became more frequent.)[10] The redrafting of the Constitution of 1977 is a moot issue by now, but there was no reason to believe that

[8] Phillip Roeder, *Soviet Political Dynamics* (New York: Harper and Row, 1988), p. 172.

[9] Robert Tucker, *Political Culture and Leadership in Soviet Russia* (New York: Norton, 1987), p. 202.

[10] See "Prizyvy Politburo TsK KPSS k 1 Maia 1991 goda," *Krasnaia Zvezda*, April 26, 1991, p. 1, for a typical example.

the new document, the USSR's fifth constitution, would have been any more respected than the previous four. The 1977 constitution, after all, is a generally humane one, and if words were sufficient guarantors of loyalty there would have been little need for constitutional reform in the USSR. Developments in the republics are disheartening as well; there is so far no serious legal-constitutional mechanism in place in Russia or the major republics, all of which at present are essentially ruled by presidential decree. The problem, whether there is an actual document or not, is that there is no *tradition* of obedience to a constitution, even among the military, precisely because Soviet socialization took place in an environment where the Party did not want the military or any other sector of society to develop loyalties beyond the Party. This process was taken to its logical extreme in the Stalin Constitution, obliterating any possibility of loyalty to anything but the Party and its Leader. Later Soviet leaders did little to rectify this situation, reflecting the low priority of the Soviet constitution as anything more than a reaffirmation of the successes of the regime and its current leaders.

Whatever the form of the new Commonwealth (and Russian, Ukrainian et al.) constitutions, it is unlikely that it will include a ban on military participation in electoral politics, one of the uniquely Soviet aspects of the civil-military relationship.

The Dual Role of the Soviet Officer

In practical terms, the denial of clear boundaries between military and political institutions opened to Soviet officers the option of legitimate participation in national politics in the roles of military specialists, Marxist theorists, and even as politicians. Huntington suggested that objective control is less likely, and military influence is increased, "if members of the officer corps assume positions in nonmilitary power structures."[11] In the USSR, military men were members of the Central Committee, the Supreme Soviet, the Congress of People's Deputies, and other governmental and Party bodies, and will without doubt continue to hold similar positions in analogous bodies to come. In 1991, 4 percent of the Congress of People's Deputies were military men, of whom half were generals; 2 percent of the last Supreme Soviet was military.[12] (By comparison with the American system, this

[11] Huntington, *The Soldier and the State*, p. 89.

[12] I am indebted to Dawn Mann and Michel Tatu for these figures on military representation in the Congress and the Supreme Soviet through the SOVSET computer network.

[245]

would be roughly akin to having eighteen senior U.S. officers in the House of Representatives and two in the Senate.) The proportions were higher still in the Central Committee of the Communist party, where military officers accounted for slightly less than 9 percent of the Central Committee between 1986 and 1990.

This attempt to coopt military elites into Party and state structures, however, carried the risk (as Gromyko's interactions with various ministers of defense and other evidence attest) of creating officer-politicians, one of the most difficult aspects of subjective control. As Arbatov wrote in frustration in 1990,

> If military men want or agree to take part in internal political struggles, and the political leadership wants or agrees to support them in these struggles, then others have to contend with the consequences: military men with the fact that they will be feared and that efforts will be made to neutralize them politically, and politicians with the fact that they will always be apprehensive about the military. And above all, society will always have to be apprehensive about a sudden undesirable turn of events.
>
> This is precisely why democracy can never develop where the previous order of things has been preserved and the Armed Forces have not been placed under the control of the political (including legislative) authorities. And at this sort of stage, naturally, the question arises of de-politicizing the army. We did not begin to contend with this until much later—until the years of *perestroika*.[13]

One expression of this dilemma came inadvertently from one of the USSR's most popular officers, Col. Gen. (and later, deputy interior minister) Boris Gromov. "And what are you," an interviewer asked him in 1989, "a general or a politician?" According to this account, "Boris Vsevolodovich smiled," and answered, "I'm trying to explain, that the times are such that anyone who cares about the fate of the Motherland is obligated to be a politician, whether an engineer, or a worker, or a soldier. There is no boundary between the army and the people."[14] Gromov was speaking as a good Marxist, correctly following the intentions of the early Bolsheviks that there would indeed be no boundaries between the army and the people. But where there are no lines between the society and its "experts in violence," the officer's conception of his role in politics is easily transformed from servant to

---

[13] Georgii Arbatov, *Zatianuvsheesiia vyzdorovlenie (1953–1986 gg.)* (Moscow: "Mezhdu-narodnye otnosheniia," 1991), p. 107.

[14] "Mezhdu armiei i narodnom net mezhi," *Krasnaia Zvezda*, March 19, 1989, p. 1.

participant, and the growth of professionalism is weakened accordingly.

The dual role of the Soviet officer is the inevitable result of both the insistence on a Marxist military and the attendant lack of a legal-constitutional definition of the role of the Soviet officer. The nature of the Party was such that participation in all Party bodies had to be, in theory, open to Party members, military or otherwise; similarly, membership in Soviet state institutions was open to all citizens. There is no analog to the American ban on holding two federal posts concurrently, or on members of the executive branch holding legislative office (which would force an officer to resign his commission before taking elected federal office). Instead, military participation in the Soviet political system was encouraged, as part of the attempt to bind the officer to society through activity in its political institutions.

The threat of the Soviet officer-politician does not lie in the remote chance that a Marshal might have succeeded in being elected president of the USSR, or that the military might cobble together a majority in the Russian parliament and vote itself a massive new budget. Rather, a practical issue arises from controlling a military institution when members of that institution are represented in the legislative process. To the American mind, this is a simple separation of powers problem: the military is under the control of the executive, and therefore an officer cannot hold a post in the legislature. Yet there is a larger conceptual danger in allowing the officer-politician to retain legislative office, in that it reaffirms to the military that there are no firm divisions between politics and the army. It reaffirms that the soldier is not a specialist in a distinct skill, separate from the politicians who must be his masters. In short, the existence of the officer-politician in the former USSR is a direct and continuing threat to the professionalism of the Soviet and post-Soviet soldier, and may in the end only encourage the remaining members of the Soviet Armed Forces to see themselves as the legitimate heirs to political power now that all other institutions in Soviet society have failed.

The present era in Soviet politics is one in which all four aspects of the system of subjective control have reached decisive turning points. Ideology is dying: while the Soviet military remains in its essence an ideological military, the Party and Marxism-Leninism itself have been abandoned in the former USSR and in most of the former socialist nations. Doctrine is irrelevant: although the Soviets formally promulgated a new military doctrine only as recently as 1987, and another round of doctrinal revision was under way in 1991, the fragmentation of the USSR, Baltic independence, the outright collapse of the Warsaw

Pact, and the transformation of Europe have all left the remnants of the high command without a coherent strategic vision. The constitution is in limbo: despite initial gains along the road to a more regularized and legal system of politics, constitutional reform has been torpedoed by the breakup of the Union. Finally, the role of the Soviet officer is in doubt: some civilian reformers, emulating Western practice, are attempting to exclude the military from Soviet politics—with the predictable result that the military resists with the political tools at its disposal—while others are welcoming reformist officers into the councils of central and republican governments.

The last decade of the century will be the last as well for the Union of Soviet Socialist Republics as it once existed. As of early 1992, the former Soviet republics are poised on the brink of complete economic collapse and, in many areas, civil war. More than ever before, the position of the Soviet Armed Forces has become central to the future of the citizens of the former Soviet Union, and to the future Russian-American relationship. The outcome of the various economic, ethnic, and political conflicts now underway in the new Commonwealth of Independent States will determine in large measure the future of international peace and cooperation.

As the situation in the Commonwealth worsens—as it is bound to without immediate economic and political triage—the costs of five decades of subjective control will become more evident to the Russian and republican leaders. First and foremost, it is now highly questionable whether the military will stand by and wait for orders from the state under all circumstances, especially as the republics begin to raise their own militias. Nor does the collapse of the August coup mean that the military has been neutralized, either in terms of capability or intentions. Indeed, one Soviet officer was overheard to remark that the August coup wasn't really a military coup: a real military coup, he grumbled, would have succeeded. (The officer's implication, of course, is that perhaps the August coup *should* have been a military-led coup.) The point is that an actual military coup—or perhaps separate rebellions among unattached units in the style of the Whites during the Revolution—may yet be a possibility, especially if fighting breaks out among the republics. In any case, the coup and the participation of the high command in it should serve as a warning to republic leaders, who may be tempted to reach for the military instrument as the economic and ethnic situation deteriorates.

Another threat to the present delicate civil-military stability may be the current departyization of the military. The Soviet Armed Forces remain one of the last cohesive institutions in the former Soviet republics, and still tend to see themselves as Soviet rather than republican. As other social and political arrangements crumble (including, perhaps the eventual collapse of the Commonwealth itself), it is to be expected that the Soviet Armed Forces—unarguably multinational, distinctly Marxist-Leninist, and unavoidably cohesive—would see it itself as a legitimate guarantor of social stability. Akhromeev was hardly exaggerating in the summer of 1990 when he said that "the Army remains the most stable institution in our society."[15] Moreover, many in the military remain committed to the idea of the inseparability of the Communist Party and the armed forces, even if it means exhuming the cadaver of the Party and dragging it behind them. Only a true believer could say, as former chief of the MPA, Gen. N. Shliaga, did in the summer of 1990, that "the only real political force, the most massive and organized which enjoys absolute authority in the Army, is the CPSU."[16] His predecessor, Lizichev, expressed similar views just six months earlier: "We must fully restore the abiding socialist values and place them at the Fatherland's service. The color of our banner has been, is, and will be red and it will always bear the words: Lenin, October, Socialism."[17] As mentioned in the preceding chapter, the idea of depoliticizing the military is anathema to political officers and combat soldiers alike, but how these loyalists will fill the void left by the Party's banning from the ranks remains unclear.

PROSPECTS FOR THE 1990S: COUPS OR CONSTITUTIONS?

The original conclusion to this book, written in early 1991, suggested that a coup in the 1990s was possible, even likely under some circumstances. Otherwise, I suggested, military influence on Soviet policy would continue to grow in proportion to the growing crisis in the USSR. Indeed, at the time, there were abundant signs that Gorbachev was making accommodations with the high command, and

[15] "Akhromeev, Other Officers Respond to Reformers," FBIS-SOV-90-157, August 14, 1990, p. 50.

[16] "General Shliaga Assails Army Depoliticization," FBIS-SOV-90-139, July 19, 1990.

[17] Lizichev was speaking at a conference of military journalists; the report appeared only in the first edition of *Krasnaia Zvezda* and was dropped from the later edition. See "Lizichev Addresses Military Journalists," FBIS-SOV-90-003, p. 106. On July 19, 1990, Lizichev was relieved of his post.

that, like Brezhnev, he was seeking a military truce at the price of civilian authority.

But the long-awaited coup has come and gone, and a bevy of new faces has moved into the Soviet (now Commonwealth), Russian, and republic defense ministries. The MPA has been all but shut down; rapid turnover is proceeding apace in every military district and in all branches of the armed forces; military units are being removed from the Baltics and other areas. All in all, it seems that the Soviet military may finally have been removed as a threat to continuing political stability in the former Soviet Union.

I find this picture overly optimistic, however. Despite the changes taking place in the central and republican defense ministries, certain Soviet-era patterns remain. As before, the minister of defense is a professional officer; one would think that the Soviets might have learned their lesson with Marshals such as Grechko and Yazov. (Shortly after becoming minister, Evgenii Shaposhnikov got his marshal's star.) Also, there is no serious proposal as yet that the military be banned categorically from political life; indeed, even the commission to remove Party organs from the military is chaired by three senior officers, headed by Volkogonov. It is no movement toward objective control to take oppositionist officers and replace them with reformist officers while leaving the overall structure of civil-military interaction intact. In other words, the personalities have changed, but the basic system of subjective control remains.

The danger here lies not only in the aggressive reemergence of the Soviet Armed Forces as a cohesive whole during a period of civil strife, but also of the problems that plagued the Soviets arising again as the Russian Republic, in particular, simply adopts the former Soviet military without serious political reform. A military guided by messianic Russian nationalism or other ethnic chauvinisms and held in check by a strong leader at the center is no better than Stalinism—perhaps worse, given the potential of modern military technology.

Is there an alternative to the participation of the Soviet military in politics, and to the consequent further entrenchment of subjective control, in the Russian Republic? In the late 1980s, there were encouraging, although halting, moves toward constitutional reform of the Soviet state in general and the Soviet Armed Forces in particular. Such moves were to no avail, largely because the political gridlock in the Congress of People's Deputies (where military officers sat side by side with their civilian fellow legislators) ensured that legislative oversight remained ineffective. In part, this was due to the tensions in the

Congress attested to by Maj. Gen. M. Surikov in a speech to fellow deputies in late 1989 about the lack of progress on a budget:

> It is embarrassing to speak about this, but for some reason the word "general" at this congress has come to sound as something of an insult. . . .
>
> I would ask, comrades, for us deputies not to be split into civilians and military. Let us unite in order to switch from words to specific deeds, so that we will not be ashamed to look our voters in the eye.[18]

Despite these tensions in the Congress (which will no doubt be replicated in the republics if military men are allowed to join the legislatures there as well), there was nonetheless an evident desire for more precise boundaries on the military on the part of the high command itself, and memories of the poor organization of the Congress may have a beneficial effect on Russian constitutional reform. This desire for a more regularized relationship confirms Huntington's assertion that the demand for clear lines of civilian authority—for objective control—usually emanates from the military itself.[19]

The Soviet case was no exception. At the February 1990 Plenum of the Communist Party, military delegates (led by Moiseev) actually supported the idea of an enlarged USSR presidency for Gorbachev, as a first step toward a more legalistic and clearer civil-military relationship. Moiseev suggested that the President of the USSR also assume the post of supreme commander in chief, whose powers would include the approval of Soviet military doctrine, programs for the development of armaments, the military budget, arms control, nuclear release authority (previously the prerogative of the general secretary of the Party), the granting of ranks above major general, and other matters.[20] In part, Moiseev and his colleagues were motivated by the rather disorganized situation in which "everyone is involved in resolving military questions in our country now" including, according to Moiseev, the Party's Central Committee, the Politburo, the USSR Supreme Soviet, the Council of Ministers, the Defense Council, the

---

[18] "People's Deputies Discuss Revitalizing Economy," FBIS-SOV-90–026-S, February 7, 1990, pp. 13–14.

[19] Huntington, *The Soldier and the State*, p. 84.

[20] "Moiseev on Presidency's Impact on Armed Forces," FBIS-SOV-90–053, March 19, 1990, pp. 87–89. Maj. Gen. Ivashov of the Defense Ministry General Department noted in April 1990 that the presidency would in fact receive these powers in the Draft Law on Defense, then undergoing revision.

USSR Council of Ministers State Commission for Military-Industrial Questions, the Foreign Ministry, and others.

Prospects, however, for the more powerful USSR presidency (or its emerging Russian analog) to translate into movement toward objective control quickly dimmed. Rather than creating a constitutional office to which the military would be loyal, the creation of the presidency was apparently one more effort to maximize the power of the single civilian leader (in the tradition of Stalin and Khrushchev) at the expense of the military. The office of president was intimately bound to the person of Gorbachev (as is the Russian Republic presidency to Boris Yeltsin), and the vestiges of that office did not survive Gorbachev's tenure as national leader.[21] The powers of Yeltsin's office will probably suffer the same fate (or be appropriated for more malefic ends) should Yeltsin likewise fall from grace.

Worse, there is no evidence that the centurions are of a mind to compromise with Nero while Rome burns. Despite the generally reasonable tone adopted by Moiseev at the February 1990 Plenum of the Central Committee about the powers of the presidency, he also lashed out at the deterioration of the army's prestige and the silencing of the military in the councils of the Party.[22] Other officers have voiced even more harsh criticism of the leadership, which culminated in Volga-Urals district commander Col. Gen. A. Makashov's extraordinary outburst at the Russian Republic Party Congress in June 1990.[23] The coda to Makashov's eruption was sounded a few days later by one retired colonel from Kishinev, who called the offices of *Krasnaia Zvezda* to say that "I think that at long last someone has said what we've all been thinking for the past few years."[24] Needless to say, Makashov was removed (and has been seen in uniform at anti-Yeltsin rallies), but the question lingers: how many other Makashovs are there? And how will Yeltsin and the other Commonwealth leaders find and remove them?

In late 1990, Nigerian leader General Olesegun Obasanjo reflected on the lessons of the coup that brought him to power. His warning was aimed at the leaders of the new democracies in Eastern Europe:

When a society is adrift, rudderless, unfocused, and obviously tottering on the brink of disintegration and disaster, in what sense can civilian

---

[21] As it turned out, the USSR presidency was scrapped in favor of a collegial, Yugoslavia-type group leadership in the new CIS in 1992.

[22] "Moiseev on Presidency's Impact."

[23] "My ne sobiraemsia sdavat'sia," *Krasnaia Zvezda*, June 21, 1990, p. 2.

[24] "Po telefonu obratnoi sviazi," *Krasnaia Zvezda*, June 21, 1990, p. 2.

leaders be said to be doing what's right for the country? The legitimacy of civilian leaders is the single most potent factor determining the propensity of the military to supplant civilian leaders.[25]

In 1991, as the Soviet Union slouched toward eventual disintegration, the mythology of Party legitimacy that served as the basis of governance in the USSR had been rejected by the Soviet populace, and the specter of chaos and civil war even now looms over Moscow. Without the ideological authority of the Party, without the popular legitimacy of the state, without even the practical gains of a "socialist commonwealth" in Eastern Europe (or the Baltics) left to bolster the claims of the new Russian government to the right to rule, it may not be long before the officers of the Soviet Armed Forces (as many still call themselves) once again determine that the civilians in the Kremlin and the new Commonwealth's capitals from Dushanbe to Kiev are no longer "doing what's right" for the citizens of the former Soviet Union.[26]

There is some hope. Although the basic pattern of civil-military relations remains in place, it is possible that senior officers like Volkogonov, Col. Gen. Konstantin Kobets (of the General Staff and, briefly, the Russian defense minister), Marshal Shaposhnikov, and others were so incensed by the behavior of the high command during the coup that they have irrevocably committed themselves to the rule of law and subordination to the state. This type of officer, representing a man in transition from Marxist to professional, may well have felt that the coup was the one line that should not have been crossed. Certainly, it now seems that the younger officers and many of the enlisted men of the Soviet military were willing to disobey their superiors and throw their support to the democratic resistance, much as one might expect American or British soldiers to do under similar circumstances. The shock of the coup, coupled with the coming generational change in the senior officer ranks, may represent the fertile ground in which a professional Soviet or Russian military may finally be nurtured.

The alternative is grim. In 1917, as he abdicated his throne, the tsar spoke of a "new and painful trial" to be laid upon Russia. Should the Soviet military reject the professional soldier's creed of noninterference in politics, and instead remain determined to protect those

---

[25] Olesegun Obasanjo, "The Military and Democracy," *Vision* (August 1990), p. 1.

[26] In discussions with several Soviet officers in late 1991, I was surprised at their continued insistence that they are "Soviet" officers first and foremost. As one put it, "As long as the Armed Forces of the USSR exist, the USSR exists, no matter what they call it."

icons—the October Revolution and the socialist Fatherland—to which they have for seventy years sworn to lay down their lives, the Soviet Union will undergo another painful trial, one that may threaten not only the course of reform in Eastern Europe but the cause of international peace. On January 11, 1992, a large meeting of Soviet officers in Moscow resulted in a blaring *Krasnaia Zvezda* headline, declaring that "officers demand clear and considered decisions from the politicians," and adding this ominous warning: "Do not force them to violate their conscience."[27] The next day, at a rally outside the Kremlin, more than ten thousand Russians protested the ignominious end of the old USSR. Carrying pictures of Lenin and decrying the transformation of the Soviet Union from a superpower to "an international beggar," the demonstrators called for the ouster of Boris Yeltsin and the restoration of Soviet rule. "The crowd," according to Western reporters, "cheered several proposals, including some from middle rank officers, that the 'army fulfill its constitutional duty and take authority into its own hands.'"[28]

We can only hope that the nascent professionalism of the Soviet officer will overcome his ideological and patriotic indoctrination, and compel him to turn away from such a course.

[27] *Krasnaia Zvezda*, January 11, 1992, p. 1.
[28] "A Cold, Lonely Rally Outside Kremlin," *Boston Globe*, January 13, 1992, p. 2.

Index

CORNELL STUDIES IN SECURITY AFFAIRS

edited by Robert J. Art *and* Robert Jervis

Library of Congress Cataloging-in-Publication Data

Nichols, Thomas, 1960–
    The sacred cause : civil-military conflict over Soviet national security, 1917–
  1992 / Thomas M. Nichols.
      p.   cm. — (Cornell studies in security affairs)
    Includes bibliographical references and index.
    ISBN 0-8014-2774-6 (alk. paper)
    1. Soviet Union—Armed Forces.   2. Civil-military relations—Soviet
  Union.   I. Title.   II. Series.
  UA770.N48   1993
  322'.5'0947—dc20   92-34543